The Great Withdrawal

Also by
Craig R. Smith

Rediscovering Gold in the 21st Century:
The Complete Guide to the Next Gold Rush

Black Gold Stranglehold:
The Myth of Scarcity and the Politics of Oil
(co-authored with Jerome R. Corsi)

The Uses of Inflation:
Monetary Policy and Governance in the 21st Century

Crashing the Dollar:
How to Survive a Global Currency Collapse
(co-authored with Lowell Ponte)

Re-Making Money:
Ways to Restore America's Optimistic Golden Age
(co-authored with Lowell Ponte)

The Inflation Deception:
Six Ways Government Tricks Us...And Seven Ways to Stop It!
(co-authored with Lowell Ponte)

The Great Debasement:
The 100-Year Dying of the Dollar and How to Get America's Money Back
(co-authored with Lowell Ponte)

Also by
Lowell Ponte

The Cooling

Crashing the Dollar:
How to Survive a Global Currency Collapse
(co-authored with Craig R. Smith)

Re-Making Money:
Ways to Restore America's Optimistic Golden Age
(co-authored with Craig R. Smith)

The Inflation Deception:
Six Ways Government Tricks Us...And Seven Ways to Stop It!
(co-authored with Craig R. Smith)

The Great Debasement:
The 100-Year Dying of the Dollar and How to Get America's Money Back
(co-authored with Craig R. Smith)

The Great Withdrawal

How the Progressives' 100-Year Debasement of America and the Dollar Ends

by

Craig R. Smith

and Lowell Ponte

Foreword by Pat Boone

Idea Factory Press
Phoenix, Arizona

The Great Withdrawal

How the Progressives' 100-Year Debasement of America and the Dollar Ends

Dustin D. Brown, Krypticeeye.com
Editing by Ellen L. Ponte

Portions of this book originally appeared in the following projects by Craig R. Smith and Lowell Ponte:
The Inflation Deception: Six Ways Government Tricks Us...And Seven Ways to Stop It! and
The Great Debasement: The 100-Year Dying of the Dollar and How to Get America's Money Back
and ***Why Cyprus Matters: Could Politicians Loot Your Life Savings Account As They Did In Cyprus? They Already Have and Have Plans to Take It All. A Savings Survival Guide.***

Portions of this book originally appeared in
The Uses of Inflation: Monetary Policy and Governance in the 21st Century by Craig R. Smith

Library of Congress Data
ISBN Number 978-0-9898471-0-0
First Edition - October 2013

Idea Factory Press
2725 E. Mine Creek Road, #1028, Phoenix, AZ 85024
*Tel. (602) 918-3296 * Ideaman@myideafactory.net*

Updates, reviews and more are posted at
http://greatwithdrawal.com

Table of Contents

Dedication

To my wonderful wife and best friend
Melissa Smith, who makes me better
each day and raised our daughters
Holly and Katie to love the Lord
with all their hearts.
Also to my Pastor Tommy Barnett,
who taught me that doing the right thing
is always the right thing to do,
and to always hold onto the vision.

Foreword
by Pat Boone

"Now we command you, brethren...
that ye withdraw yourselves
from every brother that walketh disorderly..."

– 2 Thessalonians 3:6 (KJV)

The Framers of America's Constitution put America on a straight highway into the future based on sound money, small government and individual integrity and faith.

So long as America kept faith with this standard, between the 1820s and the creation of the Federal Reserve Board in 1913, the purchasing power of our dollar over that time actually increased in value. American prosperity grew in part from keeping our money an honest medium of exchange and a store of reliable value trusted around the world.

In 1913 America began "The Great Debasement" of our currency, the turn from gold to today's Federal Reserve paper fiat money and confiscatory Progressive taxation. In less than a century the buying power of our paper dollar has dwindled to only two cents of its 1913 value, and our economy and society seem stuck and sinking in quicksand.

In this book my long-trusted friend and advisor Craig Smith and former *Reader's Digest* Roving Editor Lowell Ponte explain how this happened, and why millions of Americans and others around the world have begun a Great Withdrawal from the failed collectivist movement that has debased our values, society, politics, culture and currency.

Craig and Lowell show how this Great Withdrawal can bring an end to the failed Progressive utopian rule that has taken America on a 100-year detour away from the path of faith and freedom charted by our Framers. They map how, together and individually, we can return to America's higher road.

Pat

In his 1835 book Democracy in America, the French writer Alexis de Tocqueville imagined a future America in which our voluntary associations had died:

"I see an innumerable crowd of like and equal men.... Each of them, withdrawn and apart, is like a stranger to the destiny of all the others; his children and his particular friends form the whole human species for him; as for dwelling with his fellow citizens, he is beside them, but he does not see them; he touches them and does not feel them; he exists only in himself and for himself alone....

"Above these an immense tutelary power is elevated, which alone takes charge of assuring their enjoyments and watching over their fate. It is absolute, detailed, regular, far-seeing, and mild.

"It would resemble paternal power if, like that, it had for its object to prepare men for manhood; but on the contrary, it seeks only to keep them fixed irrevocably in childhood....

"Thus...the sovereign extends its arms over society as a whole; it covers its surface with a network of small, complicated, painstaking, uniform rules through which the most original minds and the most vigorous souls cannot clear a way to surpass the crowd;

"It does not break wills, but it softens them, bends them, and directs them; it rarely forces one to act, but it constantly opposes itself to one's acting; it does not destroy, it prevents things from being born; it does not tyrannize, it hinders, compromises, enervates, extinguishes, dazes, and finally reduces each nation to being nothing more than a herd of timid and industrious animals of which government is the shepherd." [1]

Introduction
by Craig R. Smith

I came to see the end of the world!"

– German tourist
in today's Detroit [2]

Two dreams could be dying in the bankrupt city of Detroit, Michigan and in the rest of America and the Western world.

One is an American dream of freedom that this Motor City in its heyday put on wheels and decked out in chrome, a dream that inspired the world.

The other is the collectivist dream variously known as liberalism, socialism or Progressivism. Leftists expected that their dominance in Detroit would demonstrate to the world collectivism's success. Instead, Detroit has become a scientific test proving that Progressivism's utopian ideas produce terrible results and are unworkable. In the end there can be only one.

Either we successfully reboot the original operating system of individual freedom, free enterprise and small government that America's Framers built into the U.S. Constitution, or the Progressives will by manipulation and force continue to impose their failed collectivist ideas on humankind's future.

More than 100 years ago, these collectivist ideas began to dominate Western civilization. In 1913 they took control of the United States Government and began a "fundamental transformation" of our economy, politics, culture and beliefs that continues today.

Progressives believed that government could, and should, re-make not only the world but also the very nature and society of human beings.

They aimed to replace Capitalism, private property, "selfish" individualism and God with a human-made Eden, a utopian humanist society where an all-powerful State would equally redistribute the world's wealth and power to the working class.

Detroit became the embodied symbol of this Leftist utopian dream in the United States. Through Franklin Delano Roosevelt's New Deal, labor unions seized control of Detroit's industry, and later its politics, supposedly putting the workers in the driver's seat of history.

For a brief moment following World War II, when factories in most of the world's other industrial nations lay in ruins, Detroit workers had the highest per capita income and rate of home ownership in America – and perhaps in the world.

More than three of every 10 civilian American workers during that moment were members of labor unions. The model for this was the command economy of the war, Detroit as the Arsenal of Democracy. A Cold War with the Soviet Union kept alive the spirit of unity and sacrifice Americans felt in facing a common foe.

Six decades later, much has changed.

Detroit's wheels fell off, and this Workers' Paradise of organized labor and ever-bigger government is now bankrupt and in ruins....a disaster largely caused by the same entitlement state socialist economics Progressives today keep trying to impose on the rest of America.

The Soviet Union was brought down by its internal contradictions and the failures of its own socialist economics. The Cold War is now in history's rear view mirror.

One scholar has argued that history "ended" with the permanent triumph of Western liberal democracy and free enterprise – basically capitalism with a Welfare State attached...yet which today seems to be mutating into a Welfare State with an increasingly-overtaxed Capitalist economy attached. [3]

In American private industry, scarcely more than 6 percent of blue collar workers are now union members, but more than 30 percent of white collar government workers now belong to unions.

Yet today, when public employees are given a chance to leave without penalty, a third or more are quitting unions in the very centers of the Progressive movement such as Wisconsin. Even here, a Great Withdrawal from the Left is underway.

It is no wonder that Progressive politicians are almost desperate to cut off the paths of escape for the people they tax, fleece and control.

At their peak during the 20th Century, the various akin collectivist movements – Communism, Naziism (a contraction of the German words for National Socialism), fascism, Marxism, Maoism, Fidelismo, Chavismo, socialism, the Third Way, liberal welfare statism, European Social Democracy or Progressivism – became, for millions of people, pseudo-religious cult substitutes for their lost Judeo-Christian faith.

All are now recognized by their de-hypnotized former acolytes as false gods that failed, as dead ends on the washed out road to a mirage that once looked like utopia.

The Progressive collectivist vision today is dying, and its death will cause huge changes in our world.

Today, rival groups – from Islamist terrorists to leftist ideologues – are fighting to take control of humankind's future through a power struggle whose outcome could bring either a new Dark Age or a new Golden Age.

Listen carefully and you can hear the collectivist cults' long, withdrawing roar as their high tide ebbs and people around the world lose faith in them.

The various collectivisms may still pose a military, political or economic threat as their power wanes – but fewer and fewer people take the Left seriously as an ideology anymore. History has thoroughly discredited the Left as both a moral and practical failure.

"By year 2050 there will be only two True Believer Marxists left on planet Earth," said international economist Sir Peter Bauer, "and they will be two nuns in Brazil."

The trouble is, many have likewise lost faith in the values that once made the West great – Judeo-Christian values and belief, free enterprise and the individual rights of the Enlightenment.

A century of collectivist dominance failed to create utopia – but the Great Debasement it created has undermined our moral foundations, work ethic, science, self-confidence, economy and the U.S. Dollar.

A century of Progressivism has done to the United States what British opium in the 1800s did to China – turn millions of citizens into addicts. Millions of Americans have become hooked, dependent on the entitlement state and on paper money conjured out of thin air.

America has lived for most of a century in a false economy, a hallucination conjured by this easy-money drug that gave Progressives a way to rule the United States as their own version of Aldous Huxley's Brave New World.

Brain scientists are now beginning to understand just how such mind manipulation works, and how powerfully it bypasses the rational mind to turn us into, in Tocqueville's words, "a herd of timid and industrious animals of which government is the shepherd."

We now must face the Great Withdrawal from the addiction of Progressivism and the illusory world and economy it has conjured. Detoxing from its poison could be as painful and difficult as quitting heroin cold turkey.

In the process, we will discover just how much Progressivism has warped our brains, distorted our sense of reality and impaired our rational thought and moral fiber.

The lesson Detroit teaches is that we should never depend on government alone for our healthcare, our retirement, our well-being or our safety. Detroit shows that you and your family should instead secure resources in the hands of someone you can always depend on – you.

This book in your hands is such a resource – a guide to show you and your family ways to recognize reality, survive, thrive and help restore America and its honest values amid the turbulence now descending.

We recommend that you buckle up before turning the page.

Craig R. Smith

PART ONE
Progressivism's Rise and Fall

Chapter One
Welcome to Debtroit: Where the Progressive Road Leads

"To achieve this level of devastation,
you usually have to be invaded by a foreign power....
To any American time-transported from
the mid-20th Century...were he to compare
photographs of today's Hiroshima with today's Detroit,
he would assume Japan won the Second World War
after nuking Michigan."

– Mark Steyn
Columnist & author [1]

While headed downhill on the 100th year of our drive to Progressive utopia, Americans in Summer 2013 came face to face with the burnt-out remnant of a city.

Some saw it as a warning sign, a crystal ball glimpse of what our nation's fate might be if we continue down this Statist road. A few remembered this once-proud place – and how, many decades ago, it expanded the American Dream.

The French explorer Antoine de La Mothe, sieur de Cadillac, three centuries ago here established Fort Ponchartrain, a trading post on the river strait – *le detroit* – that boats could travel between the Great Lakes Huron and Erie. This place would become a key transit point to America's West and its vast resources, a hub of trade and industry.

By 1960, the city now called Detroit had the highest average household income of all large cities in the United States. In only seven years, however, it would be sliding into dire straits and begin a steep decline and fall.

By 1964, President Lyndon Johnson's Great Society and urban renewal programs began expanding dependence on social welfare programs in Detroit, dramatically increasing the number riding for free in the wagon that working taxpayers were required to pull.

On top of these entitlements for the poor came ever-growing union wages and benefits.

What people should always remember is TANSTAAFL, science fiction writer Robert Heinlein's acronym for "There Ain't No Such Thing As A Free Lunch." You might go to a party where they are giving away ham sandwiches, but somebody paid for growing the wheat and making bread, raising the pig, and turning those products into finished sandwiches.

Who paid for the "free" welfare and rising worker wages in Detroit? Taxpayers across America, then as now, get stuck with the bill for welfare. Buyers of cars from the Big Three Michigan automakers pay the union wages and benefits via much higher car prices...prices that by the 1960s were making Detroit's cars less competitive.

On July 19, 2013, Detroit, Michigan became the largest American city ever to file for Chapter 9 bankruptcy, seeking protection from nearly $20 Billion in debt run up by nearly five decades of mismanagement, corruption and one-party Progressive political rule.

Fundamentally Transformed

"If Barack Obama had a city, it would be Detroit" has become one of the Internet's most widespread pearls of wisdom.

What once was America's fourth largest city – the Arsenal of Democracy that manufactured nearly 75 percent of our winning tanks and other large weapons during World War II, the Motor City, the throb of Motown, the pinnacle of industry whose automobiles were a global symbol of American success and power, the Silicon Valley of its era where engineers and designers dreamed of working – had by 2013 become a war zone of urban strife, poverty, decay and government profligacy known as "Debtroit."

Five decades of Obama-style Progressivism have "fundamentally transformed" this former city of dreams and prosperity into an urban nightmare, and in a Great Withdrawal more than a million of its residents have fled.

People continue to flee from there, even after President Obama, as he likes to say, "saved" General Motors and Chrysler with bailouts that cost taxpayers at least $25 Billion that will never be paid back. At least a billion of these tax dollars went to improve GM facilities in Brazil, and at least $500 Million went to GM facilities in Mexico. These dollars have fled Michigan, too.

Detroit is broke. On the day it declared bankruptcy, the city owed more than 100,000 creditors a total of more than $18.5 Billion. Its debt is equivalent to more than $25,000 from every city resident, half the per capita U.S. debt. The 2010 American Community Survey reported that the median household income in Detroit was $25,787.

Yet Detroit was once one of the world's most prosperous meccas for manufacturing. In 1950 it was home to 296,000 good-paying jobs. Henry Ford once had to recruit as far abroad as Iraq and Syria to find enough workers to assemble his cars. Ford imported the ancestors of today's sizable Michigan Arab-American population.

By 2011, only 27,000 manufacturing jobs remained in a Detroit whose population has declined since 1950 from nearly 2 million to only 701,000 in 2013.

As Detroit's population shrank, its Progressive government clung tenaciously to its size, spending, privileges and power. As a result, the biggest remaining employer by far in today's Detroit *is* the government, which has nearly 15,000 well-compensated employees – and nearly 30,000 government retirees to support with pensions and premium health care.

The city encompasses 139 square miles – bigger in geographic area than

San Francisco, Boston and Manhattan combined – yet almost a third of this land is now sparsely populated, in some areas with no more than one or two families per square block.

In some abandoned neighborhoods, weeds and vines have overgrown whole derelict houses stripped of their valuable copper wiring and water pipes by looters. The scene is like those cable shows that depict a future without humans as nature reclaims and destroys the structures we left behind.

Packs of feral dogs roam deserted Detroit streets, looking for something to chase down and devour. In one corner of the city, residents reported seeing a stalking cat more than four feet long. The wild is replacing civilization.

Detroit now has 77,000 abandoned or empty homes and at least 66,000 vacant lots, including many where homes once stood. Detroit firefighters must decide which of 32 blazes a day – nearly 12,000 each year – they will attempt to put out. Many fires are abandoned homes torched to destroy evidence of illegal occupants or crimes...or just for the hell of it to light up neighborhoods where 40 percent of the streetlights are now dark at night. [2]

Depending on Government

Need an ambulance? More than a third of those owned by the city are broken, and some of those still in service have more than 250,000 miles of wear on them.

As the *New York Times* reported, Detroit has become the one American city where many think it a waste of time to call 9-11 in an emergency. [3] The 9-11 service reportedly has been out of order for up to 15 hours at a time.

Progressives take pride in government healthcare. In today's stress-filled, on-life-support Detroit, however, the death rate from heart attacks is reportedly close to 100 percent among those who depend on the city's ambulances to get them to a hospital. Many residents, if sick or injured, now try to drive themselves to the nearest hospital. [4]

You might also urgently need an ambulance because Detroit's violent crime rate is nearly the highest in the United States. Its murder rate is 11 times that of New York City.

If you call the police for help, however, expect to wait 58 minutes for their arrival – 47 minutes longer than the national average. Less than nine percent of crimes get solved here, so for most lawbreakers crime pays.... and law-abiding citizens live in fear.

In 2012 the Detroit Police Officers Association, whose membership has fallen over the years by 61 percent from budget cutbacks, handed out a flier warning: "Enter Detroit at your own risk."

A sense of what the ruins of the Motor City are like today comes from journalist Megan McArdle's account – almost like a scene from a zombie horror movie – of getting lost in Detroit:

"It was getting dark, and I had no idea where I was or where I was going. I kept driving, figuring that eventually I'd reach either the city limits or downtown. I stopped to get gas and an elderly gentleman stared at me. 'Little girl, you do not belong here,' he said....

"Shortly thereafter, a cop pulled up next to me while I was waiting at a light, and rolled down his window.

"'Are you lost?' he said. I affirmed that I was. He asked me where I was staying.

"'Make a U-turn,' he directed me. Item: There was a no U-turn sign, somewhat tattered, directly in front of me.

"'Start driving,' said the cop. 'Don't stop at the lights until you get to downtown'....When cops start telling you to break the law, you get a little nervous." [5]

Downtown Detroit is one of the city's enclaves of relative safety. One reason: "Downtown businesses are being asked to pay for their own security patrols," reports *Time* Magazine's Rana Foroohar, "since so many police have been laid off." [6]

These remaining Detroit businesses, which according to analyst Chris Edwards of the Cato Institute are already gouged by some of the heaviest taxes in the United States, are thus expected to pay twice for a basic service the liberal government has failed to provide so it can spend tax dollars on itself. [7] This is our Progressive future.

Detroit's Great Withdrawal

A century ago migrants flocked to the burgeoning prosperity and progress of Detroit.

African-Americans by tens of thousands left the segregated South for Michigan, where pioneering civil rights activist Sojourner Truth had settled, expecting in Detroit to find jobs and dignity.

What many blacks found instead was a Detroit police force recruited in significant part from former Southern lawmen, and a city policy that pushed them into crowded, segregated neighborhoods.

In the summer of 1967, the city exploded in five days of black riots.

Forty-three people died – 33 of them African-Americans.

At least 467 were injured, including 167 Detroit police, 83 firefighters, and 17 of the National Guard troops sent by Governor George W. Romney and President Lyndon B. Johnson. More than 7,200 people were arrested.

During the riots 2,509 stores were looted or burned. The rioting damaged 412 buildings so badly that they had to be demolished. Estimates of the cost of this destruction were as high as a then-stunning $80 Million.

In "Black Day in July," Canadian songwriter Gordon Lightfoot in 1970 sang that "Motor City madness has touched the countryside...the doors are quickly bolted and the children locked inside" and "the shapes of gutted buildings strike terror to the heart."

In "Panic in Detroit," David Bowie sang in 1973 of an armed man who "looked a lot like Che Guevara."

Literally thousands of small businesses closed or moved within months of the riots.

"Before the ghetto riot of 1967, Detroit's black population had the highest rate of home ownership of any black urban population in the country, and their unemployment rate was just 3.4 percent," wrote economist Thomas Sowell.

"It was not despair that fueled the riot. It was the riot which marked the beginning of the decline of Detroit to its current state of despair," wrote Sowell in 2011. "Detroit's population today is only half of what it once was, and its most productive people have been the ones who fled." [8]

A Great Withdrawal of tens of thousands of people per year, year after year, began moving out of Detroit to the suburbs and beyond.

In that era of civil rights, integration and New Left radicalization, Progressives labeled this as "White Flight," even though much of the African-American middle class was fleeing urban Detroit, too.

This exodus, white and black, was a brain drain of those with the most skills, the ones who had paid Detroit's rising taxes. This outflow drained the lifeblood needed for any hope of economic growth.

Power Shift

After the 1967 riots, the "makers" of all races began to flee Detroit, while the "takers" stayed, increasingly addicted to free government goodies.

"In 1950, Detroit was 82% white," wrote Edward Helmore of the United Kingdom's left-liberal newspaper *The Observer* in 2013. "The 'white flight' after the 1967 race riots flipped the ratio – it's now 82% black." [9]

These changes produced a power shift in Detroit, which since 1967 has been totally dominated by one political party: the Democratic Party and its union and left-activist comrades.

In 1974, Detroit's first African-American Mayor, Coleman Young, came to power. He would remain Mayor for 20 years and fundamentally transform the city.

Young's extreme political views did not come from the civil rights movement, nor were Young's the gentle, non-violent tactics of liberal Republican Reverend Martin Luther King. Oh, had you not been taught that Martin Luther King, Jr., was a Republican?

Young had been a radical labor activist shaped by the far-left 1948 Progressive Party that nominated former Vice President Henry Wallace on a platform that condemned the United States and praised the Soviet Union.

(We analyzed this extreme left faction of the Progressive movement in our 2012 book *The Great Debasement*. This extreme faction lost in 1948, yet from the 1960s to today has gradually become a major force inside the national Democratic Party and has purged most moderate Democrats from the party.) [10]

Young's politics were also shaped by the confrontation tactics of community organizers and radical union activists, who were not pacifists.

Like many politicians, Young was quick to solidify his own political machine by using highly partisan divide-and-conquer rhetoric and tactics of racial polarization and class warfare.

These made it easy for Mayor Young not only to mobilize black supporters, but also to distract voters from his own mismanagement by blaming every problem on "white people" for taking needed tax revenues and other resources out of Detroit when they fled.

President Obama practices very similar politics of polarization and division today, as he did in the Trayvon Martin case and in many other instances. Such demagoguery mobilizes immediate support in Progressive communities, but it sets back racial reconciliation and harmony. Historians might conclude that Mr. Obama has set back race relations in America more than any President since Democrat Woodrow Wilson a century ago re-segregated the U.S. Civil Service that Republicans had integrated.

Historically, racial divide-and-conquer politics have been used by the Democratic Party since its days as the party of the slaveowners, the Ku Klux Klan, Jim Crow and Bull Connor. The particular races favored by Democrats may have changed, but not the Democrats' tactic of pitting Americans against each other by race, fomenting hatred and social Balkanization for their own partisan gain.

Progressives Raze Poletown

Mayor Young – who like Mr. Obama was a former State Senator – also practiced the pragmatic politics and power-brokering of crony capitalism. He was willing to destroy the homes of thousands of people when General Motors wanted their land to build a new factory. [11]

In 1981 Young fully supported the use of government's new "quick taking" eminent domain power and police to throw 4,200 mostly Polish-American longtime residents out of their homes and drag them from their Catholic Church in a neighborhood known as Poletown on the Detroit-Hamtramck border.

Young authorized the razing of 1,500 homes, 144 businesses, 16 churches, a school and a hospital. When some residents refused to leave their homes, Young cut them off from city services and police protection, leaving fearful Polish-Americans to face what filmmaker George Corsetti described as "a jumble of looters and demolition crews during the day and arsonists and fire trucks by night."

"The night air was always smoke-filled and people slept with guns nearby," wrote Cosetti, describing what could be parts of Progressive-controlled Detroit today. [12]

This was one of the first and most shameful uses of the Constitution's Fifth Amendment eminent domain power not to build a public road or courthouse that everyone could use, as America's Founders intended, but merely to transfer property from one private owner to another who had more political favor or clout.

Mayor Young used this power to seize the property of 4,200 industrious, mostly-middle class people so that General Motors could build a new private factory to manufacture Cadillacs, Oldsmobiles and Buicks for upper-middle class buyers.

Young soon used this imperious power to raze another neighborhood for a Chrysler factory – although he did not bulldoze its neighborhood Greek Orthodox Church as he had Poletown's Catholic Church.

Progressives, as we shall see in this book, are collectivists who have little respect for private property or individuals. Most intend to use eminent domain to enrich their crony capitalist allies so long as, by doing this, they can always expand the tax revenues and power of the government.

As New York University legal scholar Richard Epstein explores in his book *Takings*, the government confiscating someone's home in order to give it to another is, in principle, no different from taxing one person so that what they have earned can be redistributed to someone else whom Progressive politicians deem more deserving.

Both violate the Constitution's Fifth Amendment takings power, writes Epstein, unless fair compensation is given. As Professor Epstein sees this, if the government taxes you $1,000 and then gives this to individual welfare recipients, it ought to give you just compensation of $1,000 for the taking of your money. The government, of course, does not do this.

Today nearly two-thirds of every tax dollar you now pay to Washington, D.C., goes not for public roads or national defense or paying down the national debt or for the general well-being of the country, but for such "transfer payments." In other words, the primary activity of our Federal Government is now wealth redistribution. [13]

General Motors has doubtless paid more in taxes to Detroit than did the 4,200 Polish-Americans whose homes Mayor Young used eminent domain power to confiscate and destroy. GM did not, however, provide as many jobs as promised, nor, after the tax abatements Young gave GM, as much local tax revenue as expected.

Also, we should never forget that taxes on GM, like those on other companies, are passed on to their customers in higher prices. Ultimately the taxes on GM are paid not by the corporation but by the buyers of its cars.

According to journalist Ze'ev Chafets, Mayor Young expressed a desire to make Detroit a "black city." Other cities have had political machines that favored Irish-Americans and other groups, Young told Chafets, and now in Detroit it was Black Americans' "turn" to have a machine that favored them.

Mayor Young saw to it that big money projects needing government permits and approvals went through his office, according to Chafets. GM's Poletown proposal did, along with GM's concern that without the well-located building site it wanted, the auto giant might have to build its new factory outside Detroit and the reach of city tax collectors.

Was anti-white racism another of the reasons Mayor Young was willing to throw thousands of Polish-Americans out of their homes? [14]

Mayor Young for 20 years would continue to blame white flight for Detroit's problems. He may have forgotten that he evicted thousands of Caucasians, many of them elderly, who never wanted to leave their small homes and neighborhood.

In 2013 the Great Withdrawal from Detroit continued. On average, 300 residents depart every day. Hundreds of others leave the city's cemeteries each year, exhumed by loved ones who want to re-bury family members away from Progressive Detroit.

Today in Hamtramck you will find fewer Polish-Americans. Five times each day, however, you can hear the Muslim call to prayer where church bells used to chime. Mr. Obama, remembering his childhood attending mosque in Islamic Indonesia, has said he thinks the Muslim evening call to prayer is "the most beautiful sound in the world."

"Nixon Shock" Hits Detroit

One of the greatest failings of Detroit's leaders, say economists, has been that their crony relationship with the automobile industry made them too slow to diversify Detroit's sources of revenue. They failed to see how vulnerable such dependence can make a one-industry company town.

Pittsburgh, another industrial rust belt city, diversified into a variety of other businesses such as medical technology and is now thriving. Detroit was not this far-sighted.

In 1971 President Richard Nixon suddenly, by Executive Order, severed the last anchor tying the U.S. Dollar to gold. He closed the window through which European central banks could exchange their paper dollars for gold, the last vestige of America's past gold standard.

When President Nixon did this, the value of the U.S. Dollar immediately began to fall. Muslim oil producers from Indonesia to Iraq were furious, because the dollar was the global reserve currency with which their oil was purchased by all countries. They demanded more of the less-valuable paper dollars per barrel to preserve the exchange value of their oil. [15]

Detroit took a huge hit as oil and gasoline prices shot up because, unlike Japanese and European automobiles, American cars in the pre-1971 world of 25 cents per gallon gasoline had been designed for style, comfort and power, not good gas mileage.

A Ford, Not a Lincoln

President Nixon severed the dollar from gold and thereby sank the dollar's purchasing power by one-third almost overnight. His successor, Michigan-raised Gerald Ford, is remembered for two things – his Whip Inflation Now "WIN" buttons, and his "automotivated" expression "I'm a Ford, not a Lincoln."

Gerald Ford ought to be remembered instead as the President who killed the American Dream.

President Ford imposed the 55 mile per hour speed limit – not to save lives, but to save gasoline.

An earlier Republican, President Dwight Eisenhower, had championed the national highway system. His Secretary of Defense had been the President of GM, "Engine Charlie" Wilson, who told Congress: "What's good for America is good for General Motors, and vice versa."

Thanks to Ike, America was now crisscrossed with magnificent highways and freeways easily capable of being driven at 70 miles per hour or faster. American cars with their 300 and 400 cubic inch motors could cruise almost effortlessly at 80 or 90 miles per hour.

The End of Freedom Road

However, only two decades later, President Ford declared that this grand symbol of American freedom would now be chained. The new asphalt frontier would be fenced in. The Shelby Cobra that could go from zero to 60 in 4.3 seconds was no longer to be viewed with pride but as a gas-guzzler.

With our big Detroit wheels that could scarcely be held down to 55 miles per hour, a young America was now told to take its foot off the accelerator and apply the brake. That was the day the music died.

In 2013 we all know what is coming in the near future: transponders and surveillance black boxes will be required in every car. Coming, too, is the surprise of opening the mail to find automated speeding tickets not only from red-light cameras, but also because government computers detected you going three miles per hour over the limit between two robot monitors along your route.

In that same mail might come your monthly bill, as is done today in Singapore, showing which roadways you were on at what hours in the government computers....thereby turning every former "free way" into a *de facto* toll road.

By 2040 your car may be able to drive itself, synchronized and guided by government computers, and can be turned off remotely if you attempt to drive away from police or to forbidden places. (The chips to do this, and to limit your top speed, reportedly began being installed in new car electronics as long ago as 1987.) Europe in Summer 2013 announced that it will soon require chips that prevent drivers from exceeding the posted speed limit. Bye-bye, speed-unlimited autobahn.

Surely you were not fooled into thinking that Progressive-ruled government would let you retain the old, cherished American freedom to drive, were you? Surely you understand why President Barack Obama has used every power at his disposal to prevent gasoline from becoming cheap again...lest a return to the freedom of driving reawaken memories and feelings of the old American spirit.

Part of the coerced Progressive transformation of free Americans into unfree "Euro-peons" is that your car soon may be controlled by government computers, and every road of your life will be the Road to Serfdom.

Remember

Do you remember an older, freer America where the car was a cherished member of the family? We went on weekend drives just to feel the freedom of the road...and in ourselves.

Remember when the car was the first place adolescents could be themselves in a space of their own? This was where most of us learned responsibility, and that negligence has consequences...when you forgot to fill the gas tank, or check water in the radiator.

At the gas station attendants would rush to wash your windshield, check fluids under the hood, and give you a set of elegant drinking glasses – just to keep your business at 25 cents a gallon.

America back then was a nation of backyard mechanics who took pride in working on and upgrading their cars. Today computer diagnostics, controls and air pollution requirements have made this impossible for most of us. The cars today are mechanically better and more reliable. Most of today's cars are good, but few are great or excite passion as cars once did. No wonder great collectors cherish the finest old ones. We now must depend on others to keep today's cars running.

Once upon a time, a subtle part of most Americans' identity and social status was their choice of car. People thought of themselves as Ford or Chevy or Oldsmobile families, and many bought a new model every two years or so.

> Don't you gimme no Buick.
> Son you must take my word
> If there's a God in heaven
> He's got a silver Thunderbird....

Thus sang Marc Cohn in "Silver Thunderbird," his tribute to that moment in an America now disappearing in history's rear-view mirror.

> You can keep your Eldorado
> And the foreign car's absurd
> Me, I wanna go down
> In a Silver Thunderbird....

In the 1973 George Lucas film "American Graffiti," inspired by his Modesto adolescence in California's drag-racing rural central valley, the blonde dream girl cruises Saturday night streets in a sporty Thunderbird, always unattainable and just beyond the boys' reach.

(Ford would dramatically upsize their original tiny sports car so that now-married men with thickening waistlines could still fit into this image of their youth while singing with the Beach Boys of "fun, fun, fun...until Daddy takes her T-bird away.")

The America where our cars embodied style and beauty was changing. If the first imperative was now gas mileage, then cars had to become light and aerodynamic to minimize air resistance. Physics, not artistry, would be the prime shaper of cars from then on – and the rules of physics are the same for everybody. Cars that used to look very different soon began to look alike...and when all cars look alike, one brand looks pretty much like all the others.

American consumers suddenly began looking for cars that delivered more miles per gallon. Lifelong fans of Fords and Chevys were test-driving Toyotas and Volkswagens that were better built and more reliable than many models from Detroit.

Customers were told: "Never buy a car made on Monday" by workers still hung over from weekend drinking and too secure in their union jobs to care how carefully they worked.

American auto makers were slow to improve their technology and quality, and began to lose market share.

A popular term of that era was "built-in obsolescence," the widely-held notion that companies such as General Motors were deliberately making their cars to break down or rust out faster, so that customers would have to pay sooner for repairs or a new car.

The idea of built-in obsolescence was a libelous insult to both makers and buyers, because it implied that short-sighted companies were deliberately making inferior products to pick the pockets of gullible, captive customers.

What made this insulting term at least a tiny bit plausible, however, is that for a golden decade or so after World War II, nearly 99 percent of the cars on America's roads and new Interstate Highway System were made by America's auto companies. Millions of families were voluntary hostages to their favorite American car brand and would not consider foreign competitors.

(From 1954 to 1987, these included American Motors, headed for a time by George Romney, and its proud brands such as the Rambler, Pacer and Gremlin. Lee Iacocca's Chrysler bought AMC from Renault in 1987 to obtain its Jeep brand.)

And because of the cost pressures of high union wages and benefits, the Big Three for a time maintained profitability by putting less value into some models of their automobiles. In a land where backyard mechanics still worked on their cars, this deterioration in quality was soon widely noticed.

The pride Americans had taken in their cars began to slip, and "Made In USA" on cars from around Detroit began to be seen no longer as a boast but as a warning label. Being branded a Chevy or Ford family began to make people feel like cattle herded by loyalty to companies that were no longer loyal to them.

Soon the Big Three car makers would fight back not only by improving their products, but also to cut costs by moving a sizable share of their manufacturing out of heavily-unionized Michigan. [16]

In fact, so many managers moved from Michigan to oversee this outsourcing that sunny El Paso, Texas acquired its own semi-pro ice hockey team to entertain homesick expat Detroiters who now lived in Texas but crossed the Rio Grande River into Juarez weekdays to supervise Mexican workers making American cars. Like many other proud American inventions, much of our car making has gone over the border to Mexico and Canada.

Spending the Future

How did Mayor Young and his Progressive successors spend Detroit's limited and shrinking tax resources? As one example, Young erected a statue downtown that honored famed Detroit native and world champion boxer Joe Louis, who became a national hero to both whites and blacks by beating German boxer Max Schmeling in 1938 as World War II approached.

This statue, however, does not include the world champion's face. It depicts only Louis' horizontally-extended arm and clenched naked – not boxing-gloved – fist, akin to what in that era was called the "black power salute." Mayor Young, said some critics, was using scarce taxpayer money to make a potentially polarizing ideological statement. [17]

Another investment by Detroit's Progressive government is described by Mark Steyn: "'The Howdy Doody Show' ended its run in 1960.... The city's Institute of Arts paid $300,000 for the original puppet – about the cost of 300,000 three-bedroom homes." [18]

Steyn's reference, strangely enough, contains a shocking grain of truth. Homes have been on the market in Detroit for $1, and many for as little as $500, yet they remain unbought. This is how much five decades of one-party Progressive rule have debased value and values in Detroit.

In our 2010 book *Crashing the Dollar*, we discussed how the vice president of quasi-governmental lender Fannie Mae was considering the deliberate destruction of thousands of homes as a way to reduce their supply and boost the market price of housing. His ideas sounded like federal farm programs begun during the New Deal that restricted or prohibited the planting of crops to prevent surpluses and thereby raise their market price in a world where many are starving.

The City of Detroit, we noted, was then preparing to bulldoze housing to increase the property values of remaining homes. And we continued with information that the press has never, to our knowledge, reported:

> *"Meanwhile, liberals find ways to feed the vultures of the Great Unraveling. During the crisis savvy contractors from around the country have been snapping up abandoned homes in Detroit for anywhere from $1 to $2,500. They then turn to the government and offer to rent these homes to the poor.*
>
> *"The government obliges, taking over responsibility for each home while paying the contractors at least $700 per month out of taxpayer money. In less than four months the contractor owns the property, owes virtually nothing in property taxes because of each house's low purchase price, and thereafter pockets at least $8,400 per year as pure gravy from houses bought for as little as $1.*

"It helps, of course, to be a favored government insider seeking such opportunities. But in cases like Detroit's, one new idea of entrepreneurship in America consists of finding and milking government programs at taxpayer expense.

"This is the brave new world that community organizers such as Barack Obama created, a bleak and bankrupt urban rustbelt wasteland in which the government-privileged few pick the pockets of the many working taxpayers." [19]

Perhaps this sweetheart deal for Progressive insiders has been replaced by others, because in 2013 even $1 Detroit homes no longer always sell.

Where Progressivism Leads

"Detroit is America's first Third World city," wrote Detroit-area native Chafets in his book *Devil's Night and Other True Tales of Detroit*, whose title refers to an orgy of mayhem and destruction that repeatedly erupted in Detroit on the night before Halloween. [20]

Detroit's strangely alien quality was featured in a 2011 SuperBowl ad by Chrysler, punctuated by the driving song "Lose Yourself" by Detroit rapper Eminem. The ad's theme was "Imported from Detroit," as if it were a foreign country.

Five decades of Progressive rule have warped politics in Detroit far to the left. A study by the nonpartisan Bay Area Center for Voting Research, which analyzes the leanings of every American city, ranked Detroit the *Most Liberal* city in America – more liberal than Berkeley or Oakland, California, or Washington, D.C.

"Detroit is perhaps the most striking example of a once thriving city ruined by years of liberal social policies," wrote economist Thomas Sowell. [21]

After nearly 100 years of labor organizer class warfare and 50 years of racial polarization, Detroit has been turned into a hostile and toxic environment for capitalist investors. These investors have left and taken their capital with them. Its remaining residents now look to government for jobs and handouts.

The worst victims of Progressive rule are its citizens.

Detroit's public schools annually spend approximately $14,000 per student, which enriches the powerful Detroit Federation of Teachers union.

"Yet little value is received in return" for Detroit imposing "the highest property tax on homes, the top commercial property tax and the second-highest industrial property tax," according to Cato Institute analyst Michael Tanner. Detroit's "per-capita tax burden is the highest in Michigan."

"In 2009, Detroit public-school students turned in the lowest scores ever recorded in the national math-proficiency test," wrote Tanner. "More than a third of students fail to graduate. In many ways, Detroit is a model of tax-and-spend liberalism." [22]

Detroit has also closed down two-thirds of its public parks, so children have both bad schools and few safe or pleasant places to play. Progressivism has turned Detroit into a place unfit for raising well-adjusted, success-oriented, ambitious and hard-working children.

Detroit's Welfare State, meanwhile, has effectively infantilized many of its residents in a culture of dependence on paternalistic government. By one estimate, 60 percent of Detroit's children are living in poverty. Less than half of Detroit residents over the age of 16 have jobs. An estimated 47 percent of the residents of Detroit are functionally illiterate. [23]

Welcome to the world Progressivism creates, a world that could be America's fast-approaching future.

Echoes of Excellence

Can Detroit be saved? Optimists point to a few small silver linings in today's dark clouds over the Motor City. Many believe that when you hit rock bottom, there is no place to go but up.

The chance to buy a home outright in Detroit for the cost of one month's rent in Manhattan is starting to attract young urban pioneers. Abandoned neighborhoods that today look like ghost towns might soon instead become a new Wild West frontier for brave opportunity seekers.

Bankruptcy might give Detroit a fresh start and a chance to pull out of its Progressive-induced economic death spiral – at least if voters stop re-electing the kinds of self-serving, demagogic politicians who caused this nightmare. If Progressives remain in power, however, then few will invest in Detroit's future. Why bail out a boat without fixing the holes in the bottom that keep sinking it?

Things are looking up for General Motors, which as of 2013 is selling more cars in China than in the United States. As we noted, with its fungible billions in Obama bailout money, GM has invested in new facilities – including $500 Million in Mexico and $1 Billion in Brazil....great news for unemployed American workers and gouged taxpayers. The Federal Reserve's near-zero interest rates also helped America's Big Three automakers invest lots more in car-making robots so that fewer human workers will be needed in the future. [24]

In June 2013 *Consumer Reports* for the first time in 20 years ranked an American car – the 2014 Chevrolet Impala – as the best sedan in its category. The magazine described it as among the highest-rated vehicles they have ever reviewed, adding that this new Impala model – based on the same platform as the Cadillac XTS – "is competitive with cars that cost $20,000 more." [25]

The Impala test-driven by *Consumer Reports* was not built in the United States – but on GM's Oshawa assembly line in Ontario, Canada. When in full production, however, it is scheduled also to be built for American consumers at the GM facility in Detroit-Hamtramck on confiscated land where Polish-Americans once lived.

With the average American car now between 11 and 13 years old, demand for new cars has been increasing. This, however, does not mean that Detroit can ever return to its glory days of prosperity based solely on the auto industry.

Michael Sivak of the University of Michigan's Transportation Research Institute in July 2013 released a study showing that Americans are now driving less.

"This is the first time we've ever seen a drop like this," said Sivak, who attributes the decline in driving not only to a low economy and high gas prices, but also to telecommuting, public transportation, urbanization and the nation demographically aging. Older people tend to drive less than younger people. [26]

The Volt Revolt

The quality of some American cars has improved greatly because ultimately companies that make things must respond to the discipline of consumers and the market – or die. This is vital – unless they, too, become crony capitalist dependents on government for money and favors.

In apparent cooperation with the Obama Administration's push for green energy technology, General Motors since 2009 has forged ahead with its mostly-electric vehicle the Chevy Volt, also assembled at its Detroit-Hamtramck facility.

This is clearly a car consumers do not yet – and might never – want. They have voted with their feet against it. Sales have been meager at best, despite huge federal subsidies, price discounts and dirt-cheap lease offers.

In 2012, Reuters did an analysis with experts and concluded that GM could be losing more than $49,000 on each Volt it sells. GM said that Reuters' number is too high, but acknowledged that it loses money on each Volt. Analysts have doubts that GM can ever recoup its costs, even if, as GM hopes, it can start to break even on the Volt by 2015. [27]

"The Volt is basically the Chevy Cruze with a big battery," says business radio host John Ransom. "That means a buyer can pay around $28,000 for the privilege of buying a car that goes 38 miles on a full battery charge and has all the amenities of a car that costs $5,000 less even after Volt discounts." [28]

GM says its Volt can go more than 300 miles when its small internal gasoline engine charges its battery. Relying heavily on that engine, however, reduces gas mileage below what a buyer could get from a conventional Honda Accord.

The Volt can be charged in a homeowner's garage for as little as $1.50 per day, or $547.50 per year, its promoters say. They seldom mention that its battery is expected to last approximately eight years, and then will need to be replaced at a cost of more than $8,000.

Is the Volt worth its high cost to green our world and clean our air? Ironically, an electric car might cause more pollution than a clean gasoline or natural gas vehicle, recent scientific research suggests. [29]

The electricity in a Volt owner's garage is not environmentally immaculate. That juice comes from a polluting power plant. And even more energy is required to produce and dispose of the Volt's battery and other parts.

However, instead of letting consumers decide such matters, the Federal Government, with its monopoly of force and ability to both print money and confiscate what it wishes, can ignore the will of the majority and impose policies and subsidies as politicians and their appointees wish. Crony capitalism is not free market capitalism.

Another example of Progressive foolishness was Mr. Obama's "Cash for Clunkers" program, which deceived people into junking their old cars without making clear that their cash incentive would be taxed. This program needlessly destroyed working cars, and disposed of them in a far more environmentally destructive way than free market recycling would have done.

The more power government has, the more risk we run that a handful of self-righteous leftist politicians will impose their often-wrongheaded biases on our nation's economic decisions and our lives.

For some, the biggest reason nowadays not to buy GM, Chrysler or Ford cars is that every dollar spent on them enriches the United Auto Workers, and, through this union's huge political contributions, the Democratic Party.

Dollars spent on Chrysler cars and trucks go not only to help elect Progressives, but also to enrich the foreign company that, thanks to President Obama, now owns Chrysler – the Italian automaker Fiat. This, apparently, is what Progressives mean when they speak of saving "American" companies.

The Great Withdrawal will see consumers increasingly redirect their purchasing dollars, their marketplace "green votes," away from politicians for whom they would never vote. Such politicians find it easy to tax and spend ever more money in ways a majority of Americans disapprove.

As of August 2013, polls found that only 35 percent of Americans supported President Obama's economic policies, a rating similar to President Herbert Hoover's after the start of the Great Depression. He is destroying the confidence needed to encourage investment in new jobs, or to expand businesses.

Breaking Free

Many across America will be watching with bated breath to see what happens in Detroit's bankruptcy. If the courts permit Detroit to escape its debt in either municipal bond obligations, or public employee retiree pension and health insurance costs, or both, then another "fundamental transformation" of our politics and economy could grow from this legal precedent.

Dozens of cash-strapped cities will rush to shake off contracts and bond obligations if the courts allow this.

President Obama's auto company bailout shoved aside secured bondholders and redistributed their rightful share to the United Auto Workers, a major contributor to Democratic campaign coffers. (Mr. Obama as of mid-2013 has also stuck America's taxpayers with a $25 Billion loss for this sweetheart gift to his UAW comrades.)

This created a terrifying legal precedent for investors. Bonds had been the backbone of investment in America. "Gentlemen prefer bonds," said financier Andrew Mellon. Bonds were sometimes called a "graveyard for a dying dollar" because they paid investors a low interest rate in exchange for an absolute guarantee that investors would never lose their principal.

President Obama, with one imperious gesture to benefit a huge campaign contributor union, destroyed faith in this centuries-old bond guarantee. As a result, today bonds are viewed as an investment with uncertain risk.

America's bond markets have been uneasy. In a move TrimTabs called "unprecedented," investors in June 2013 withdrew $80 Billion from bond funds. "The herd is scrambling for the exit," wrote TrimTabs CEO David Santschi about this bond-shaking great withdrawal. [32]

Mr. Obama has dangerously undermined what had been one of the most stable and secure cornerstones on which American investment stands.

What will happen amidst the larger economic shocks that soon could be coming?

This chilled the investment environment for bondholders, who were cheated by Mr. Obama's high-handed action and the threats he reportedly used to enforce his will. It also may have given Progressives in city governments the idea that they, too, could stiff bondholders. [30]

Kevyn Orr, the emergency manager of Detroit appointed by Michigan's governor, has followed the Obama precedent by indicating that Detroit might not honor its general obligation municipal bonds, which cities pledge to secure if necessary by increasing taxes. Such bonds traditionally have been thought of as almost entirely safe by investors.

If Detroit can get away with paying such bondholders only pennies on the dollar for their investment, then the future cost that Detroit and other cities must pay to raise revenue by selling bonds could increase dramatically.

Bond buyers weigh a bond's cost, predicated in interest rate, with the amount of risk they assume by buying it. Detroit has threatened to increase this risk, and hence the interest-rate cost, merely by talking about repaying bondholders less than their investment. The first mention of this possibility triggered an immediate $1.2 Billion "hemorrhage," as one expert described it, from muni bond funds. [31]

If Detroit prevails in shortchanging bondholders, this will make bonds more costly, as an alternative to immediate taxation, for potentially hundreds of cities. [33]

Who do Progressives think voluntary bond buyers are – involuntary, captive taxpayers who live only to be milked by our politicians? Do they understand the consequences if investors take their money elsewhere? Do they recognize that money can move instantly into foreign investments?

Americans have already paid a huge price for electing a Chief Executive who had never before worked as an executive anywhere, and a Commander-in-Chief with zero military command experience. God only knows what will happen if he faces an even larger crisis that requires a steady, skilled leader.

If Detroit likewise prevails in cutting promised pensions, and especially healthcare benefits, this also could hugely impact the cost and confidence workers have with their pensions nationwide.

"The bill for promises past is now so large for some cities and towns that it is crowding out money for the most basic of services – in the case of Detroit, it could not even afford to run its traffic lights," warned famed investment advisor Meredith Whitney.

Whitney sees "five more towns like Detroit in Michigan alone" and many more nationwide, where Detroit's aftershocks will be staggering. [34]

Sharply reducing pensions might even ignite street protests as have erupted in 2013 in Cyprus, elsewhere in Europe and in Brazil. If this happens, Detroit might soon acquire the nickname "Debt-riot."

Bailing Out a Sinking Ship

Detroit may look to Washington for help in the form of something like an auto bailout for this very Democratic city in a political swing state. The AFL-CIO in July 2013 called on President Obama to bail out Detroit.

Detroit has 47 different public employee unions, at least one of which reportedly has only one member. The Detroit Water & Sewer Department has a farrier (a horse-shoer) who receives $56,000 in pay and benefits every year, even though the city has no horses in this department to shoe.

Salaries and benefits for current employees eat up 36 percent of Detroit's revenue, and legacy obligations such as pension contributions and healthcare for retirees consume another 39 percent. This leaves only 25 percent of the government's revenues for everything else. [35]

"Detroit gave unions the keys to the city, and now nothing is left," writes *Forbes* columnist Kyle Smith.[36] We could also say that in Detroit's Progressive government everything is left....far left.

As Smith notes, the Detroit branch of the Service Employees International Union (SEIU) now requires that those who receive Medicare payments to care for aging and ill relatives or friends, pay union dues. Do you tend an aging parent? In Detroit, you and your family could be forced to pay dues to this radical, Obama-supporting public employees union.

In Detroit, SEIU has, with government complicity, greedily extracted more than $34 Million in coerced union dues from Medicare checks that were supposed to help those in need. Welcome to what Progressives mean by compassion, such as putting the Internal Revenue Service in control of Obamacare.

Michigan recently became a "right to work" state, to give its workers choice. However, we can expect Detroit's Progressive unions to tighten their death grip on workers until forced to let go.

When asked if Mr. Obama had indicated a bailout was coming, Detroit's current Mayor, basketball great David Bing, in late July 2013 replied: "Not yet."

Tin Cup

"The moment Detroit is bailed out, every other city will line up with its tin cup," opined syndicated *Washington Post* columnist Charles Krauthammer.

President Obama eventually will bail Detroit out, probably with already-allocated money from the immense emergency slush fund left over from the financial crisis of 2008-2009. This will never officially be called a bailout, however, said Krauthammer, and will channel money to Detroit's Progressive government "through sleight of hand." [37]

Sixty to 100 such cities, most with Democrat Mayors, have been running up expenses and obligations far in excess of city revenues...and many of these will ask to be bailed out if Mr. Obama finds leftover funds to rescue Detroit.

With control of Congress hanging on the 2014 elections, which of these cities can President Obama refuse? What political tradeoffs will Democrats face if they bail out corrupt or incompetent politicians with taxpayer money?

The Obama Administration already channeled most of its bailout spending to Democratic cities and states, and one likely purpose of Obamacare has been to get Progressive politicians and union bosses who recklessly underfunded their health plans off the hook. [38]

What will people think in prudent, honest states and towns who see their pockets picked to keep Progressive big city mayors and governors in power?

Many of the cities deep in debt have practiced questionable bookkeeping, as we now know Detroit did. By some expert estimates, the cost of bailing these cities out of their unfunded pension shortfalls alone, if accounted for honestly, is at least $1.4 Trillion and could be as much as $4.4 Trillion or more. [39]

Good for Gold

City pension and healthcare costs could sink many cities if unpaid...and risk voter removal of their Progressive leaders.

Yet on the other hand, it might plunge the entire U.S. economy into another Great Depression or Recession if Washington picks up a potential $7 Trillion tab for local and state Progressive corruption, profligacy and mismanagement.

The Federal Reserve is responsible for the value of our money. A sudden added $7 Trillion burden dumped on top of the current $2.9 Trillion Fed Balance Sheet of U.S. debt paper has the potential to bring down the economy and the U.S. Dollar.

Progressives now fear the possibility of a domino-like effect as one city's bankruptcy triggers another, which triggers others.

"We're going to see more Detroits, and eventually the government of the United States will be somewhat similar to Detroit, because people will give up their confidence in us," retired Texas Congressman Ron Paul told CNBC in July 2013.

"If 10 cities declare [bankruptcy] tomorrow and the Feds say 'Well, we've got to bail them out,' that could do great damage to the dollar," said Paul. Such bankruptcies will push the U.S. to print more and more money as it bails out these debts.

As a result, said Congressman Paul, "you're going to see gold go up. And, eventually, if we're not careful, it could go to infinity, because the dollar will collapse totally."

For gold owners, wrote CNBC reporter Alex Rosenberg, the Detroit bankruptcy might in that way look like "very good news indeed." [40]

The Progressive method of operation was, and is, that when the economy is good, they raise taxes and expand government. When the economic cycle turns negative, the politicians blame others, refuse to reduce government – and, increasingly, use the bad economy as a reason for expanding government and spending even more.

This ideology becomes a one-way ratchet by which everything is used to expand government, every expansion of government becomes permanent, dependency on government grows, and taxes must keep increasing to feed this ever-fattening parasitic beast that produces nothing.

"Detroit's ruling class is a parasite that has outgrown its host," writes Kevin Williamson, a journalist and the author of *The End Is Near and It's Going to Be Awesome*. [41]

Yet the politicians are self-deluded into thinking that their partisan redistribution of other peoples' earnings is the same as creating wealth. Politicians seem to think that they can get whatever they want from people – work or campaign contributions or votes – with ultimately-unkept promises of fat pensions, Cadillac health care and welfare benefits tomorrow and forever.

"It is illegal for a private corporation to do what Detroit did," writes John C. Goodman, President of the National Center for Policy Analysis. [42] The head of a private company could go to prison for what are now routine financial manipulations by government.

Recent Detroit city officeholders have gone to prison for corruption, including Mayor Kwame Kilpatrick and City Council member Monica Conyers, the wife of Democratic Congressman John Conyers, a member of the Progressive Caucus in the House of Representatives. No matter how corrupt their officials are, however, many who depend on government in Detroit and other cities will vote to re-elect the politicians who provide their welfare checks, government jobs or other benefits.

We must never forget where the polarized Welfare State crony politics of Progressives inevitably leads. In 2009 in Detroit, 65,000 people lined up for applications for a share of free federal stimulus money ostensibly to help the homeless or those facing foreclosure.

If equally divided, the $15.2 Million being offered would provide less than $219 per applicant, although the government's aim was to select approximately 3,500 people who would receive more. This was, in effect, a lottery in which at most only five percent of applicants would win.

Ken Rogulski, a reporter with WJR radio in Detroit, interviewed some of the people standing in line. The answers he got speak volumes:
Rogulski: "Why are you here?"

Woman #1: "To get some money."

Rogulski: "What kind of money?"

Woman #1: "Obama money."

Rogulski: "Where's it coming from?"

Woman #1: "Obama."

Rogulski: "And where did Obama get it?"

Woman #1: "I don't know, his stash. I don't know. (Laughter) I don't know where he got it from, but he's giving it to us, to help us."

Woman #2: "And we love him."

Woman #1: "We love him. That's why we voted for him!" [43]

If you had money to invest, would you risk it in a city like Detroit where the above interview reflects the prevailing mindset of the voting majority?

"You will find men who want to be carried on the shoulders of others, who think that the world owes them a living," said Henry Ford, one of the greatest pioneer builders of Michigan's auto industry. "They don't seem to see that we must all lift together and pull together."

The Perennial Progressive / Socialist Agenda

"The proletariat will use its political supremacy
to wrest, by degrees, all capital from the bourgeoisie,
to centralize all instruments of production
in the hands of the State....in the beginning,
this cannot be effected except by means
of despotic inroads on the rights of property....

1.
Abolition of property in land and application of
all rents of land to public purposes.

2.
A heavy progressive or graduated income tax.

3.
Abolition of all right of inheritance.

4.
Confiscation of the property of all emigrants and rebels.

5.
Centralization of credit in the hands of the State,
by means of a national bank with State capital
and an exclusive monopoly.

6.
Centralization of the means of communication
and transport in the hands of the State.

7.
Extension of factories and instruments of production
owned by the State; the bringing into cultivation of wastelands, and the
improvement of the soil generally in accordance with a common plan.

8.
Equal liability of all to labour. Establishment of
industrial armies, especially for agriculture.

9.
Combination of agriculture with manufacturing industries;
gradual abolition of the distinction between town and country,
by a more equable distribution of the population over the country.

10.
Free Education for all children in public schools.
Abolition of children's factory labour in its present form.
Combination of education with industrial production...."

– Karl Marx and Friedrich Engels
The Communist Manifesto, 1848. [44]

Chapter Two
Spinning Our Wheels in Quicksand

"It is well enough that people of the nation do not understand our banking and monetary system, for if they did, I believe there would be a revolution before tomorrow morning."

– Henry Ford

Detroit is the first major American city in the 21st Century to declare bankruptcy, but it almost certainly will not be the last.

More than 60 American cities have budgeting shortfalls, underfunded pensions and health care obligations, and other problems that, in varying degrees, resemble Detroit's. Chicago, Baltimore, Philadelphia, and even New York City are among those facing serious financial problems.

Detroit requested a financial bailout from both the state of Michigan and the Federal Government after receiving financial assistance from both.

The Federal Government in 2008 rushed to bail out major banking institutions on the theory that they were "too big to fail." The challenge posed by Detroit is whether any city this large can be allowed to fail.

The Chapter 9 bankruptcy of Detroit has raised serious questions among those who work for cities and depend on government pensions, as well as among those who provide financing to cities by buying municipal bonds. Such uncertainty had, as of August 2013, already raised the cost of bond financing for utilities in Puerto Rico – with more such problems to come.

The Progressives' reason to bail out one of their most iconic cities, a Detroit that in many ways fulfills the Progressive dream, is obvious. One risk from such a bailout, however, is that it creates a precedent that other Progressive cities may seek to follow.

Detroit's Domino Effect

Put simply, most Progressive cities are welfare city-states in which a large percentage of the population lives on government money, either as government dependents or government employees.

When Detroit declares bankruptcy and cannot cover its obligations, this makes it harder for other cities to borrow money via municipal bonds. Two or three such insolvencies could set off a domino effect, with each falling city bringing down the next weakest.

If Detroit is able to extract billions of dollars from Michigan and the Federal Government to cover pension shortfalls caused by local politician recklessness, then other cities might continue to behave recklessly in expectation that taxpayers elsewhere can be squeezed to bail them out.

In the private sector, companies and investors face "moral hazard," the risk that a mistake or misjudgment can cost a company everything it has. Such risk is what deters imprudence and profligacy.

In the public sector, however, Progressive politicians are playing with tax dollars taken by coercion from others. Their main risk is being voted out of office, but in a welfare city-state these tax dollars can be used to buy enough dependent votes to stay in power.

One-Party City-States

This is a major reason why most big cities are monolithic one-party governments, and why without the scrutiny of a viable two-party system their absolute power can lead to absolute corruption.

The ruling politicians here routinely spend taxpayer money to bail out their supporters, so we should not be surprised that liberal politicians expect Progressive comrades in state capitals or Washington, D.C., to bail them out, too.

How much might a bailout of the 60 or so most Progressive, profligate cities and states cost?

A precise number is difficult to determine, because many of these cities engaged in either wildly optimistic or cynically deceptive bookkeeping practices. The more deeply investigators look, the more reckless debt they usually find.

In 2012 the States Project, a joint analysis by Harvard's Institute of Politics and the University of Pennsylvania's Fels Institute of Government, calculated that if we add all the promises made to retired public employees and money borrowed without taxpayer approval to the $2.5 Trillion known obligations in bonds and debt security, the total real indebtedness of profligate state and local governments in America might be more than $7 Trillion. [1]

If taxpayers nationwide get stuck paying even a significant fraction of such local and state debt, this potentially could tip the entire United States economy into recession or worse. Such is the fatal sequence of Progressivism, the metastasizing of the entitlement and regulatory bureaucratic state.

Handoff Debts

The other domino effect comes from the expectation that debt can always be passed on to somebody else. Millions of citizens have been taught to be dependent on handouts from local politicians.

In part because of this dependence on the Welfare State, 27 percent of Americans have no savings at all, 46 percent have savings of less than $800, and 76 percent of Americans now live paycheck to paycheck.

This makes us a fragile society where a majority of citizens have almost no savings, no reserves to fall back on in a natural emergency, social breakdown, terrorist attack or other crisis.

This unwillingness of millions of people to provide even minimal reserves for themselves makes all the rest of us more vulnerable to social breakdown.

We have become a society, as Tocqueville foresaw, in which millions of infantilized government dependents look to the paternalistic Progressive local politicians to take care of them.

Those left-liberal politicians, in turn, are also welfare recipients who expect to be saved by a safety net of state funding.

Today, many cities, with begging cups in hand, turn to their state governments. Michigan has several cities in economic dire straits almost as bad as Detroit's, which may be only the first of many large dominoes to fall.

Michigan is home to many conservative towns and suburbs whose politicians have been thrifty and financially responsible, so why should their taxpayers be expected to bail out profligate Progressive communities such as Detroit and Flint?

As politicians advance their political careers from local to state government, their Progressive politics have come to dominate entire states such as California. The once-Golden State now spends far in excess of its tax revenues. This state's legislature long ago began looting the tax revenues of cities and counties. California's lawmakers have already driven the state deep into debt and obligation.

A domino effect of city bankruptcies could tip the entire state of California into insolvency. The state politicians have seemed unconcerned about this, apparently because they believe that the state's huge delegation of 53 representatives in Congress will have enough clout to force the Federal Government to bail out the entire state of California.

Chain of Dependency

The Progressive Welfare State, in other words, has made tens of millions of Americans dependent on government programs. It has made local liberal politicians dependent on state governments.

And in this chain of welfare, Progressives have also made state governments heavily dependent on handouts from Washington, D.C. A recent analysis by the Tax Foundation shows that more than 36 percent of Michigan's state government general revenue, and more than 32 percent of California's, are now federal aid. [2]

Alaska is the most independent such state, getting only 24 percent of its state government's general revenues from federal aid. Mississippi is the least independent, with 49 percent of its state general revenue coming from Washington, D.C. Such money, of course, almost always comes with puppet strings attached. [2]

If President Nixon had not closed the gold window in 1971, this casual pattern of money transfers would be impossible. As economist Alan Greenspan, later to chair the Federal Reserve, wrote in 1966:

"[T]he gold standard is incompatible with chronic deficit spending (the hallmark of the welfare state)....The welfare state is nothing more than a mechanism by which governments confiscate the wealth of the productive members of a society to support a wide variety of welfare schemes....

"Gold stands in the way of this insidious process. It stands as a protector of property rights," wrote Greenspan. "If one grasps this, one has no difficulty in understanding the statists' antagonism toward the gold standard." [3]

Redistribution of the Wealth

Progressives have poked fun at conservative states that get more each year in federal benefits than their taxpayers pay in federal taxes. They point out that several major liberal states send more dollars to Washington than they get back in benefits. [4]

The sophistry in this left-liberal argument is that federal assistance to any state may be mandated for spending in ways Progressives, not Conservatives, would approve. Little may go to help the people whose income was taxed away and sent off to Washington.

This costly round-trip money travel to Washington, D.C., and back has undermined the federalism that America's Framers designed to give the states and Federal Government their own spheres of power. Many states are now welfare wards of Washington, D.C., and can be punished with funding reductions or cutoffs if they balk at federal commands.

As we discussed in our 2011 book *The Inflation Deception*, each member of the County Board of Supervisors in San Diego, California, was elected by voters to represent their interests. Yet when it comes time to allocate taxpayer money, 95 cents of every dollar in this county's budget is earmarked, mandated, guidelined or otherwise directed as to where and how it must be spent by the Federal Government in Washington, D.C., or by the state government in Sacramento.

The people's locally-elected Supervisors have discretion over how to spend only five percent of the county's total budget. The decentralized federalism established by America's Framers is being replaced with ever-increasing centralized, bureaucratic control.

A century ago, Progressives crusaded against what they called business monopolies and concentrations of wealth. Today we can clearly see their real goal: to transfer all power and wealth to the biggest, greediest and most destructive monopoly of all, the Federal Government.

A Numbers Game

If our national economy is healthy and vibrant, the Federal Government might be able to bail out a number of cities and perhaps even one or two states. If our economy remains weak, on the other hand, we might not only be unable to bail out cities and states, but also be unable to avoid sliding into recession or depression as local and state governments begin a domino collapse.

So how healthy is the U.S. economy?

This is hard to assess for at least two reasons. The first is that our economy now rests entirely on "the full faith and credit of the United States Government."

We have a faith-based economy based on a faith-based dollar, not an economy grounded on anything tangible or solid as our money was before the Progressives took power in 1913. The value of the dollar itself changes, usually slowly but sometimes rapidly. It has no solid foundation of reliable fixed value, as it did under the pre-1913 gold standard.

If people here or abroad lose faith in our dollar, or lose the confidence to continue buying and selling because of uncertainty about our economy or government policies, the system could collapse overnight like a house of cards.

The second reason our economy is hard to evaluate is that 95 percent of the economic data we have about the United States Government comes *from* the United States Government.

We used to assume that all such data would be honest and objective, not politically manipulated or massaged for partisan or ideological reasons. Today this has changed. Official economic data coming out of the departments of the current Administration ought to be taken with at least a large grain of salt.

In August 2013, CNBC analyst Rick Santelli questioned whether government's changing ways of calculating inflation have become a way to "fudge the numbers."

"Listen, I don't believe the government's calculations. There, I said it," said Santelli. "I don't have better numbers; I have common sense."

"There's a difference," Santelli continued, "between real life and the government." [5]

Here is one example why. During the summer of 2013, politicians were looking with trepidation towards September when the Federal Government's official debt ceiling was expected to be reached.

Would a political fight over this or future debt ceilings lead to another government "shutdown," a brief publicized closure of a few government jobs that Progressives could use as symbols to extract maximum partisan advantage? Which side, the punditocracy pondered, would be hurt more if this happened?

Unless politicians could agree to raise that limit, all Federal Government borrowing, in theory, would have to cease when the ceiling was reached.

Off the Books

Then something strange happened. As Cybercast News Service reported, the national debt had been rising faster than expected and was within only $25 Million of hitting the debt ceiling when suddenly in May 2013 the official government debt numbers froze – and remained absolutely unchanged by even a penny for month after month after month.

Obviously the government continued to spend and run up debt of at least $3 Billion each day during these months. Yet somehow, mysteriously, like the sun standing still in the sky over Jericho, the official debt clock stopped moving so that government could continue to function prior to Congress' return from vacation.

If the government for reasons of political convenience or expediency is willing and able to manipulate a key economic statistic this important, can we rely on any official number concerning unemployment, income, or other factors?

Washington has another favorite way to do sleight of hand with debt, by using a method that might land private business owners in jail if they used it.

A huge portion of actual federal debt is simply kept off the books of the official budget and is seldom mentioned. These ultimate expenses that taxpayers must eventually pay include Treasury debt, housing-related commitments, student loan guarantees, backing for the Federal Deposit Insurance Corporation, debts to the Federal Reserve, various government trust funds, and long-term obligations to Social Security and Medicare.

Quicksand Trap

In 2013 Economics Professor James D. Hamilton of the University of California San Diego did an independent analysis of this (with advice from former Congressional Budget Office chief Douglas Holtz-Eakin and others).

Dr. Hamilton calculates that total Off-Balance-Sheet federal liabilities, as of 2012, added up to $70.1 Trillion.

This, he noted, is "6 times the size of the reported on-balance-sheet debt" of the United States Government. [6]

Add this to the almost $17 Trillion in immediate debt, and combined federal debt is already at least $87 Trillion, which Washington pays for at temporarily near-zero interest rates with annual total federal tax revenues of only about $2.5 Trillion.

The Federal Government is currently paying out in expenses, including benefits, more than it takes in as tax revenues. The $7 Trillion in debts run up by Progressive cities and states could be enough to break Uncle Sam's economy if taxpayers nationwide get stuck with it.

Who is Uncle Sam planning to stick with a debt 10 times bigger than this, with the bill for his $70.1 Trillion concealed debt? We already know the answer. This tab for the Progressives' orgy of wild spending and vote buying will almost certainly be passed on to you, your children and your grandchildren to pay.

Bottom line: the Federal Government is trapped so deep in its own $87 Trillion quicksand hole that it has little ability to bail anybody else out – except, of course, by agreeing to turn their debt into *our* debt.

The Stimulus That Failed

Our economy should appear robust and vibrant, if the theories of the late British economist John Maynard Keynes are accurate.

During the past five years our government and Federal Reserve have pumped more than $6.5 Trillion worth of stimulus money into the economy. This is the greatest dose of economic stimulus ever given to any economy at any time in human history. We are awash in liquidity and therefore, Keynes predicted, we should be swimming in prosperity.

The reality is quite different. After more than $6.5 Trillion of stimulus, our economy in the 2nd Quarter of 2013 was unofficially measured to be growing at an anemic 1.7 percent (later "adjusted" by foreign trade gimmickry to 2.5 percent). During the entire tenure of Progressive President Barack Obama, average annual Gross Domestic Product economic growth has averaged only 1 percent....and this is misleading, because 39 percent of GDP is actually federal, state and local government spending, not genuine productivity in the economy.

Yet even this low number may be too high. The reason is that it is calculated using another number called a "deflator" to offset the effect of inflation on growth. The official government position during these years has been that inflation is running at 2 percent or less.

The trouble is, when we look at the analysis of independent economists such as John Williams of ShadowStats – and when we look at the higher prices we pay for food at the supermarket or gasoline at the pump – it is obvious that real-world inflation is higher than 2 percent. ShadowStats has calculated, using the older pre-politicized, pre-gimmicks statistical methods, that real-world inflation in 2013 was running between 7 percent and 11 percent.

Inflation, of course, devours economic growth. This means that if government claims that we have 2.5 percent economic growth but is factoring in only 2 percent inflation in its deflator, then with real-world inflation of 7 percent to 11 percent, our actual economic growth falls to between *Minus* 2.5 percent and *Minus* 6.5 percent.

The Concealed Recession

If this is correct, then we have been in negative growth since President Obama took office in 2009. And negative growth for two consecutive Quarters is the definition of a recession.

Could it be that the United States never escaped from the 2008 Recession? This would be consistent with even official numbers that otherwise seem hard to explain.

Unemployment has remained stubbornly high for the past five years, with more than 20 million Americans unable to find needed full-time work. Nearly 40 percent of the unemployed are classed as long-term unemployed, people who have not found a job for six months or longer.

With many potential employers now saying they will not even look at the application of someone who does not currently have a job – and with long-term unemployment eroding job habits and skills, the prospects for the long-term unemployed to find full-time work are small.

Jobs are being produced, but roughly 77 percent of these are part-time or temporary jobs. In fact the second-largest private employer in the United States is now Kelly Services, a temp worker provider to other companies.

The Affordable Care Act popularly known as Obamacare is one reason for the decline of full-time and drastic increase in part-time jobs. This law requires employers with more than 50 employees working 30 hours or more per week to pay for employees' health insurance. This has given employers a huge incentive to replace full-time employees and to hire instead part-time employees to escape the Obamacare mandate.

Progressives idolized France with its 35 hour workweek and Welfare State. Mr. Obama is now rapidly transforming America to a 29.5 hour workweek, with government benefits compensating for low-paying, part-time jobs. Next stop: the zero-work lifestyle of free government goodies – and total dependence.

The Invisible Soup Line

During the Obama years, for every low-paid hamburger-flipper job, two people have signed up for SNAP, the Supplemental Nutrition Assistance Program still unofficially known by its original name, Food Stamps.

People logically ask where the soup lines are if we in fact are in a recession or depression. Such soup lines were certainly visible in large cities and small during the Great Depression of the 1930s.

Thanks to the Food Stamp program, today's soup line is invisible – yet it is the largest and longest in American history. Today's soup arrives as a benefit card in the mail. The people using such cards, if stood only two feet apart, would make a depression soup line more than 17,500 miles long, a line that would stretch more than 70 percent of the way around Planet Earth.

The Obama Administration authorized extensive advertising in both English and Spanish to recruit people to this government program, producing more than a 50 percent expansion in what critics say was designed to create dependency on government and the Progressive politicians who support such giveaways.

Food Stamps originated in an unholy alliance between Big City Progressive Democratic politicians and rural farm state Republicans. Both stood to benefit from this welfare program – urban Democrats from giving away food for free, and Republicans because this program justified juicy taxpayer subsidies for farmers, whether they own family farms or giant corporations.

Both parties eagerly supported Food Stamps for many decades. Only in 2013 did the Republican majority in the House of Representatives vote to cut this from the Farm Bill – which as critics said should have been called the "Food Stamp Bill" because more than 70 percent of the spending it authorized went not to farmers but to Food Stamps.

SNAP, now with 47.5 million enrollees, is only one of 15 subsidized food programs offered by the U.S. Department of Agriculture. One or more of these programs in fiscal year 2012 were used by 101 million Americans, nearly one-third of our nation's entire 316 million population, at a cost to taxpayers of $114 Billion.

The 101 million beneficiaries of these food programs, noted the Cybercast News Service, are more people than America's entire 97,180,000 full-time private sector 2012 workforce. [7]

ZeroHedge.com in April 2013 reported that the official government numbers of those counted as unemployed – more than 11 million – combined with those defined as "not in the work force" – nearly 90 million – added up to more than 101 million working-age Americans without a job. [8]

American Dreamers

Part of the American Dream has always been that children would grow up and become more successful than their parents. Today, however, 21.6 million young people between ages 18 and 30 live at home with their parents – the highest proportion of stay-at-home young Americans since World War II. [9]

Many fulfilled their family's dream by going to college, but in the process the average graduate has left carrying student loan debt of more than

$25,000. Traditionally, the goal of going to college was to improve one's prospects for getting a good job and earning a good living. However, nearly half of these recent college graduates have been unable to find work commensurate with the college degree they earned.

The 54 percent of recent graduates who did find such jobs now face a greater long-term prospect: they may spend the next 40 years or more looking up a promotion ladder at the backside of an older person above them who cannot afford to quit... and so works on and on past conventional retirement age.

The ladder to promotion for today's young college graduates may be more crowded and slower-moving than for any previous generation.

A 2013 survey by Wells Fargo found that one of every three recent graduates regretted going to college.

The Obama Administration eagerly took control of 90 percent of college loans, and then set about telling beneficiaries of the remaining 10 percent how to avoid paying their lenders.

Student loans now total more than $1 Trillion, a debt greater than everything now owed on credit cards in the United States.

The Federal Government is now more than $16 Trillion in immediate debt, yet somehow finds the wherewithal to become a lender of another $1 Trillion to students who have little or no credit history. The default rate on student loans is currently around 17 percent, with losses borne by the taxpayer.

A Progressive Trap

Researchers at Ohio State University recently found that approximately one in four college students – especially those from lower-income homes – felt an increase in self esteem from running up large credit card debt. This ability to run up huge debt, the students said, made them feel more important. [10]

The researchers did not say how many of these students planned a career in politics. A love of running up debt, at least with other peoples' money, is the prime qualification for a modern politician.

The researchers did find retrospectively that by the time these students turned 30, they no longer viewed indebtedness positively.

The Obama Administration has offered to cancel student loan debt for those who seek certain careers in the government or become employees, activists or community organizers for approved – which is to say, Politically Correct – nonprofit organizations.

Many of America's colleges and universities are bastions of Progressivism and the political Left. So consider how President Obama's student loan policies serve his ideology:

(1) By enabling unemployed people to attend college, Mr. Obama removes them from the unemployment rolls and thereby makes his economic policies appear more successful.

(2) By funding student loans, Mr. Obama funnels hundreds of billions of taxpayer dollars into institutions of higher learning that are home to America's Left and serve as its main indoctrination centers in Progressive ideology. (It is almost no longer a joke to say that when an American university boasts of having a diverse faculty, it means that its professors include a gay Marxist, a Latino Marxist, a transsexual Marxist, an African-American Marxist, a Lesbian Marxist, and even an occasional White male Marxist.)

(3) By providing student loans, Mr. Obama encourages dependency on, and a compliant attitude towards, Big Government. He sends a message that if you want to be able to afford college, kids, you had better not become a Republican or Tea Party activist. This will not look good on your college or student loan application. It may increase your chances for obtaining a student loan if you are associated with Progressives and Left-wing causes. President Obama's Progressive trap thus turns young people into the government's acolytes and indentured servants.

(4) By offering to cancel student loan debt – but only for those who turn their backs on Capitalism and instead go to work for government or the Left – Mr. Obama turns higher education into a recruiting tool to build an anti-free enterprise army of voters, shock troops and government dependents.

Every new government employee or beneficiary becomes a tax drain on private free enterprise – and tips the balance of power in America away from the free market and towards Big Government.

Uprooted

For the young college graduate who chooses not to work for government or a Politically Correct nonprofit, future prospects are challenging. High unemployment has suppressed wages. In fact, the longtime chairman of the Federal Reserve Board Ben Bernanke has said that elevated unemployment holds down wages and thus prevents inflation from getting out of hand.

Those carrying student loan debt of $25,000 or more may suffer from not only high payments but also a low credit score. If all they can find is temporary work, then their chances of getting the credit to buy a new car, and especially a home, will be slim.

As a result, the Millennial generation is buying fewer new cars and fewer homes than generations before them.

Homes are selling and prices are rising, according to government statistics, but this now comes from different sources than in the past – from older buyers and foreign investors who see America's depressed real estate market and low interest rates as an opportunity.

Corporations are also buying up homes cheaply to offer as rentals. In 2013, the investment fund Blackstone alone rushed to buy 16,000 homes from Miami to Phoenix for $2.5 Billion to manage as rentals.

This is part of what Bloomberg described as companies "seeking to transform a market dominated by small investors into a new institutional asset class that JPMorgan estimates could be worth as much as $1.5 Trillion." [10]

As many as two million homes might already be owned by private equity companies. CNBC reported that "housing is the new stock market." [11]

As of August 2013, 60 percent of home sales were reportedly for cash, not the usual means available to young first-time buyers.
The 20th Century American Dream of owning your own family home

with a white picket fence is rapidly disappearing.

In its place is the Progressive Obama-era American Dream of a rented apartment paid for, if you are lucky, by working more than one part-time job, without benefits, in a big city where even small paychecks may be hit with big taxes to buy off all the welfare voters who keep Progressives in power.

A Rare Tax Break

Congress in an earlier era was delighted to include a home mortgage-interest deduction in the income tax code. This was one of the few tax breaks available to ordinary Americans who had no fancy accountants or tax lawyers.

Today's politicians, eager for money to expand Big Government, now call this deduction an $85 Billion per year "tax expenditure" and talk among themselves about how wonderful repealing this tax break could be.

Progressives believe that all wealth should be expropriated and redistributed to their choice of who is "most deserving." They therefore hate giving tax breaks to anyone, especially those unequally rich enough to be able to buy a home.

Progressives ideologically dislike bankers even more than they hate most other Capitalists. This is why in the San Francisco Bay suburb of Richmond, the government is now preparing plans to use eminent domain power to take away the banks' lender mortgages in order to benefit homeowners who put their homes up as loan collateral. If this succeeds, it would set a precedent that might be used by politicians across the country – and which could then drive up the cost of getting future mortgages.

The Irrevocable Deduction

Outside of a few dozen congressional districts gerrymandered to ensure the perpetual re-election of Progressives, few politicians would dare to go before a crowd of home-owning voters in their districts and propose repealing the mortgage-interest deduction.

If this tax break were repealed, the immediate effect would be that far fewer people could afford to buy a home – and therefore home prices would fall.

(In the long run, ending this deduction would reduce homes to their true market value, without a special tax incentive, and this would produce a more realistic economy undistorted by politicians favoring one particular investment or industry.

This, arguably, would be healthier than what we have today, and a true free-market economy would salute it. People would diversify their savings into more investments and be safer, while spreading more of their money around the economy. However, the immediate effect of ending this deduction would probably be disadvantageous to those who bought their homes under today's value-distorting tax rules.)

This mortgage-interest deduction encouraged and enabled people to buy a home of their own, and to make their home their largest single investment by turning their nest into their nest egg. This made social sense because a community of homeowners tended to be a stable, rooted community.

Living In Your Piggy Bank

A man's home was his Castle, the saying went. This tax break helped working Americans achieve a sense of accomplishment and pride, knowing that they had bought a tangible, valuable investment in America – proof that dreams can come true here. It rewarded the work ethic.

Home ownership also had the advantage for the local tax collector of putting people's savings into an investment they could not easily pack up and carry away in one night. Property taxes became a stable and reliable cornerstone of local government revenue, based on an asset the government could easily seize or tax-lien if homeowners failed to pay their taxes on time.

A Baby Boom generation grew up thinking that the family home was an ideal form of savings and investment whose value always increased, and never decreased. During the decades following World War II, when America had become the most powerful and prosperous nation on Earth, this belief proved true, especially in golden places like California.

During the early 2000s, an investment bubble in housing sent home prices into the stratosphere. Millions were tempted to turn their astonishingly valued homes into piggy banks, as lenders offered home-equity loans not just on the homes' actual value but for 125 percent or more of the appraised value. Few Americans at the time understood that the Federal Government had been twisting the arms of bankers, using regulatory threats to persuade lenders to reduce their previous standards and requirements.

Liar Loans

Big government wanted home loan money to flow, especially to those who in the past would have been unqualified for mortgages. As we documented in our 2010 book *Crashing the Dollar*, banks felt compelled to make what they variously called "liar loans" – based only on the claimed, not verified, income of borrowers – or "Ninja" loans to customers with no income, no job and no assets.

Hundreds of billions of dollars in loans, to comply with political demands, were given to people who paid little or nothing down for homes and hence later felt they had nothing to lose by leaving when the bubble burst and their homes lost value.

Rather than pay an underwater mortgage for more than a home was now worth, millions walked away from their debt. This flooded the market with vacant homes and accelerated the plunge in home market prices, punishing those who honored their agreement and rewarding deadbeats who did not.

Many of these deadbeats, as we noted in *Crashing the Dollar*, understood that the Federal Government had for political reasons strong-armed banks into giving them mortgages regardless of their credit-worthiness – and would almost certainly do so again, as President Obama resumed doing in 2013.

Bankers anticipated the housing bubble going bust, and bundled their shaky mortgages and insured them with major companies such as AIG. The banks then sold these bundles to unsuspecting buyers in the U.S., Iceland, Norway and elsewhere around the world where American companies and real estate had been trusted. When the bubble burst, AIG, despite being one of the world's biggest insurance companies, had nowhere near enough money to cover the losses.

Bailouts for Bundlers

The Federal Government and Federal Reserve provided many hundreds of billions in liquidity to prop up major banks deemed "too big to fail," expecting that these banks would quickly resume lending.

The banks in most cases lent the money they received back to the Federal Government itself, risk free, in exchange for a small percent of interest on money that had cost the banks virtually nothing. After all, the government could always repay debt by printing new money.

However, between vague new government regulatory threats and their losses, the big banks for years greatly tightened their requirements for lending money to homeowners and small businesses. This tightening caused, and is still causing, a major economic contraction.

After the housing bubble burst and home prices plummeted – in some regions falling by half – average home-owning families lost 39 percent of their net worth. Generation X families lost even more, by some estimates as much on average as 55 percent of their net worth.

Those in the Millennial generation saw the shattering effect of the housing collapse on the hopes, dreams and lives of their parents.

Many recent Millennial college graduates have already decided to postpone marriage and having children because of the problems in this age of Obamanomics. Many are still seeking a secure depository for the fruits of their own lives. And in 2013 the Progressive media was telling them how fashionable and smart it is to choose to remain childless.

The long-term consequences of this societal shift will be to create a nation with fewer people decades from now to pay the Social Security taxes when those now 34 or younger reach retirement age – if retirement for them is possible at all.

In 2012, say some analysts, we crossed an economic line. Those entering the workforce thereafter, on average have zero hope of ever collecting from Social Security as much as they will be expected to pay in as taxes.

The Casino

We are assured every day by the sellers of stocks that the market is thriving and reaching record highs. The long-promised green shoots of prosperity and economic recovery are really here this time, they say. We should be buying stocks again.

By mid-August, 2013, the annual Wall Street harvest time known as earnings season was almost done. On the S&P 500, with 87 percent of companies having reported, the all-important Earnings Per Share (EPS) data was clear. EPS had grown in the Second Quarter by a solid 4.1 percent. *Laissez les bons temps rouler*, as they say during New Orleans Mardi Gras. "Let the good times roll."

The devil, however, hides in the details. When analysts looked more closely, they discovered that EPS growth was Minus 8.4 percent in the energy sector, Minus 1.3 percent in Industrials, Minus 1.1 percent in Telecom, Minus 4.8 percent in Info Tech, and minus a grim 11.6 percent in Materials.

The main reason earnings per share were up was a powerful 28.1 percent increase in Financials. The banks appeared to be coming on far, far stronger than the rest of the market, showing what seemed to be strength in their ongoing 10-year deleveraging of debt. The real reason for this apparent strength, said market skeptics, was that the banks' EPS growth was a result of "accounting gimmickry" that will not last. [11]

Bottom line: If this outlier Financials earnings per share of 28.1 percent is set aside, then the average S&P 500 earnings for the Second Quarter of 2013, like those for the First Quarter, are negative. This is one more indication of an economy less healthy than it appears at first glance to be.

The New York Stock Exchange hit (non-inflation-adjusted) record highs in Summer 2013, but it did so while the Federal Reserve Board's QE3 was continuing to pump $85 Billion per month – more than a trillion dollars per year – into the economy.

"This is an A-rod stock market," said CNBC's Rick Santelli, referring to star Yankees batter Alex Rodriquez, accused of using a professional baseball-prohibited performance-enhancing drug.

"Can the market still hit," asked Santelli, "when it's no longer taking the juice?"

Even the most enthusiastic stock market bulls are skeptical of future market growth without continued Fed assistance.

When Fed Chair Ben Bernanke so much as hinted during Summer 2013 that the Fed's ongoing flood of liquidity might soon taper off even slightly, the market plunged by more than 500 points in two days.

The Fed's easy money in the stock market casino has been more than a stimulant. It is a drug that causes many disturbing side effects. Withdrawal from this drug could have devastating effects on our economy.

The Perennial Progressive / Socialist Agenda

"We ask that the government undertake the obligation above all of providing citizens with adequate opportunity for employment and earning a living.

"The activities of the individual must not be allowed to clash with the interests of the community, but must take place within its confines and be for the good of all.

"Therefore, we demand:

"...an end to the power of the financial interests.

"We demand profit sharing in big business.

"We demand a broad extension of care for the aged.

"In order to make possible to every capable and industrious [citizen] the attainment of higher education and thus the achievement of a post of leadership, the government must provide an all-around enlargement of our entire system of public education ...

"We demand the education at government expense of gifted children of poor parents ...

"The government must undertake the improvement of public health – by protecting mother and child ... by the greatest possible support for all clubs concerned with the physical education of youth.

"We combat the ... materialistic spirit within and without us, and are convinced that a permanent recovery of our people can only proceed from within on the foundation of the common good before the individual good."

– From the political program
of the Nazi (National Socialist) Party
adopted in Munich, February 24, 1920

Chapter Three
The 100-Year Detour

"The people never give up their liberties but under some delusion."

– Edmund Burke
British Political Philosopher

In 1913, America took a hard left turn off the road our Founders designed and onto an uncharted road into the future. We left behind the faith our forefathers had in individual freedom to follow an alien collectivist ideology called Progressivism.

Since that fateful turn, America has been on a 100-Year detour.

This Progressive path has brought America into two World Wars, a Great Depression, a Cold War as well as several regional conflicts, and a Great Debasement of our social values and the U.S. Dollar.

This detour has lately led America into a swamp of Europe-like chronic high underemployment where our wheels have gotten stuck in a stagnant economy.

We are lost. Night is falling. The Progressive detour has brought us to the smoking ruins of Detroit. If we press on into the darkness, we know that cliffs are all around us.

We are a long way from home, the secure home America's Founders built for their descendants in the Constitution. Most Americans can sense our growing distance from what America once was.

To help find our way home, we need to understand where we are, how we got here, and what the words and ideas used by today's ruling Progressives such as President Barack Obama really mean on their signposts along this Leftward downhill road.

Progressives Take Power

In 1912, Progressive Democrat Woodrow Wilson was elected president in a three-way race that split the numerically superior Republican vote between incumbent William Howard Taft and former President Teddy Roosevelt, running as the standard bearer of the Progressive Bull Moose Party.

In 1913, the year Wilson took office, he and a Progressive Congress rammed through three huge deviations from our Founders' direction.

The 17th Amendment to the Constitution that year ended the election of U.S. Senators by state legislatures and gave that power instead to direct election by voters. This, say critics, weakened the power of states in the Constitution's carefully designed balance between the Federal Government and the states. This in some ways distanced the voice of the People farther from the Congress, which makes and spends our taxes.

The 16th Amendment in 1913 overturned the Framers' prohibition of an income tax. Progressives promptly enacted the income tax that is with us today. The courts had repeatedly struck down as unconstitutional all attempts to impose an income tax, so to get this Progressive tax President Wilson had to amend the Constitution.

Progressives in 1913 also created the kind of Central Bank popular in Europe that American Presidents such as Andrew Jackson had successfully fought against. This new Progressive entity, the Federal Reserve System often referred to today simply as The Fed, was given the authority to "furnish an elastic currency."

The Federal Reserve, of course, is scarcely more a part of government than Fred Smith's Federal Express shipping company. It is essentially a cartel of private banks that have been given the power, with government cooperation, to conjure an unlimited quantity of U.S. Dollars, unbacked by anything, out of thin air.

Politicians had been unable to print unlimited quantities of inelastic dollars backed by a fixed quantity of gold. Overnight the Fed greatly shrank the amount of gold required to be behind dollars and banks, making the money supply far more stretchable.

In 1933, Progressive President Franklin Delano Roosevelt would effectively end the gold standard for U.S. citizens by making it illegal for them to own monetary gold or to enforce the "gold clauses" that up until then had made contracts inflation-proof and independent of government money.

The last vestige of the gold standard, which allowed European and certain other foreign central banks to exchange their paper dollars for gold at a fixed rate, was killed on August 15, 1971, by President Richard Nixon. Mr. Nixon faced demands by France and other nations that possessed more paper dollars than the U.S. had gold in Fort Knox.

Taken together, these three Progressive changes greatly increased the centralized power and revenue of the Federal Government in Washington, D.C. The almost limitless expansion of government is something that Progressives, then and now, crave.

A Power-Mad Philosophy

Progressives advocate what they see as social progress, and they have little compunction about imposing such progress via the power of the State.

Like the utopia envisioned twenty-four centuries ago by the Greek philosopher Plato in his *Republic*, the Progressive utopia is a society in which every facet of life is controlled by a ruling elite superior to those they govern.

Plato's imaginary all-wise "philosopher kings" regulated the life of the citizens of *The Republic* right down to what music people were permitted to hear, lest they be corrupted by the wrong vibrations in the air.

One of today's Progressive "philosopher kings" is New York City Mayor Michael Bloomberg, a billionaire Nanny Statist obsessed with controlling what people are permitted to eat, how large a soft drink they may buy in a restaurant, and much more.

Almost all of today's Progressives exhibit similar clinical symptoms of megalomania. They regard themselves as superior to the rest of us, and therefore as entitled to impose their ideas on us.

They generally accept the Darwinian assumption that humans are just one of many species of animals in a natural environment where no God exists, that we are merely the result of billions of years of evolution.

Progressives generally regard those who believe in God as inferior and lacking in intelligence. Progressives routinely accuse religious believers of "imposing their morality on others."

Yet Progressives and other leftists, ironically, never hesitate to impose *their* morality on others via laws, rules, and government redistribution of wealth taxed away from those they envy and transferred to those Progressives favor.

Priests with White Robes

Progressives embrace science, perhaps because its white-robed practitioners are the closest thing today's atheist collectivists have to a religious priesthood possessing deep knowledge and authority.

Progressives believe that if Science and State are given limitless power, they can create a new Eden and a perfect human species free from greed, want and war.

In this human-made paradise the only God will be Humankind. The genetically-modified vegan lion will lie down with the genetically-modified fearless lamb, and re-tribalized Age of Aquarius hippies will beat their swords into iPhones.

To bring about their vision of the future, Progressives have no compunction about sacrificing us as expendable pawns in their coercive social engineering.

Because only the collective matters to them, Progressives have been willing to sacrifice more than 120 million individual human beings to advance the cause of Communism or Naziism during the last 100 years.

In the United States, Progressives, eager to perfect the human race via science, embraced eugenics, the idea that we should breed humans as we do race horses and other animals to amplify their "best" traits and weed out what Progressives saw as defects.

The Real Nature of Progressives

President Woodrow Wilson supported the eugenics movement, later discredited because fellow collectivist Adolf Hitler based his racist theories and genocidal mass murder on it.

Yet eugenics was a fashionable Progressive cause in 1907, when Woodrow Wilson "campaigned in Indiana for the compulsory sterilization of criminals and the mentally retarded," recounts historian Paul Rahe, "and in 1911, while governor of New Jersey, he proudly signed into law just such a bill." [1]

The co-founder of Planned Parenthood – which thanks to Leftist lawmakers has received ample taxpayer funding and for decades has been America's largest abortion services provider – was Margaret Sanger.

Sanger was one of the most outspoken Progressive leaders of the eugenics cause. The Public Broadcasting System reported that Sanger in 1920 said that "birth control is nothing more or less than the facilitation of the process of weeding out the unfit [and] of preventing the birth of defectives." [2]

Sanger, embraced as a heroine by today's Progressive feminists, believed that she and other eugenicists had a shared mission to "assist the race toward the elimination of the unfit." [3]

In her book *The Pivot of Civilization*, Sanger called for coercion to prevent the "undeniably feeble-minded" from having children. [4]

"Three Generations of Imbeciles Are Enough"

Progressives continue to lionize their ideological comrade Supreme Court Justice Oliver Wendell Holmes.

In his 2006 book *How Progressives Rewrote the Constitution*, New York University Law Professor Richard A. Epstein wrote:

"Holmes had some sympathy for the great Progressive cause of eugenics; his notorious decision in *Buck v. Bell* [1927] declared that '[t]hree generations of imbeciles are enough,' and thus allowed the state to railroad a helpless woman of normal intelligence and poor background into forced sterilization." [5]

Progressive Justice Holmes elsewhere wrote: "It is better for all the world, if instead of waiting to execute degenerate offspring for crime, or to let them starve for their imbecility, society can prevent those who are manifestly unfit from continuing their kind." [6]

"No Jews Need Apply"

Surely today's Progressives could not so arrogantly play God, could they?

Yes, they could, even in President Barack Obama's White House. Mr. Obama's first Science & Technology Advisor was John P. Holdren, an appointment heralded by the liberal media as proof that the new President's views were far advanced beyond those of troglodyte Republicans.

Holdren in the 1977 book *Ecoscience*, which he co-authored with Paul and Anne Ehrlich, raised the possibility of controlling population size by "Adding a sterilant to drinking water or staple foods" or by "Involuntary fertility control....A program of sterilizing women after their second or third child."

Under President Obama, this was the mind shaping and controlling America's science and technology policies. [7]

Holdren's co-author Paul Ehrlich became famous as author of *The Population Bomb*, which predicted that global overpopulation would cause mass famines and world wars late in the 20th Century. Like almost all

Progressive doomsaying, his prediction proved false.

Ehrlich in subsequent speeches discussed the use of such a sterilant in food and water supplies, with government in control of the only antidote. Ehrlich proposed that those wanting children could enter a government lottery to win a dose of antidote, so that no political favoritism would be involved.

Given the megalomaniacal lust for power that tempts Progressives to sterilize the rest of us in the first place, however, imagine a future Adolf Hitler with his citizenry thus sterilized. This would be a dream come true for Hitler. Genocide would for him be as easy as the government deciding which Aryans would receive the antidote, and whose DNA would be weeded out of the gene pool by refusing them the reproductive antidote. No Jews need apply.

Un-Man-ing America

When Progressives decide to play God by re-engineering society, they often create unintended consequences. Or are these huge earthquake faults splitting American society apart being created by collectivist design?

President Obama's anti-free market economic policies have caused fear, uncertainty, and economic stagnation in the real economy – if not in the stock market casino buoyed by more than $1 Trillion each year in paper stimulus money.

These Progressive policies have caused devastating high and long-term unemployment in America. One aspect of this that few analysts have noted is that the Obama unemployment is highly asymmetrical by gender.

"In the worst economic times of the 1950s and '60s, about 9 percent of men in the prime of their working lives (25 to 54 years old) were not working," wrote *New York Times* Economix reporter David Leonhardt in April 2011. "At the depth of the severe recession in the early 1980s, about 15 percent of prime-age men were not working." [8]

"Today [April 2011], more than 18 percent of such men aren't working," writes Leonhardt. "That's a depressing statistic: nearly one out of every five men between 25 and 54 is not employed."

Two years later male unemployment had grown even worse, according to Nicholas Eberstadt of the American Enterprise Institute. In an analysis titled "The Astonishing Collapse of Work in America," Eberstadt in July 2013 found that 30 percent of adult American men – nearly one in three – today is neither working nor seeking work. In 1953 this number was only 14 percent. [9]

Over the past 60 years, the labor force participation rate for adult men has fallen by about 16 percentage points, Eberstadt writes, to 64.5 percent. Today 76 million men are working, but at Eisenhower-era levels this would have been 96 million men employed.

The "great bulk of the change is due to an exodus out of the labor force – that is to say, to a massive long-term rise in the number of adult men who are neither working nor seeking work," writes Eberstadt, author of the 2012 book *A Nation of Takers: America's Entitlement Epidemic*. [10]

Men on Strike?

Why is this tectonic shift in male employment happening? Eberstadt offers little explanation, noting that "America's leadership has not yet paid serious attention to the collapse of work in modern America."

We know this: the rise of the Progressive welfare state, especially since the Great Society entitlement programs of the 1960s, has redefined the role of the man in American society.

Men used to be the family breadwinner, the provider, the person who went to work and brought home the bacon. Government has all too often taken over this role of the male spouse, thereby coming between men and women.

Women with small children were in many cases able to obtain more government benefits *without* a husband than with one, and to that extent a man could be an "anti-provider" who reduced family income.

In today's hard times caused by Obamanomics, many men have given up on finding jobs that pay well. In up to 40 percent of American households, working women have become the primary breadwinner.

In her 2013 book *Men On Strike: Why Men Are Boycotting Marriage, Fatherhood, and the American Dream – and Why It Matters*, practicing psychologist Helen Smith writes that many men have soured on marriage and work because "[T]he new world order is a place where men are discriminated against, forced into a hostile environment in school and later in college, and held in contempt by society." [11]

"Maybe there is no incentive [for men] to grow up anymore," writes Smith. "It used to be that being a grown up, responsible man was rewarded with respect, power and deference. Now, not so much."

Another Great Withdrawal

The "new world order" Smith refers to, of course, is the Progressive world order that, indeed, polarizes the relationship between men and women and favors feminism over old-fashioned masculinity. With government reducing the value of their traditional role as provider, many men are left to seek other ways to become valuable.

This male Great Withdrawal from work, marriage and other traditional male roles is clearly re-defining America's society and economy. What would the ancient Greek playwright Aristophanes, who came from conservative island culture and saw Athens decaying, see in today's America?

Aristophanes twenty-four centuries ago in his play "Lysistrada" depicted the women of Athens going on a sex strike to make their men stop making war. What would he make of today's America where, according to Smith, millions of men are going on a different kind of sex and work strike, a Great Withdrawal, and are being infantilized by the Progressive State?

As sociologist Charles Murray reported in his 2012 book *Coming Apart: The State of White America 1960-2010*, upper and upper-middle class Whites are becoming more traditional in their behavior, even if they espouse Progressive ideas. Their divorce rate and recreational drug use is falling. [12]

The lower and lower-middle class, by contrast, has lost much of its work ethic and traditional values. The middle class in general has, in inflation-adjusted dollars, been stuck at roughly the same income for the last 30 years. The old pride in being a man is waning.

Slacker Nation

From Murray's data, it appears that the bottom third of White America is becoming a slacker nation. Without decent job prospects or education, millions of men no longer see much wrong with living off government checks that in 35 states pay as much or more than minimum wage, or off the paychecks of their wives or girlfriends.

More than 50 years of Progressive propaganda designed to undermine whatever stigma these people used to feel about taking welfare has succeeded.

Nearly 100 years of Progressives teaching class warfare has taught slackers to believe they are entitled to money taxed from the rich who somehow cheated them out of a better life.

The work ethic of working-class Whites was the foundation on which America's industrial success was built, writes Murray. The erosion of working-class morality, and today's 40 percent rate of White out-of-wedlock births, may be burning this bridge back to the old style of manufacturing that was a key to American success in an earlier era.

The new era for the higher end of the White spectrum will mean private schools, gated communities, and jobs in finance and high tech and consulting. These people will do very well, at least until the economy crashes.

Most Whites used to think of themselves as middle class in an America of widely-shared values, morals and work ethic. What Murray sees is a widening fault line as perhaps 20 million working-class mostly-White males have become slackers and stopped working, or now work "off the books" in America's underground economy; many of them increasingly have more in common with the culture and status of minorities, Murray suggests, than with upper-middle class Whites.

At both ends of the White spectrum birth rates are falling. By unmanning working-class White males, the Progressives have reduced their desirability as mates and fathers. This may be a new kind of "birth control" imposed economically by the Progressives, an echo of eugenics inherent in their collectivist, control-freak ideology.

Upper-middle class Whites, by contrast, are graduating from grad schools with student loan debt and intense competitive pressure to establish their careers. These driven people, male and female, are now postponing marriage, first-home buying, and starting a family. This will reduce total fertility, leaving them with fewer – yet very well cared for – children. This, too, could be seen as a Progressive way of reducing the White birthrate in America.

They Blinded Us With Science

The Progressivism of Margaret Sanger lives on in Planned Parenthood. Since the 1973 Supreme Court ruling *Roe v. Wade*, an estimated 55 million lives have been ended by abortion in the United States, roughly the same number of additional productive citizens we need today to keep our collapsing social programs solvent. President Obama is a strong supporter of Planned Parenthood.

President Obama as an Illinois State Senator supported making legal what might be called "post-natal abortion" – the killing of a baby that had slipped outside its mother's body, and therefore been born, before an abortionist could kill it inside his or her mother. Princeton University Progressive ethicist Peter Singer has proposed giving parents six months *after* a baby is born to decide whether its continued survival is in their, and its, best interests.

When you hear Progressives demanding that we give vast new regulatory powers over private property plus another $100 Trillion to Big Government to deal with planetary warming (that measurements indicate ended 18 years ago) – all because some government-funded scientists say so - remember who Progressives really are and what they really want.

When you hear Progressives promoting Obamacare and its "death panels" that have the government power to decide who lives and who dies, who gets treatment and who will be denied, remember who Progressives really are and what they really want.

When you hear President Obama grabbing control over America's health care system, energy sector, auto industry, banking industry, student loans

– and, soon, as we shall show you, your private retirement accounts – in the name of re-engineering American society into the kind of authoritarian monarchy America's Founders fought a revolution to escape, remember who Progressives really are and what they really want.

Progressives Versus America

America's Founders fought a revolution to throw off the power of England's King George III. The U.S. Constitution and its Bill of Rights were crafted precisely to restrict and limit the powers of government, to in Thomas Jefferson's phrase "bind [the rulers] down with the chains of the Constitution."

The first litmus test of whether someone is a Progressive can be to mention the Constitution. Progressives despise its restrictions on government, and will respond that this work of America's Framers is old, obsolete, written for an 18th Century world of unsophisticated farmers with muskets.

Americans of that era were generally well-educated, knew English and some Latin, had studied the history of Greece and Rome as well as the Bible, and thought deeply about the issues and ideas humans have faced for thousands of years. It's true that they were not distracted by today's constant media noise, by Politically Correct news, by the prescription and other drugs now used by 70 percent of Americans, or by Attention Deficit Disorder or Economic Deficit Disorder.

The Constitution, a Progressive will usually say, should be recognized as a "living document" that Progressive judges can reinterpret for our own time, i.e., that Liberal judges should be allowed to change completely by bending our founding document's carefully crafted words into pretzels.

Progressives are dragging us backward from a Government of Laws to a Government of Men as Progressive judges rewrite the Constitution with each ruling, and President Obama "nullifies" laws by selectively enforcing or ordering government agents not to enforce them.

Circumventing the Constitution

In *How Progressives Rewrote the Constitution*, Professor Epstein considers the Supreme Court's Progressive majority ruling in *Wickard v. Filburn*. [13]

In this 1942 case, Ohio farmer Roscoe Filburn had grown bushels of grain not to sell, but to feed to his own cattle. This violated the New Deal's Agricultural Adjustment Act designed to limit how much farmers could grow as a way of propping up crop prices, the government charged.

By the Progressive pretzel logic of this case, Filburn had broken this law by not needing to spend money to buy grain sold by other farmers. Federal jurisdiction to impose such a law, Progressives argued, came from the government's constitutional power to regulate interstate commerce.

By growing his own grain on his own land to feed his own cattle, Filburn had interfered with the price of grain being sold across state borders, thereby lowering consumption from the "free marketplace." The high court ruled against Filburn and ordered him to pay a fine of $0.49 for each of 239 bushels he had produced in excess of the law's quota.

By such sophistry, Progressives began stretching the Constitution's Commerce Clause to justify federal power over nearly everything in the United States, e.g., to regulate a window washer in a building where the renter of one office sent an occasional business letter to people in other states. [14] This and similar interpretative power grabs by Progressives obviously exceeded, contorted and circumvented the intent of the Framers.

The Road to Serfdom

Progressives have method in their madness for power and their desire to unleash government.

"Progressivism has always been part of a broader global movement," write John Halpin and Conor P. Williams in their history of the Progressive Intellectual Tradition in America, done for the left-liberal Center for American Progress. [15]

Many of Progressivism's tangled philosophical roots are more European than American.

The foremost value to America's Founders, as it is to most Americans today, for example, is individual liberty. We did not wish to be "citizens of the world," as President Obama described himself in his first Berlin speech, but to be citizens of the greatest country on Earth.

America was made great and exceptional by people who left their collectivist homelands behind and came here looking for liberty and opportunity. American exceptionalism is as genuine as the "entrepreneur gene" many of our ancestors carried in their DNA, as we detailed in our 2011 book *The Inflation Deception*. This gene moved them to become part of the mostly-self-selected American People, our nation of faith and free enterprise.

Progressives, by contrast, identify more with the French Revolution than with the American Revolution; their primary value is not liberty but equality, by which they mean equality of outcome, not equality of opportunity.

This apparently is part of what drives the unrelenting Progressive passion to use government power to redistribute wealth.

Progressive Roots

America's Founders had a particular view of human rights, as Thomas Jefferson set to words in our Declaration of Independence: "We hold these Truths to be self-evident, that all Men are created equal, that they are endowed by their Creator with certain unalienable Rights, that among these are Life, Liberty and the Pursuit of Happiness...."

The Progressive view is very different, and reflects the predominantly-European culture of the late 19th and early 20th Centuries out of which Progressivism and other similar collectivist ideologies of the Left such as socialism, national socialism (i.e., Naziism) and Communism came.

These ideologies were born in a post-Enlightenment, post-French Revolution culture in which it was fashionable to believe that "God is Dead." Therefore any Jeffersonian talk about people being endowed with unalienable rights by a divine Creator was unacceptable.

Freedom is not "something that individuals have as a ready-made possession," wrote Progressive educator and philosopher John Dewey. It is "something to be achieved."

"Natural rights and natural liberties," wrote Dewey, "exist only in the kingdom of mythological social zoology." [16]

As Progressives see it, "freedom is not a gift of God or nature. It is a product of human making, a gift of the state," as University of Dallas Professor of Politics Thomas G. West explains.

"Man is a product of his own history, which he collectively creates himself," writes West. "He is a social construct." [17]

To America's Founders, the People created the government, which is supposed to be their servant. They wanted a government of, by and for the People to protect our freedom, to create independence and not dependence as Tocqueville feared. They certainly did not want a government of the lawyers, by the lawyers, and for the lawyers and elites.

To Progressives, we did not create the government. The government – the collective – created us, and we are to be the State's expendable, obedient servants.

The purpose of the State is the "perfection of humanity, the civilization of the world," wrote Progressive political scientist John Burgess, who believed that the State is "the perfect development of the human reason and its attainment to universal command over individualism; *the apotheosis of man"* [i.e., man becoming God]. [18]

Social Morality

If this godless Progressive view of the universe seems to be on the same wavelength with Marxism, you should not be surprised. Progressives, like Marxists, are collectivists.

During President Bill Clinton's sexual scandals during the middle-late 1990s, Democratic Party official Steve Grossman was asked by a reporter about morality. Grossman immediately replied that President Clinton was "the most moral politician I know."

In Progressive-Speak, the coded language used by acolytes of this ideology, what Mr. Grossman apparently meant is that two kinds of morality exist – individual bourgeois morality such as marital fidelity, and social morality that involves advancing the crusade for ever-bigger government.

Mr. Clinton's bourgeois immorality with an intern scarcely older than his daughter is irrelevant, Grossman seemed to be saying. Someone can follow society's conventional rules in his personal life, but anyone not helping to advance the cause of socialism and Progressivism is socially immoral. What Grossman deemed important was that President Clinton had greatly advanced the cause of Progressivism.

Transforming America

In the years leading up to 1913, as we explained in our 2012 book *The Great Debasement*, America was undergoing a huge transformation that changed both of its major political parties, our government, our economy and the fate of the U.S. Dollar forever. [19]

Thirty-two million of America's 92 million people, according to the 1910 Census, lived and worked on farms. Their way of life was being replaced by agricultural machines so rapidly that within a century America would be producing four times more food than we consume with only two percent of Americans farming. Fifty-four percent of Americans lived in communities of 1,000 or fewer people.

People from rural farms and foreign lands were flocking in pursuit of happiness to factory towns and big cities. Most found jobs and a rising standard of living, yet they also found cities run by corrupt political machines, and industries owned by the corporations and Trusts of the wealthy and powerful.

As Progressives saw it, the very nature of humans and their work had been changed by industrial capitalism.

This was no longer the age of medieval guilds in which skilled craftsmen had their own tools and knew how to turn a piece of raw leather into a finished shoe.

Alien Nation

On a Henry Ford assembly line, the worker was now a man who turned one nut on one bolt. It had been Ford's genius to break down the process of manufacturing an automobile into tiny, simple individual tasks. This produced enormous efficiency, but it reduced the individual worker to little more than a machine.

Psychologists would later describe this phenomenon as alienation, concluding that none of the workers on an assembly line felt a craftsman's pride in the finished automobile. Taking pride in one's work evaporates in the collective, a corrosive acid to individualism.

Assembly line workers found themselves in a difficult position. They arguably were not skilled workers, because the tasks they performed were remarkably simple and did not involve a craftsman's skill at creating a product from start to finish. What could such a worker say to justify getting a raise?

Felix Frankfurter explained his Progressive view of this in the *Yale Review*:

"'Collective bargaining' is the starting point of the solution.... It is...belated recognition of economic facts – that the era of romantic individualism is no more. These are not days of Hans Sachs, the village cobbler and artist.... We are confronted with mass production and mass producers; the individual, in his industrial relations, [is] but a cog in the great collectivity...." [20]

Do you begin to see why collectivist Progressives call union negotiations "collective" bargaining?

Labor unions, unlike medieval guilds, offered an alternative as workers confronted an age of growing corporations and enlarging government: collective bargaining.

Unions would represent all the workers in a factory simultaneously, bargain for higher wages for all based on rising corporate profits, and threaten to have all the workers go on strike unless union demands were satisfied.

What this meant in practice was that unions use the threat of intimidation, violence and work disruption to demand what in free-market terms was a higher-than-market price for labor that could be easily replaced.

This was made possible by Progressive governments that politically sided with labor unions, and by politicians who found it to their advantage to obtain campaign donations and worker votes. Progressive politicians embraced union leaders who encouraged class warfare and confrontational strikes, which repeatedly elicited violence between workers and property owners.

Standard of Living

The result in American politics has been what Union critics see as a money-laundering operation. Progressive politicians empower unions to extort dues from their members and money from corporations. Union bosses then kick back a fat slice of this money in campaign contributions to the politicians, thereby helping re-elect them.

Workers for many years benefited from this. At General Motors, for example, the average assembly line worker now costs the company, by one estimate, at least $114 per hour in wages and benefits.

General Motors went from being a company that made automobiles to a company that pays pension and health benefits and occasionally also builds a car.

This fulfilled one Progressive hope: that the standard of living of workers would improve. Indeed, unions for a time raised industrial workers to middle or even upper-middle class income. Ironically, this also lifted many workers into a middle-class tax bracket and made workers more responsive to Republican arguments for lower taxes.

Detroit, as the perfect embodiment of industrial unionism, shows us what followed. Because its workers were being paid a higher-than-market income, competition soon offered American consumers better cars at lower prices.

In America many people are workers but all people are consumers. By driving prices to a higher-than-market level, organized labor extracted higher worker wages from the pockets of consumers, most of whom earned less than union members.

The only way to sustain such an overpriced system would be by restricting competition with import tariffs, special taxes, or other government power that gave unionized companies a monopoly advantage in the marketplace.

For a time, the giant Detroit automakers got more money to pay their workers by squeezing value out of the cars they sold, by making cheaper automobiles.

This opened the American market for foreign automakers such as Japan's Toyota, Honda and Nissan that produced cars of higher quality and dependability than were coming off the unionized assembly lines in and around Detroit.

Foreign automakers soon began opening their own factories in the United States, mostly in right-to-work states where unions did not have entrenched political power or legal advantages.

One of the things that made this possible was a new technology called air-conditioning, which allowed factories in semi-tropical Southern states to create cooling breezes, not sweatshops, for their assembly line workers.

The Wages of Progressivism

Today, a typical foreign auto manufacturing facility in the South pays roughly $80 per hour in wages and benefits for a non-unionized worker to produce its cars, compared to nearly $120 per hour that it costs General Motors to employ a unionized worker in Michigan.

That wage differential comes not from a higher quality of work, but from the ability of unions to coerce corporations in what union critics see as little different from an organized crime protection racket. Union opponents have said that we should not be surprised at the many historic examples of unions in collusion with organized criminals, because the two are actually similar in their methods and aims.

From the outset, blue-collar industrial unions have faced an inevitability. Because Henry Ford had the genius to simplify each assembly-line task, those tasks can be done not only by unskilled labor but also by skilled machines.

In England more than a century ago a movement arose called the Luddites. Their concern was that their jobs could be taken by machines such as mechanical looms.

One form of protest undertaken by Luddites was to remove their wooden shoes and throw these into the gears of factory machines, thereby jamming and damaging them. These wooden shoes were called *sabots*, and their use to jam the machinery of industry came to be called sabotage.

Organized labor from its outset has gotten its power from the threat to jam and halt factory operations, not just from the quality of work done by its members.

For union leaders, the added wages and benefits they gain beget more coerced dues paid to the union, bigger political donations to Progressives, and more political influence via politicians whom many rank-and-file union members might never have given a contribution to voluntarily. Coercively-unionized workers were a means to an end for union bosses.

The higher that union wages have gone, the more incentive companies have had to replace such workers with robots. This has been facilitated by the Federal Reserve holding interest rates close to zero, which has made it easier for large companies to invest in robots.

The Dawn of Progressivism

Back in 1913, the spirit of the age was "progress" and change. Scientists and inventors were remaking the world with electric light, gasoline-powered vehicles, radio communications, phonographs and flying machines.

In this era of upheaval, from Russia to rural America, many well-intentioned people began asking if government and society could be improved. Many wondered if the old ruling elites should remain in control of this new world.

"Progressivism" became the umbrella label that brought together populists suspicious of private or public concentrated power and wealth, a variety of social reformers, and recent immigrants, some of whom came to America bringing European socialist ideas of class warfare and expropriating the rich.

"This Invisible Government"

In 1912 former Republican President Teddy Roosevelt, after being denied his party's nomination, sought re-election to the White House on his own Progressive Party ticket.

His "Bull Moose Party" platform advocated women's suffrage (unlike either of his rivals, Progressive Democrat Woodrow Wilson and Republican incumbent William Howard Taft). It also called for a National Health Service; social insurance for the disabled, elderly and unemployed; an eight-hour workday; an inheritance tax; and a constitutional amendment permitting a Progressive income tax, among many other things.

Above all, Roosevelt's Progressivism centered on his "New Nationalism" – his ideal of a paternalistic, muscular central government to regulate businesses, create great national projects such as the Panama Canal and national parks, extend American values to other lands, and protect working people and the middle class.

"To destroy this invisible Government, to dissolve the unholy alliance between corrupt business and corrupt politics is the first task of the statesmanship of the day," declared Roosevelt's 1912 platform.

Power-loving Progressives

Democratic Progressive Woodrow Wilson won the presidency with 42 percent of the national vote. Roosevelt split the 50 percent Republican vote, winning 27 percent of the popular vote to his one-time friend President Taft's 23 percent. Socialist Party candidate Eugene V. Debs won 6 percent.

The following year, 1913, the Great Debasement began. President Wilson would transform America forever by signing an income tax law. He also signed the act creating the Federal Reserve System, the quasi-private entity that has grown to control America's banking institutions, money supply, economy and more in fulfillment of an evolving Progressive ideology.

Wilson signed into law the Clayton Antitrust Act to regulate corporations and trusts, and the Federal Trade Commission Act giving government far-ranging powers to intervene in business.

Most remember Woodrow Wilson, who was President of Princeton University, as America's only academic intellectual President.

Most also remember that Wilson took the United States into World War I only months after being re-elected in November 1916 under his slogan "He Kept Us Out of War."

After that war, Wilson and his "Fourteen Points" helped establish the League of Nations, forerunner of today's United Nations. The U.S. Congress, unwilling to surrender any of America's sovereignty to the international body, refused to ratify Wilson's agreement to join the League.

Wilson was fashionably Progressive, pro-organized labor and anti-Big Business. Yet his smug Progressivism was also eager to impose his eccentric morals on others.

Wilson cracked down on the free speech of those who opposed his entry into the war. Recreating his own version of the Alien and Sedition Acts that Thomas Jefferson had abolished, Wilson unleashed his Attorney General A. Mitchell Palmer, who rounded up 10,000 "reds" and other radicals and deported many of them.

Wilson, born in Virginia and raised in Georgia, was the first Southerner to be President since 1869. His father was a slaveowner and Confederate chaplain. One of Wilson's earliest boyhood memories was of standing next to Robert E. Lee and looking up at the Confederate general's face.

As a Progressive president, Wilson re-segregated the federal civil service that Republicans had racially integrated. African-American federal employees were required to eat in segregated dining rooms and use "Blacks Only" bathrooms.

Wilson also enthusiastically praised and encouraged Americans to see the D.W. Griffith movie "Birth of a Nation," which was openly pro-Ku Klux Klan.

Yet Wilson's racism did not necessarily extend to other racial or ethnic groups. While President, after his first wife died, Wilson wed a direct descendant of famed Native American princess Pocahontas.

Wilson's Democratic Party has always used racial polarization politics to gain and hold power. What is amazing is that those who have historically been this party's most abused victims are today its most loyal voters.

Evolving Progressivism

In 1920, following World War I, voters restored Republicans - Warren G. Harding and then Calvin Coolidge - to the White House. The war's economic undertow pulled America into what could have become the Great Depression.

Instead of responding as Progressive Franklin D. Roosevelt did 12 years later with massive government programs and stimulus spending, Harding and Coolidge simply got government out of the free market's way. Unhindered, the economy quickly recovered, and the economic downturn turned into the prosperity and good times of the Roaring '20s Jazz Age in less than two years.

In 1924 a second Progressive Party emerged, led by charismatic Republican Robert LaFollette, the energetic reformist Senator of Wisconsin. Where Teddy Roosevelt wanted to regulate giant corporations, "Fighting Bob" LaFollette hated them and sought to stamp them out. He had also been an outspoken critic of America's involvement in World War I.

This second wave of Progressivism came after the Russian Revolution. Many Progressives felt energized by the revolutionary idea that old social orders, including capitalism, could be swept aside and replaced with something that claimed to be better. Most would later become deeply disillusioned as they recognized the real nature of the Soviet Union.

Where Teddy Roosevelt's Progressive Party was largely made up of White Anglo-Saxon Protestant (WASP) social reformers and was critical of those who considered themselves "hyphenated Americans," LaFollette's Progressive Party was much more oriented to blue-collar organized labor, and to racial and ethnic minorities as well as recent immigrant groups who very much still thought of themselves as hyphenated.

Part of LaFollette's vision of something better was a future that put academic social planners in control. To this end, he encouraged the University of Wisconsin-Madison to play a significant role advising the state government.

In the 1924 campaign, the charismatic, emotional LaFollette was endorsed by the American Federation of Labor (AFL) and the Socialist Party of America.

He got 17 percent of the popular vote nationwide, yet won only the 13 Electoral Votes of Wisconsin, where his sons would later create a small dynasty of state officeholders. LaFollette finished second in 11 Western states. After this election his Progressive Party was finished and disbanded.

Following World War II, in 1948 a third Progressive Party arose to challenge President Harry Truman. This party's standard-bearer was Henry Wallace, who had been FDR's Vice President before Truman.

Less than six months after FDR replaced Wallace with Truman, President Roosevelt died. Truman became President.

The 1948 Progressive Party was by any measure radical. Socialist Norman Thomas and several other prominent leftists resigned from the party over what they called undue Communist influence on Wallace.

The 1948 Progressive Party Platform blames the United States for the dawning Cold War, and urges friendly relations with the Soviet Union, whose army was then occupying Eastern Europe. (See Platform excerpts on page 142.)

The problems in America, this 1948 platform said, were caused by "Big Business control of our economy and government.... Today that private power has constituted itself an invisible government which pulls the strings of its puppet Republican and Democratic parties.."

The 1948 Progressive Party platform called for government expropriation of the property of private corporations, and denounced anti-Communist investigations by Congress.

In the presidential election, Henry Wallace won 2.4 percent of the popular vote and zero Electoral Votes.

Today's Progressives

Many of today's Fourth Wave Progressives developed their political ideas from the anti-Vietnam War, Civil Rights and New Left movements of the 1960s and 1970s. Their views resonate with the Social Democratic political parties of Europe, which describe themselves as democratic socialist in ideology.

The members of the Congressional Progressive Caucus are almost all Democrats. In past years this caucus openly embraced the group Democratic Socialists of America (DSA), of which labor leaders such as recent AFL-CIO President John Sweeney were proud card-carrying members.

Beginning with President Ronald Reagan's run for re-election in 1984, the Communist Party USA ceased running its own candidates and directed its followers to cast their votes for the Democratic Party candidate. The CPUSA presumably does this to avoid splitting the Progressive political Left coalition.

The Democratic Party certainly does not seek CPUSA support, nor does such support suggest in any way that Democratic candidates share Communist views.

America's Communist Party is either terrified of the Republican Party since Ronald Reagan, or it accepts today's Progressive-dominated Democratic Party as now far enough to the left that its policies are acceptable to the CPUSA.

In 2007 then-Senator Hillary Clinton during a presidential debate was asked if she described herself as a liberal. "No," replied Ms. Clinton, "I consider myself a proud modern American progressive, and I think that's the kind of philosophy and practice that we need to bring back to American politics."

"Progressive" has become a fashionable designer label to wear among Democrats nowadays, in part because it is remarkably vague.

Judging by its three previous waves of evolution, the label called Progressive suggests that its wearer's thinking might be at least one part Progress, one part anti-Big Business populism, one part democratic socialism, one part class warfare, one part smug "We Know What's Best for You" Nanny

Statism, a large dose of social engineering, and a small pinch of liberalism.

Self-Righteous Leftists

So what do today's Progressives believe?

The chief political values of traditional Americans have always been liberty, rugged individualism, self reliance and responsibility, family and values.

The foremost ideological values of Progressives, as we have said, in some ways seem to come more from the French Revolution than the American Revolution. Progressives primarily desire equality and fraternity, i.e., a belief that the collective, the group (however defined at any given moment) matters more than the individual.

In a Progressive world, everyone is equally special – which means that nobody is special. Exceptional qualities, ideas and achievements are weeds in the Progressive garden of Egalitarian Eden, where individuality is to be torn out by the roots and removed. Thou shalt not eat from the tree of "I."

By equality, Progressives a century ago and today do not primarily mean equal treatment and rights under the law. They seek to use government power to end all inequality, especially of wealth.

Yet, paradoxically, Progressives have always been eager to have government treat people unequally in order to impose their egalitarianism. They are delighted to confiscate wealth from the successful so government can redistribute these riches while taking a hefty percentage for itself.

The successful, as Progressives like to say, are merely "winners in life's lottery" – a phrase that disparages the achievers as merely lucky, not meritorious. As to the poor, in a folk song made popular by singer Joan Baez, "there but for fortune go you and I."

Progressives fight racism by using reverse racism – laws and government policies that discriminate in favor of members of one race over others in matters of preferential college admissions, hiring, quotas and other opportunities.

To achieve egalitarian "leveling" of society, Progressives have always been eager to make government heavier and heavier in order to crush down whatever individualistic nails stand out from the masses.

To fight business "monopolies," for example, Teddy Roosevelt and Woodrow Wilson paradoxically were happy to expand the power of the biggest monopoly of all, the government.

"Equal" Yet Superior

Progressives claim to support the ideal that all people are equal. Yet at the same time Progressives regard themselves as morally and mentally superior to those who hold other values and ideas.

As we have learned during the past 100 years, were it not for their double standards, Progressives would have no standards at all.

Again, Progressives almost by reflex accuse Conservatives, especially Christians, of "trying to impose their morality on everybody."

However, nearly all Progressives believe that their superior morality and intelligence entitles them to impose their values onto everyone else through the force of government.

Paternalistic Progressives

This Progressive mindset could be heard in the 1984 Democratic Convention speech of then-New York Governor Mario Cuomo. Boiled down to its essence, Cuomo's message was that we are all one big family, and that government is the parent who should decide how much each family member must pay into this collective, and how much each will receive from it.

In Cuomo's paternalistic Progressive society, government is the master parent, not the public servant, and we are children who must accept their inferior place and bow to the State's superior Progressive wisdom.

Political science has a formal term for the kind of social-political system Governor Cuomo and other Progressives advocate. That term is feudalism, the system of rulers, castles and subservient serfs of the dark and medieval ages.

The biggest difference between then and now is that feudal serfs typically were forced to pay only 10 percent of everything they produced to the lord of the local castle.

In today's Progressive neo-feudalism, average Americans are forced to pay federal, state, local and hidden taxes, including inflation, of 55 percent or more of what they earn to our Progressive governments.

In medieval England when the rulers King John and his agent the Sheriff of Nottingham turned rapacious, legend tells that a hero we remember as Robin Hood seized money the government had stolen – and returned it to its rightful owners, the taxpayers.

Back then, a starving peasant would be put to death for killing and eating a wild deer in Sherwood Forest – because these deer, like everything else in nature, were defined by law as the King's property.

Eco-ideology

Today's radical environmentalist Progressives have gone even farther in their craving for power. Even after a Democrat-controlled U.S. Senate voted against his measure to give government total control over the "greenhouse gas" carbon dioxide as a "hazardous pollutant," President Barack Obama had his Environmental Protection Agency assert that it had regulatory authority to control all sources of this gas.

As you read this, you are naturally exhaling carbon dioxide, a by-product of human breathing. President Obama therefore has asserted his Administration's power to directly regulate and control you and all other carbon-based life forms – from trees to elephants – that breathe Earth's air.

Progressives use both taxation and regulation to force their values onto others. Do not be surprised if you soon must pay a breathing tax. President Obama opened the door, in effect, to changing the traditional Presidential song "Hail to the Chief" to "Exhale to the Chief."

Progressive Nanny Statism also continued in New York City Mayor Michael Bloomberg, who has imposed government restrictions on every individual's access to salt, sugar and foods containing trans-fats – not only for children in public schools, but also for adults in private restaurants.

A judge threw out Mayor Bloomberg's restriction on the size of soft drink a customer may buy. We applaud this judge, but we know that many Progressive-appointed judges hold the opposite view...and that such judges often put their ideology above the views of elected lawmakers.

To the left of Mayor Bloomberg are even more extreme Progressives who believe that those who disagree with them on issues such as global warming should be fired, denied media access, and occasionally turned into targets for intimidation and violence.

A Genuinely "Progressive" Income Tax

In 1913 the 16th Amendment became part of the U.S. Constitution. It permitted creation of an income tax. The Federal income tax law enacted immediately thereafter was "Progressive," imposing heavier tax on those with larger incomes.

The income tax passed Congress amid promises that it would tax "the rich," a technique that has been used ever since to enact nearly every tax expansion such as the Alternative Minimum Tax (AMT), which beginning in 2013 increased the taxes of more than 30 million Americans.

In 1913, when one lawmaker proposed putting a 7 percent tax ceiling into the income tax law, colleagues ridiculed him by saying "If we did that, then some fool would try to raise the tax that high."

The 1913 income tax imposed a marginal tax rate of 1 percent on the first $20,000 of income for married joint filing taxpayers, according to the Tax Foundation. That tax rose to 2 percent on incomes up to $50,000; 3 percent on up to $75,000; 4 percent on up to $100,000; 5 percent up to $250,000; 6 percent on up to $500,000; and 7 percent on any income above $500,000.

We need to remember that the 1913 dollar had not yet undergone 100 years of the Great Debasement, as our dollar has. Our numbers appear in 1913 dollars. To see best-selling author and head of the Landmark Legal Foundation Mark Levin's discussion using inflation-adjusted amounts that reflect today's debased dollar, go to his 2013 book *The Liberty Amendments*. [21]

Remember, too, that in 1913 the average American earned $740 a year.

A one-percent income tax on this 1913 American, even with zero deductions, would have been $7.40, less than three days' income each year.

That average American's $7.40 income tax in 1913 would today, if increased by inflation alone, be somewhere between $151 and $370. Sound good?

If you pay vastly more than this today, it is because the Progressives' Great Debasement has destroyed the value of your dollars. Your tax in 1913 would not jump to 2 percent until you earned $20,000 – the equivalent in 2012 of earning $453,292.

To reach 1913's top marginal tax rate of 7 percent, you needed to earn $500,000, which – as calculated by inflation alone by the Tax Foundation – in 2012 dollars is $11,332,304.

Progressive and neo-Marxist economists dismiss such comparisons by arguing that wage inflation has kept up with price inflation. This argument is misleading for a host of reasons.

We need to keep at least three realities in mind:

(1) The Progressives have used the very inflation their Great Debasement created to force average Americans into confiscatory tax brackets once used to tax only the wealthy.

The issue is no longer how much you "earn," but how much the government lets you keep for yourself. Under their divide-and-conquer politics, nearly half the working-age population now pays no income taxes. Those who do pay carry a much heavier-than-equal share of the burden.

(2) If income has kept up with inflation, then why must both husband and wife work in today's average American household – when the income of one earner used to be enough?

Many millions with fixed or limited incomes have not been able to keep up with the Progressives' deliberate inflation. An even more grim reality is that in most families one spouse is working just to pay the taxes and other costs, visible and invisible, now imposed by Progressive government.

We believe that it is unhealthy for a society if half the population shoulders a hefty tax burden, while the other half pays little or no tax. To make the world more equal, there should be a ceiling, an upper limit - both annually and lifetime - on how much tax anyone should ever be required to pay, an "Alternative Maximum Tax."

All those people who nowadays pay little or no income tax should be required to pay something, anything, so that everyone has a sense of helping pay for the system, and of sacrificing so that money becomes to you more than abstract numbers, and government assistance more than freebies.

(3) Back in 1913, the gold standard was still in effect. With its fixed exchange rate around $20 per ounce, a person could readily convert $500,000 in U.S. Dollars into 25,000 ounces of gold – or 25,000 $20 gold coins.

At gold's August 2013 price of around $1,425 per ounce (and adding no numismatic value for what in 1913 were everyday, circulating coins), $500,000 in such 1913 gold coins would in September 2013 be worth approximately $35,625,000.

The average American has always earned less than this, of course, but in 1913 any savings could easily be done in the safe, value-growing medium of gold numismatic coins, beyond the reach of the Great Debasement.

From 7 to 94 percent

The new income tax increased drastically in 1917, the year the United States entered World War I. Tax brackets multiplied dramatically. Suddenly married joint filers were required to pay 2 percent on income up to $2,000 ($35,059 in 2012 dollars, adjusted for inflation), and 4 percent on earnings to $5,000 (approximately $87,648 in 2013 dollars).

The top marginal tax rate in 1917 had soared to 67 percent on all income above $2 Million (just over $35 Million in 2013 dollars). However, with Rockefeller Trusts and cleverly-designed tax avoidance plans, few paid the full 67 percent - *if* they jumped through loopholes.

The greed of Big Government Progressives has been insatiable. By 1936 they pushed the top marginal income tax rate to 79 percent, then to 94 percent in 1944, backing off to "only" 91 percent from 1946 until the mid-1950s.

The top rate was still 70 percent when President Ronald Reagan was inaugurated in 1981; in two terms he drove the income tax top rate down in stages to 28 percent in 1988, producing a huge, long-lasting economic environment of growth and prosperity.

When Progressives regained power under President Bill Clinton, they rushed to jack the top tax rate back up by more than 41 percent – to 39.6 percent in 1993. Many old loopholes stayed closed.

Progressives screamed when Republican President George W. Bush in 2003 lowered the top tax rate to 35 percent – still 25 percent more than it had been under President Reagan.

President Barack Obama vowed that if re-elected in 2012, he would greatly increase tax rates on payers in upper income tax brackets – and would slash a wide range of deductions and tax credits to push government's take from taxpayers even higher.

In this Mr. Obama has kept his word, soaking the upper and upper-middle class with additional taxes. The predictable result: high unemployment and underemployment, and a weak economy, as Keynes warned.

Prosperity is almost as predictable and attainable. Cutting taxes is a proven stimulant. Texas is business-friendly, has no income tax, is prosperous, and in recent years has created nearly half the new jobs in America.

Progressive politicians like President Obama insist on intensifying their class war against the rich, even though poor and middle class Americans by the millions are the chief victims of Mr. Obama being a (Class) Wartime President who devastates the economy.

Slamming Shut the Gold Window

During World War I, Progressive President Woodrow Wilson had effectively restricted the gold standard. This made it more difficult to convert paper gold certificates into gold itself, and harder for some to take monetary gold out of the United States without the approving signature of one or more high government officials.

People suddenly found that their escape hatch from debased fiat dollars into the secure safe haven of gold had been slammed shut and locked, at least until after World War I. Within 13 years, that door would be closed, and remain locked for more than four decades.

American lawmakers discussed creating an income tax during the War of 1812 and actually imposed one temporarily during the War Between the States.

Democrats enacted an income tax in 1894 that imposed a 2 percent tax on all incomes above $4,000 – which meant that the tax would hit roughly the top 10 percent of households in America. The U.S. Supreme Court struck the tax down because the Framers had in the Constitution wisely prohibited any tax that targeted individuals by requiring that all taxes be apportioned among the states.

A Hidden Agenda

Prior to the Progressives, those who supported an income tax did so to fund the government – during wars in 1812 and 1861, or to offset revenue lost from reducing a tariff in 1894.

In 1848 in *The Communist Manifesto*, Karl Marx and Friedrich Engels proposed 10 steps to destroy the capitalist bourgeoisie, the class of business people and the wealthy. Nine of these 10 steps have already, either entirely or in part, been implemented in the United States. (See these 10 steps on page 44.)

Three of Marx's and Engels' steps:

1. Restrictions should be put on inheritance of wealth, at least by "rebels" who oppose the State.

2. All banking and credit should be centralized under government control.

3. Government should impose a heavily-graduated "Progressive" income tax that confiscates much more money from the rich than from others.

Today's Progressives are quick to say they are not Marxists or socialists. Many, however, share the Marxian hatred for the wealthy and for prosperous business people, and for some of the same reasons held by socialists.

Most Progressives, including President Barack Obama, openly favor government redistribution of wealth. In then-Senator Obama's phrase to the citizen who came to be known as Joe the Plumber: "Things just work better when we spread the wealth around."

(Note the planted assumption here that it is "*the* wealth," not *your* wealth, not the property of someone who earned it and rightfully owns it. Wealth in Barack Obama's phrase is a collectively-shared entity, the way one would speak of "the desert" or "the ocean.")

If some are needy, the Progressive assumption goes, then it is not only ethically acceptable but also morally imperative to take the excess wealth from those not in need and give it to the poor. "From each according to his ability, to each according to his need," wrote Marx in his 1875 *Critique of the Gotha Program*, which presumes that the State knows everybody's ability and true needs.

From a conservative and libertarian view, this Progressive ideological point of view poses many ethical problems. This redistribution of wealth is coercive.

It puts the coercer in the morally-dubious role of deciding whose need warrants such expropriation of wealth from one and redistribution to another. The person arrogant enough to do this, as Adam Smith noted, is precisely the person least fit to do so wisely or justly.

The Negative Income Tax

Let's acknowledge an unpleasant truth about Progressives, who tell us they care about the poor.

Progressivism needs to keep the "poor" poor in order to justify its many expansions of government in their name, including a steeply-graduated income tax of the sort Marx wanted to impose on the rich. To Progressives, the poor are a means to an ideological end.

Today, more than 70 cents of every tax dollar spent on government programs for the poor never reach the poor. The bulk of this money goes to support an array of social workers, community organizers like the young Barack Obama, $100,000-a-year politically-selected consultants, and others who justify their own substantial income and power through spending this government money.

In 2013 the government will spend an average of $61,830 on every three-person family in poverty, according to research by Michael Tanner of the Cato Institute. [22] The Welfare State spends roughly $1 Trillion each year to keep fighting a failed 60-year War on Poverty that poverty, and government-enriched Progressives, keep winning.

As the late Nobel laureate economist Milton Friedman once proposed, why not give this money – or some large fraction thereof – to the poor family directly? If government did this, every poor family's income would exceed the national average. A small step in the direction of this Friedman "negative income tax" idea is the Earned Income Tax Credit.

Progressives will not accept Friedman's idea, however, because it would eliminate the bureaucratic and politician middlemen in the deal. That would no longer expand and empower the government, which has always been the real purpose of redistributionist programs.

"Welfare is the price we pay to keep the poor *in their place*," a famous Progressive intellectual who has worked at the highest levels of a Democratic Administration in Washington, D.C., once privately told one of us. This is the true, unmasked mindset of today's ruling Progressives.

In his 2013 best-seller *This Town: Two Parties and a Funeral – Plus Plenty of Valet Parking – in America's Gilded Capital*, veteran journalist Mark

Leibovich shows how Washington, D.C. is no longer a town of selfless public servants. [23]

"People now come here to get rich," writes Leibovich, who gives details of how our Capital's lobbyists, consultants and others – the kind of people candidate Barack Obama promised would have no access if he was elected – have been having the biggest, fattest financial years in their history.

The ever-bigger money magnet of our "gilded capital" Washington, D.C., has greedily cranked up its power and taken for itself America's earnings that once would have expanded companies and created jobs in Detroit, Milwaukee and Philadelphia. That money instead has made the upscale counties around D.C., the wealthiest in America, and has left millions of Americans across the country unemployed, hopeless and hurting.

Pockets of Freedom

Our Progressive rulers are happy to tend the poor, many of whom as Alexis de Tocqueville foresaw, have been "fixed irrevocably in childhood," infantilized by dependency on the State, and have been reduced "to being nothing more than a herd of timid...animals of which government is the shepherd."

On the other hand, Progressives hate the rich. The real reason for this is not inequality, but because the rich are pockets of freedom, like tiny nations independent of collectivist control.

The rich, as we noted in our 2012 book *The Great Debasement*, can give asylum and refuge to those seeking freedom from the monolithic rule of Politically Correct Progressive orthodoxy:

"The Koch Brothers for many years funded the libertarian think tank the Cato Institute that advances alternatives to Progressive Big Government ideology."

"Rupert Murdoch funds the Fox News and Fox Business cable channels as well as the *Wall Street Journal, New York Post* and other outposts of free thought."

Progressives relentlessly seek ways to strip the wealthy of their money, not only to enrich government but also because this would eliminate nearly every independent bastion of non-Progressive free thought.

If wealthy conservatives were eradicated, all that would then remain is an all-powerful government, government-funded leftist universities, and today's sycophantic and partisan Progressive mainstream media. If this happens, the last vestiges of the Enlightenment will be snuffed out, and a long Dark Age of unfree human thought will be imposed.

Progressive Judgment

Progressives tend to see business and the profit motive as evil. They imagine that business people sit around all day counting their money, chanting "Greed is Good," and cheating customers.

The reality, as 18th Century British author Samuel Johnson observed, is that "A man is seldom more innocently occupied than when he is engaged in making money."

The Capitalist succeeds or fails by risking his own investment money in a realm of voluntary transactions. No one is forced to buy his product or service. Those who believe he cheated them will never be his customers a second time, so he has every incentive to deal honestly with them.

To succeed in the marketplace, the business person must strive to provide the best product and service at the best price to customers, who "are always right" and can take their business elsewhere. He makes his income by peaceful persuasion, without resort to force or coercion.

Progressives say they favor freedom and choice, but they want government to interpose itself between people who freely choose to swap goods, services and money with one another. Progressive freedom apparently does not extend to these forms of human interaction that we call enterprise or trade.

Compare this to what Progressives deem superior to Capitalism: government.

"Government is not reason, it is not eloquence – it is force," goes a statement widely attributed to George Washington. "Like fire, it is a dangerous servant and a fearful master."

Government does use coercion, force and the threat of force, to take whatever it wants from its subjects – their liberty, property, earnings – and to redistribute what it takes to the ruler's cronies and favorites.

Government makes almost nothing – except war. What it spends is taken at gunpoint, in one way or another, from others.

As we have said, Progressives such as Teddy Roosevelt accused Capitalists of forming "monopolies." In a free marketplace, monopolies are almost impossible to sustain without the assistance of government's coercive power.

Not surprisingly, today's Progressives are eager to give total power to the ultimate monopoly and the wealthiest, greediest, most coercive entity in society – the government.

A Wealth Tax

In 2013 the Progressive income tax has become not a tax on income but a tax on the upper-middle and upper classes. Those with the top 10 percent of incomes now pay more than 70 percent of all income taxes. Progressives such as President Obama obsessively demand that taxes on "millionaires and billionaires" be raised even more to force the successful to "pay their fair share."

This Karl Marx-approved tax that Progressives pushed into law in 1913 has always violated the Equal Protection principle of the Constitution. It imposes radical inequality today by putting no burden on millions of Americans, while placing a crushingly heavy burden on other Americans.

This Progressive tax also violates American values in other ways. It penalizes success and disproportionately targets achievers for audits. And it rewards failure and sloth with far less onerous taxation. By transferring a huge share of capital from the productive to the unproductive, it is in the long run a form of economic and national suicide.

Who's the Fairest of Them All?

A truly "Progressive" income tax – one that helped produce progress and prosperity for all, as we argued in *The Great Debasement* – would do one of two things. Either it would impose no added burden on success whatsoever, or – if progress is really the goal – would turn the tax rate tables upside down so that taxes got progressively lower as a person's income increased.

Such a "truly Progressive" income tax would reward people for working harder by moving them into lower, not higher, tax brackets as they earned more money. This would stimulate immense prosperity that would benefit all...all, that is, except those feeding at the trough of gigantic government.

Progressive Newspeak

Progressives have developed a special jargon to advance and obscure their agenda. This jargon has much in common with Orwellian doublethink used in George Orwell's dystopian novel 1984, where future serfs were taught reflexively to think that peace is war and freedom is slavery.

In the Orwellian mind of Progressives, giving someone a tax cut is a government "expenditure" that must be "offset" by raising other taxes.

Government spending is an "investment." And slowing the rate of government growth while continuing to spend more than before is called a "spending cut."

Roads and other infrastructure may, indeed, enhance commerce, but they are no substitute for voluntary investment in the free marketplace.

Progressives, motivated by politics and an ideology of redistributing wealth, are more likely to build a bridge to nowhere with taxpayer money than a bridge of optimal social utility and efficiency.

They also create an unhealthy collectivist mindset in some radical Progressives that "if you have a successful business, you didn't build that," that all success must be credited to, and hence belongs to, the collective and the State.

"Government is not a business," wrote *New York Times* columnist and Keynesian economist Paul Krugman, and therefore it need not balance its books or justify its income and outgo like a business.

Any business person caught playing the phony bookkeeping games our government uses every day would go to prison. Professor Krugman is correct, however, that we should never think of government as an "investor" in the noble sense we would ascribe to businesses.

Progressives made a major effort through the McCain-Feingold Campaign Finance Law to restrict or prohibit campaign ad funding by corporations on the grounds that "a corporation is not a person." The U.S. Supreme Court struck down this blatant attempt to stifle the views of companies.

If corporations are not persons, we continue to ask, then how does government justify taxing them? Was not a founding idea of the American Revolution "No taxation without Representation?" We do not allow corporations to vote in our elections. Progressives tried to silence all corporate political free speech during election campaigns. How, then, can a corporation have representation that legitimizes making it pay taxes? Just a thought inspired by the Orwellian surrealism of Progressivespeak, the speech and thought of Progressives.

The Beehive

In 1912 Woodrow Wilson, a founding father of today's Progressive State, delivered a speech titled "What Is Progress?" that reveals much about the mindset and values of his ideological comrades. [24]

He described how inside the "house" of America he and other Progressives were fashioning a new and superior structure that would replace it.

"[A] generation or two from now," said Wilson, "the scaffolding will be taken away, and there will be the family in a great building whose noble architecture will at last be disclosed, where men can live as a single community, co-operative as in a perfected, co-ordinated beehive...."

Yes, a beehive, the perfect embodiment of a collectivist society. We admire bees for their industriousness. However, in nature the hive is a place where almost all the workers are nominally female, yet only the Queen

Bee has offspring.

It is a place with almost no males except a few drones, whose job is to mate with the Queen once during her courting flight. Thereafter, these drones are prevented from re-entering the hive and, without honey, quickly die. Does this sound like the new American slacker society of unemployed males about which Helen Smith wrote in *Men on Strike*?

Bees have been around since the time of the dinosaurs, scientists tell us. Their society is durable.

Yet the bee has scarcely changed during all that time. Most bees are collectivist species that make no progress, as we use the term. They are thus a fitting symbol for back-to-feudalism Progressives such as Woodrow Wilson and Barack Obama.

"Liberalism is just
Communism sold by the drink."

– P.J. O'Rourke

On June 4, 2013, Becky Gerritson testified before Congress about IRS demands made to her small Alabama Tea Party Group, one of perhaps 150 or more such targeted Conservative groups (excerpts):

"In September 2008, when we had our first $700 billion bailout, we, along with millions of Americans, were VERY concerned! That bailout was confirmation that our government was out-of-control. But just a few months later, in January of 2009, we learned that our government was going to spend another $787 billion. This money went to foreign nations, failing banks, and unproductive industries. We were worried and knew we had to do something to sound the alarm...

"We knew that the government had gone far beyond its habitual, deficit spending. The government was mortgaging America's future...

"In the spring of 2009, we learned others were organizing "Tea Party" events around the nation to educate and empower concerned citizens who believed their government was out of control...

"...we are patriotic Americans. We peaceably assemble. We petition our government. We exercise our right to free speech. And we don't understand why our government tried to stop us...

"I am not here today as a serf or vassal. I am not begging my lords for mercy. I am a born-free American woman – wife, mother and citizen – and I'm telling MY government that you have forgotten your place.

It is not your responsibility to look out for my well-being or monitor my speech. It is not your right to assert an agenda. The posts you occupy exist to preserve American liberty. You have sworn to perform that duty. And you have faltered...

"The IRS wanted us to identify our volunteers...
"They wanted us to provide detailed contents of all speeches ever given, the names of all of our speakers, and their credentials...

"Government agents made invasive and excessive demands for information that they were not entitled to...

"The individuals who sought to intimidate us were acting as they thought they should, in a government culture that has little respect for its citizens...

"Many of the agents and agencies of the federal government do not understand that they are servants of the people. They think they are our masters. And they are mistaken...

"I want to protect and preserve the America I grew up in, the America that people cross oceans and risk their lives to become a part of. And I am terrified that it's slipping away..."

PART TWO
Progressive Control

Chapter Four
Addictionomics

*"Every form of addiction is bad,
no matter whether the narcotic
be alcohol, morphine or idealism."*

– Carl G. Jung
Memories, Dreams, Reflections [1]

*"You are not friends, or you would not
try to give us what makes us fools."*

– Arikara Native American
rejecting a gift of liquor from
Meriwether Lewis during the
Lewis & Clark Expedition [2]

Aldous Huxley began to write his 1932 dystopian novel *Brave New World* as a parody of then-popular Big Government Progressives and collectivists such as socialist H.G. Wells, author of *A Modern Utopia* and *Men Like Gods*, who believed that through science they could create a perfect society and perfect people.

One means of social control in Huxley's *Brave New World* was not fear or intimidation but soma, a drug that tranquilized and produced euphoria in almost every character in the novel.

At one point in *Brave New World*, a crowd of people runs out of soma and starts to go into frenzied panic. A global government truck arrives and sprays the calming drug over the crowd.

"There will be, in the next generation or so, a pharmacological method of making people love their servitude, and producing dictatorship without tears," Huxley told a California medical school audience in 1961.

Such a drug, he said, could produce a "painless concentration camp for entire societies, so that people will in fact have their liberties taken away from them, but will rather enjoy it, because they will be distracted from any desire to rebel by propaganda...or brainwashing enhanced by pharmacological methods." [3]

Brave New Money

In *Brave New World*, most people were happy. They practiced free love and had the "feelies," movies that electrically induced artificial emotions and feelings. Soma gave them a life of sensual pleasure, serenity without pain, and even pseudo-religious experiences. The soma, along with their mental programming as infants, also apparently dulled those parts of the brain that think, raise hard questions, let people perceive reality, or crave freedom.

We, of course, would never live in Brave New World, would we? In today's America more than 70 percent of us are taking at least one pharmaceutical drug, and 50 percent of us regularly use more than one. Many of the foods we eat cause a variety of drug-like changes in our bodies, including stimulants such as coffee, tea and chocolate. What else in our lives is mind-altering?

"At Harvard Medical School, neuroscientist Hans Breiter has compared activity in the brains of cocaine addicts who are expecting to get a fix and people who are expecting to make a profitable financial gamble," writes *Wall Street Journal* columnist Jason Zweig in his book *Your Money & Your Brain: How the New Science of Neuroeconomics Can Help Make You Rich.*

"The similarity isn't just striking," writes Zweig. "It's chilling."

Dr. Breiter's MRI brain images suggest, Zweig writes, that "once you score big on a few investments in a row, you may be the functional equivalent of an addict – except the substance you're hooked on isn't alcohol or cocaine, it's money." [4]

At the heart of what money means to us are great mysteries about what persuades people that certain pieces of paper are worth trading a large portion of our lives for.

Economist Irving Fisher identified one of these mysteries in the title of his 1928 book *The Money Illusion*, as we explained in 2011 in *The Inflation Deception*. Fisher's theory is that we tend to value paper currency not at its real purchasing power, which can vary, but at its numerical face value.

Our economic decisions are not entirely rational, Fisher found, which runs counter to the Enlightenment view of how the marketplace works. Because of this, his theory was rejected for more than 60 years by most mainstream economists.

Today, however, new scientific research is finding evidence that the Money Illusion influences much of our economic behavior.

Which, for example, would you prefer – a two percent raise in an economy with one percent inflation, or a four percent raise in an economy with five percent inflation?

Oddly enough, researchers find that a major proportion of people tend to choose the bigger numerical raise even though even-higher inflation wipes it out.

The two percent raise would have been far more remunerative, in accord with the old principle: "It's not what you make; it's what you (in purchasing power) keep." Yet money illusion deludes our irrational minds with a larger number.

Number Our Daze

Writing about the pervasive power of "money illusion" in their book *Animal Spirits: How Human Psychology Drives the Economy, and Why It Matters for Global Capitalism*, University of California Berkeley Nobel laureate economist George A. Akerlof and Yale University economist Robert J. Schiller remind us that money is more than "a medium of exchange" and "a store of value."

Money, they write, is also a third thing, "a unit of account," meaning that "people think in terms of money" and the quality and quantity of its units. [5]

Our accustomed units of money such as U.S. Dollars, British Pounds or the Euro become measures of our idea of value – much as Americans think of distance in terms of inches, feet and miles, while Europeans think in millimeters, meters and kilometers.

The units that Americans and Europeans use for distance are fixed and unchanging. Miles can thus consistently be converted into kilometers, or vice versa, by the same formulas today or 10 or 100 years from now.

Economists, according to Akerlof and Schiller, used to assume that money has a similar convertibility and that currency was merely a "veil" – that "people saw through inflation and it had no effect on real transactions." New research suggests otherwise.

"We believe that, in going from nominal dollars to real dollars, something will be lost in translation," they write. "Such losses would be the consequences of money illusion."

Minding the Casino

Our units of money, when under the influence of a variety of factors that include inflation and the psychologies of inflation expectation and money illusion, keep changing....shrinking or stretching like rubber in how our minds perceive and attach value to them.

Think of this as a variant of why gambling casinos have gamblers in their table games play with casino chips instead of actual money, or how banks provide credit cards that allow someone to spend and spend without needing to hand over even a single actual dollar bill. Both of these methods can distort a person's sense of reality and judgment about the transactions he or she is making.

Currency trading is an entire investment specialty based on wagering how one currency will rise or fall relative to another. We can use the objective, mechanical brain of a computer to calculate the results of such transactions.

Nevertheless, political human brains will manipulate the supply of dollars via inflation, and all-too-human emotional brains influenced by uncertainty and money illusion will respond with a subjective desire for greater numbers of dollars, even when inflation has made a larger number of dollars worth less. This is the psychological manipulation, the illusion, that has kept people working for the past 30 years with no increase in real, inflation-adjusted pay. They get more and more dollars that, because of deliberate inflation, each have less and less purchasing power.

Supply and Demand is a natural law of economics, but this does not mean that either scientists or economists fully understand all the factors that give green pieces of paper their power to stir human demand. This power reaches beyond mere convertibility or exchange value.

The Wealth Effect

"Inflation is the true opium of the people," wrote Austrian economist Ludwig von Mises, "and it is administered to them by anti-capitalist governments and parties."

Among the first effects and symptoms of inflation is an illusion of prosperity, abundance and well-being that tricks most of the people sometimes, and some people all of the time. When this sweeps through an economy, it is called the "wealth effect," an artificially-induced "high" that Federal Reserve Chair Ben Bernanke has openly acknowledged he hopes to produce by injecting stimulus money he has conjured out of thin air into the economy.

This effect of inflation is addictive and requires ever-increasing doses of stimulus money. Soon thereafter, it is followed by a crash when people lose faith in their paper money. A hangover then ensues that can last for years, even decades. [6]

This inflation deception happened in Germany's Weimar Republic after World War I, where vast quantities of paper money run off the printing presses first intoxicated, then addicted, and in its hyperinflationary crash devastated the society as people needed wheelbarrows full of money to buy a single loaf of bread.

Social values were destroyed in the upside-down Weimar world where hard work and thrift led to poverty, while irresponsible borrowing made wastrels wealthy as they paid off debts with devalued worthless currency. Weimar's hyperinflation and moral breakdown thus paved the path to the depravity of Adolf Hitler.

In a healthy, productive society, each working person, on average, produces at least as much as he or she consumes. The money a person earns for productive work is an honest claim on goods and services in the marketplace.

One of the fundamental problems with inflation is that politicians concoct vast quantities of paper money in excess of what people are actually producing.

This concocted cash is created so that the politicians can give themselves and other unproductive people a dishonest claim on available goods and services that others worked to produce.

This effectively transfers much of the earnings of productive people into the pockets of the unproductive, while bidding up the price of everything for consumers.

Those who get the biggest gain from such newly-made fiat money are the ones who receive it first. They can buy at the lower old prices, before the marketplace adjusts by the irrevocable Law of Supply and Demand to the larger supply of paper dollars available to buy things.

As these new dollars go from hand to hand, they lose value because sellers recognize this growing supply of dollars as a sign that the value of dollars is in decline.

Your Brain on Inflation

Researchers at California Institute of Technology and Stanford University in 2008 reported finding that the higher the price tag that tasters saw on a bottle of wine, the more "pleasantness" they experienced from drinking it.

People often respond better to a higher-priced product, expecting that the price is based on higher quality. What makes this research experiment unusual was that its 20 participants responded while a sophisticated MRI monitored their brain activity.

The researchers identified more than half a dozen precise regions within the brain that seem to have a hedonic response of "experienced pleasantness" to higher prices.

One of these researchers, Antonio Rangel of Cal Tech, working with scientists at the University of Bonn in Germany, reported finding evidence that the brain's medial prefrontal cortex "exhibits money illusion."

Their study, published in 2009 in the *Proceedings of the National Academy of Sciences* of the United States of America, suggests "that money illusion is real in the sense that the level of reward-related brain activity [in this cortex] in response to monetary prizes increases with nominal changes that have no consequence for subjects' real purchasing power." [7]

If money illusion is real, these researchers write, then potentially "central banks can affect production, investment, and consumption through changes in monetary policy that have an impact on the inflation rate."

If the money illusion influences people to respond favorably to larger numeric quantities of money – even when that quantity has lower purchasing power – then, they note, this might be a possible cause of bubbles in markets such as housing.

If the money illusion exists, they write, this could become a factor in setting wages for workers. Employees under money illusion might care more about nominal wages (and promised future benefits) than about real wages.

"The existence of money illusion is important," they write, "for the understanding of the relation between income, inflation, and subjective well-being. Importantly, even small amounts of money illusion can have substantial effects...[in which] small deviations from rationality imply big and lasting effects in aggregate outcomes." [8]

Some researchers in this field call Money Illusion "the Inflation Illusion."

Such new scientific approaches, along with those from emerging disciplines such as neuroeconomics, are providing powerful new insights into money, inflation, and how we might be manipulated. These and other studies already suggest some disquieting realities.

Addictive Dollars

The effects of money and the money illusion, and by extension an increase in the quantity of money as is seen in inflation or hyperinflation, vary widely from one individual to another – but research now suggests that in some people money apparently has the ability to:

– Cause changes within the brain and body, likely by stimulating the release of pleasure-inducing neurotransmitters. (Might this help explain why some people become shopaholics for certain high-priced merchandise?)

– Bypass or diminish our ability to think rationally, thereby subtly changing our perception of reality as well as our judgment and decision-making processes. (This effect in some cases could be akin to the hallucinatory "high" caused by intoxicating alcohol or other perception- and judgment-altering drugs.)

– Create cravings for ever-increasing quantities of money, a response akin to addiction and chemical dependency.

Future scientific studies should pursue how far this parallel between the mental and physiological effects of drugs and inflation goes. From what the evidence already suggests, a few such questions about inflation to consider are these:

– Does inflation cause bipolar disorder, an emotional and physiological roller coaster ride of extreme ups and downs in which "irrational exuberance" is followed by feelings of sickness, weakness, disorientation, stress, anxiety and depression?

– Does a causal link exist between economic depressions and widespread emotional depression, and between the health of the economy and the physical and mental health of many people living in that economy?

– Could this mean that by treating and curing a distorted economic consciousness in individuals, we can cure economic problems in society – and vice versa?

– Does the diminishing value of money during inflation, or a person's inability to increase income as fast as prices rise, cause something akin to a drug user's withdrawal symptoms? In what ways can today's unreal economic policies induce symptoms of a Great Withdrawal in America?

The Money Drug

"Pecuniary *[i.e., of, concerning or consisting of money]* motives either do not act at all – or are of that class of stimulants which act only as Narcotics," observed poet Samuel Taylor Coleridge.

Both cash and cocaine can trigger release of the neurotransmitter dopamine in the brain, a chemical associated with excitement and pleasure that in tiny natural doses reinforces learning and memory, as when a person does something successful for the first time.

In unnaturally large amounts, things such as cocaine that elicit dopamine become addictive and destructive.

Perhaps this is one of the reasons why the Bible warns that "the *love of* money," an addictive, obsessive or near-idolatrous fixation on money, "is a root of all kinds of evil. It is through this craving that some have wandered away from the faith and pierced themselves with many griefs." (Emphasis added.)[9]

Society is more than the sum of its individual members, yet it embodies a kind of democracy of the prevalent values, habits, beliefs, strengths and weaknesses of a majority of its people. As the ancient Greek philosopher Plato said, society is "man writ large."

This may help explain why some societies are prosperous while others remain poor. [10]

High on Inflation

"When the alcoholic starts drinking, the good effects come first," wrote Nobel Laureate economist Milton Friedman in 1992.

"[T]he bad effects come only the next morning, when he wakes up with a hangover – and often cannot resist easing the hangover by taking 'the hair of the dog that bit him.'" [11]

"The parallel with inflation is exact," continued Friedman. "When a country starts on an inflationary episode, the initial effects seem good. The increased quantity of money enables whoever has access to it – nowadays primarily governments – to spend more without anybody else having to spend less. Jobs become more plentiful, business is brisk, almost everybody is happy – at first. Those are the good effects."

"[T]hen the increased spending starts to raise prices," wrote Friedman. "Workers find that their wages, even if higher in dollars, will buy less; businesses find that their costs have risen, so that the higher sales are not as profitable as had been anticipated, unless prices can be raised even faster."

"The bad effects are emerging: higher prices, less buoyant demand, inflation combined with stagnation."

"As with the alcoholic," wrote Friedman, "the temptation is to increase the quantity of money still faster, which produces the kind of roller coaster the United States has been on."

"In both cases, it takes a larger and larger amount, of alcohol or of money, to give the alcoholic or the economy the same 'kick.'"

"The parallel between alcoholism and inflation carries over to the cure," wrote Friedman. "The cure for alcoholism is simple to state: stop drinking. But the cure is hard to take because this time the bad effects come first, the good effects later."

"The alcoholic who goes on the wagon suffers severe withdrawal pains before emerging in the happy state of no longer having that almost irresistible desire for another drink."

"So also with inflation," Friedman continued. The initial effects of a slower rate of monetary growth are painful: lower economic growth and temporarily higher unemployment without, for a time, much reduction in inflation."

"The benefits begin to appear only after one or two years or so, in the form of lower inflation, a healthier economy, [and] the potential for rapid noninflationary growth."

Detox

In the early 1980s, noted Friedman, then-Fed Chair Paul Volker and President Ronald Reagan took the United States, cold turkey, off the insane, near-suicidal double-digit inflationary binge President Jimmy Carter's Progressive policies unleashed.

Many of the evils threatening our world and economy today have their origins in the four-year ruinous reign of Mr. Carter, now second only to Mr. Obama as the least competent and most destructive president in American history.

President Carter, in effect, stole half the life savings' purchasing power of the American people. President Obama's policies are on track to steal every remaining penny of the life savings of Americans, to crash the U.S. Dollar and leave the U.S. economy wrecked beyond hope of repair or recovery.

It took great political and moral courage for President Reagan to restore sanity to the economy and soundness to the dollar. For millions of innocent Americans this wringing out of epidemic inflation caused pain, loss, temporary unemployment and hardship. He was detoxing America from getting hooked on President Carter's monetary morphine.

Millions of less innocent Americans, Friedman suggests, had "the absence of a real desire to end the addiction."

Inflation robs those who work hard, are thrifty and live sober, responsible lives. It punishes those who defer their pleasures and invest in building a better future.

Inflation rewards those who borrow and buy instead of saving, because it lets speculators repay their debts with debased, cheapened dollars.

"Many of us are not unhappy about inflation," wrote Friedman. "Naturally, we would like to see the prices of the things we buy go down, or at least stop going up. But we are glad to see the prices of the things we *sell* go up."

"One reason inflation is so destructive," Friedman continued, "is because some people benefit greatly and others suffer; society is divided into winners and losers."

"The winners regard the good things that happen to them as the natural result of their own foresight, prudence, and initiative. They regard the bad things – the rise in prices of the things they buy – as the fault of forces outside their control."

"Almost all of us will say that we are against inflation," wrote Friedman, when "what we generally mean is that we are against the bad things about it that have happened to us."

The drug of inflation, wrote Friedman, thus makes us "schizophrenic."

Upping the Dosage

"Easy money is the opiate of the American economy," wrote University of Maryland economist Peter Morici in July 2013, and "like the addict, it needs ever larger doses to stay on task."

"Last September, the Fed nearly doubled purchases of long-term securities," wrote Morici, "but growth has since slowed to about 1 percent.... With growth slowing, the Fed may have to pump even more cash into the economy with diminishing results."

"Sooner or later the recovery could falter," warned Morici, "and much like Europe, a few pockets will prosper but much of the rest of the country, like Spain and Italy, will sink into double-digit unemployment." [12] Even if we survive the withdrawal symptoms of quitting the Progressive drug of easy money, will we be able to go from its depressed "New Normal" to America's healthy Old Normal? Or will we forever be Progressaholics?

Chapter Five
The Herd Inside Our Heads

"You never want a serious crisis to go to waste ....crisis provides the opportunity for us to do things that you could not do before."

– Rahm Emanuel
President Barack Obama's
first White House Chief of Staff
Wall Street Journal, Nov. 19, 2008

"Every collectivist revolution rides in on a Trojan horse of 'emergency'."

– Herbert Hoover

For Native Americans of the Western Plains, hunting buffalo with puny arrows was difficult and sometimes deadly to the hunter. The Blackfoot and other tribes devised an easier, although ecologically destructive, way to kill their prey and obtain a year's worth of meat in mere minutes.

As Lewis and Clark described, a swift-footed young brave wearing a buffalo head and hide would move between a grazing herd and a nearby cliff. At a prearranged signal, the hunting band would stand up and rush towards the herd from the opposite sides.

As the animals panicked, the young brave who appeared to be a buffalo would start running towards the cliff. Being herd animals, the buffalo would follow him and start to stampede. At the last moment, the brave ducked into a rock shelter. The onrushing frightened buffalos, unable to see the danger or stop, charged over the cliff to their doom.

Government by Crisis

Progressives long ago mastered the ancient art of herding people by using, or creating, crises.

"The whole aim of practical politics," wrote journalist H.L. Mencken almost a century ago, "is to keep the populace alarmed – and hence clamorous to be led to safety – by menacing it with an endless series of hobgoblins, all of them imaginary."

Why do you think that the January 2013 panic-driven congressional agreement to authorize $41 in new government spending for every $1 in spending cuts was urgently needed? Ironically, it was to prevent America from "*going over the fiscal cliff,*" which lawmakers and the public were told would be a nightmarish disaster for the economy.

This is what being "bullish" means today – to be buffaloed cattle who are herded and stampeded by the powers that be for their financial or political benefit.

America was once a democratic Republic, yet Progressives are turning us into a "crisis-ocracy."

Progressive politicians no longer gain and wield power through reasoned debate and calm compromise – but through the politics of emotion, crisis, panic, fear and emergency decrees.

Crisis, real or concocted, is an easier way to move the public than old-fashioned honest consensus-building. It has also become an easier way to move politicians, many of whom privately confess that our system needs crises to overcome partisan stalemate.

"The perfection of interest-group politics," wrote Federal Circuit Court Judge Richard Posner in his 2010 book *The Crisis of Capitalist Democracy*, "seems to have brought about a situation in which...taxes can't be increased, spending programs can't be cut, and new spending is irresistible." [1]

To restore the Republic, we can and must immunize ourselves against such political manipulation of our minds, money, values and votes.

Our first step to escape the emerging crisis-ocracy – which could also be called a "panicracy" – government by panic – is to understand how it works.

Panicracy's President

President Barack Obama was elected by precisely such tactics. As we documented in our 2011 book *The Inflation Deception*, weeks before the 2008 presidential election the United States suffered "a financial Pearl Harbor" attack as half a trillion dollars from mysterious overseas sources made a coordinated assault to undermine key U.S. Institutions, including Bear Stearns and Lehman Brothers. Both broke under vicious bear raids. [2]

The presidential race was put on hold as senators, including Republican standard-bearer John McCain and his Democratic rival Barack Obama, rushed to Washington, D.C., amid demands that Congress authorize an immense bailout fund to prevent collapse of the nation's largest banks and investment houses.

Congress hesitated and then – after weeks during which no collapse occurred – agreed to authorize nearly a trillion dollars in emergency money for entities lawmakers were told were "too big to fail." The nation's top bankers were locked in a room until they agreed to accept huge government loans – and the political strings that came with this money.

We were told on three successive weekends that if this gigantic authorization did not pass, doomsday and global collapse would happen on Monday morning. Yet only, after nothing happened on two Mondays, on the third such weekend – and after another $80 Billion in pork for key lawmakers was added to the legislation – did the astronomical spending measure pass.

Much of this "urgent" money allocated in the name of emergency then sat idle for months or years, gradually being used as a political slush fund to reward crony capitalists, unions and politicians friendly to the Obama Administration.

In this atmosphere of media alarm and uncertainty, the wheels of commerce slowed and the economy slid into recession. A frightened electorate shifted from McCain to Obama, who came to office as head of a one-party government with Democrats also solidly in control of both the House and Senate.

Emergency Powers

President Obama promptly used emergency powers and government money to seize control of General Motors and Chrysler, taking both into bankruptcy to shed their debts.

Mr. Obama shoved aside the secured bondholders who by law had first claim on company assets during bankruptcies, then threatened and intimidated those who dared to challenge his high-handed behavior.

He then transferred a large share worth $26.5 Billion of the ownership of these companies to the left-liberal United Auto Workers union, a major campaign contributor to Democratic politicians. This was, noted critics, the behavior not of an elected American president but of a caudillo dictator in a Central American banana republic.

This set the stage for all bondholders, municipal or corporate, that were fully-secured to be left swinging in the financial wind with the stroke of the President's pen. This sent shockwaves to every future purchaser of bonds – other than U.S. bonds – for we are told America would have to be bankrupt for its bonds to be worthless. America will never go bankrupt, of course. Its Progressive leaders will just bankrupt the People.

President Obama's high-handed re-writing of the rules concerning bonds is only one of many, many examples of this Progressive ruler putting himself above the law.

When the Democrat-controlled U.S. Senate rejected the President's budget 95-0, a bill that would also have given him the power to regulate carbon dioxide (which we carbon-based human life forms exhale after every breath), President Obama had his Environmental Protection Agency set about imposing such power via regulation.

Mr. Obama is the first President ever held in contempt of court for illegally obstructing oil drilling in the Gulf of Mexico in defiance of a court order. He blocked uranium mining on federal land in northern Arizona and has attempted unilaterally to shut down coal operations in Appalachia.

Approximately 80 percent of the $90 Billion budgeted for solar and other alternative energy goes to companies such as Solyndra whose leadership included major Democratic campaign donors.

President Thomas Jefferson once said that "great issues should not be forced on slender majorities." Obamacare was rammed through using parliamentary gimmickry after a special Massachusetts election had cost Democrats their ruling Senate majority – so socialized medicine was forced onto Americans not with a slender majority, but with no filibuster-proof legislative majority at all.

In the House of Representatives, Democratic Speaker Nancy Pelosi forced an Obamacare vote by lawmakers who were given no time to read the final legislation. "We have to pass the bill so you can find out what's in it," Ms. Pelosi, who grew up as daughter of the Democratic machine political boss in Baltimore, haughtily told them. Welcome to Progressive democracy and the politics of forcing lawmakers to buy every pig in a poke, with its details and defects hidden from view. In the January 2013 Fiscal Cliff law, Senators reportedly were likewise given 3 minutes to read a 150-page bill before voting on it.

In election year 2012 President Obama refused to negotiate with congressional Republicans over immigration reform. Then, on June 15, he imposed his own version of the DREAM Act by Executive fiat, allowing millions of illegal immigrants – including criminals – to remain in the U.S. and obtain work permits. This allowed illegals legally to take jobs here while 23 million American citizens were unemployed or underemployed. This defiance of law won enough Hispanic votes to secure Mr. Obama's re-election.

Mr. Obama also issued an Executive directive that allowed state welfare departments to waive the requirement that welfare recipients must seek work. This slapped aside the "Workfare" law signed in 1996 by President

Bill Clinton that had reduced welfare rolls by half.

This not only encouraged more welfare dependency, but also meant that the unemployment rate would "improve" from above 8 percent into the high 7 percent range for the first time during Mr. Obama's presidency.

This gimmick did not create a single new job. However, because those who stop looking for work for four weeks are no longer counted as unemployed, this trick allowed Mr. Obama weeks before the 2012 election to claim that his economic policies were succeeding. It was a crisis-ocracy-conjured illusion.

The Fed Fumble

Between them, the Federal Government and Federal Reserve injected more than $6 Trillion in stimulus money into the economy. Economists in both institutions expected that this much money – some taxed from achievers, but most conjured by the Fed out of thin air as paper fiat money – was, by the "multiplier" in Keynesian theory, supposed to produce $1.50 in economic stimulus for every $1 redistributed from rich savers to poor spenders by increasing money's velocity in the marketplace.

Keynes apparently was mistaken about stimulus and its multiplier effect, according to research by economists Ethan Ilzetzki of the London School of Economics and Enrique G. Mendoza and Carlos A. Vegh of the University of Maryland. They studied how it worked in 44 different countries and found that the Keynesian fiscal multiplier can be effective in emerging countries with low debts, fixed exchange rates and closed economies.

In advanced nations like the United States with high debt, floating exchange rates and open economies, however, Keynesian measures are often much less effective.

And because American banks borrowed stimulus money and promptly re-lent much of it at a profit to the U.S. Government, the velocity of this money in the economy did not speed up. It slowed down, making worse the very economic slowdown that Keynesian stimulus was supposed to prevent.

In July 2013 a former Fed Governor, Laurence Meyer, told CNBC that the velocity of money in the economy means nothing. "Money doesn't appear in any modern macro model," he said. "We're beyond that now."

The Keynesian magic never happened. As we predicted and document in our *The Inflation Deception*, this flood of unearned trillions into the marketplace created an "anti-stimulus." [3]

Instead of creating prosperity, the Fed's stimulus fumble made business people slow down their hiring and investing out of fear that a tidal wave of inflation would inevitably follow.

The feared inflation tsunami *is* coming, because politicians can no more repeal the Law of Supply and Demand than they can repeal the Law of Gravity. Inflation is the price of government creating a mountain of dollars to exchange for the same old basket of goods, and our stagnant 1-2 percent economic growth is already being eaten up by real inflation that is running around 7 percent. The inflation is all around us as asset inflation, frozen money waiting to thaw and ignite, and exported obligations.

The Stealth Recession

We never left the 2008 Great Recession, in our opinion. And legitimate data – not massaged, manipulated government data – backs up our opinion 100 percent.

The American economy is already devastated by debt now bigger than our $16 Trillion annual Gross Domestic Product (nearly 40 percent of which now comes from federal, state and local government spending, not actual productivity of goods or services).

During President Obama's first four years, the Federal Government share of America's GDP rose from 19.5 percent to a peak at approximately 25 percent as the government grew relative to our economy by 25 percent.

Twice as many Americans are now employed by government as work in all of manufacturing combined. At least 49.1 percent of U.S. households now include one or more persons who receive a government benefit. Under Mr. Obama we have become a nation in which at least 43 percent of working-age adults pay no income tax, and who therefore are likely to see government as a free goody-dispensing machine.

We have undergone the "fundamental transformation" this former radical community organizer desired, into a southern European-style Welfare State with chronic high unemployment, low productivity, stagnant growth, and therefore an addictive dependence on ever-more wealth redistribution by an ever-growing government.

No wonder that Yale Law Professor Jack Balkin has said: "The American Presidency is currently on steroids, and will continue to be for a very long time to come."

The Crisis-ocracy Trap

Our politicians and Fed now find themselves caught in a trap of their own making. The economy is now addicted to ever-increasing doses of cheap, near-zero-interest stimulus money, yet such spending debases the dollar and will ultimately destroy our economy, unless stopped.

The politicians need more and more wealth to redistribute to buy their re-elections, but putting heavier taxes on the backs of the productive is already reducing productivity, jobs and economic growth.

In the wake of Hurricane Sandy's devastation of New Jersey, we saw President Obama and other politicians promise everything to victims and then deliver almost nothing. What did emerge in January 2013 was a pair of emergency aid packages that added up to $60 Billion. More than half of this amount, said critics, was political pork for special interests that did nothing to help Sandy's victims....but that passed because of their tragedy. Such emergency "Christmas spending trees" used to be the exception for politicians. They are now the norm.

The U.S. Senate refused to pass a new budget for nearly four years because, after Republicans regained control of the House of Representatives in 2010, getting a new budget through Congress would require compromise and cuts in the absurdly-high spending levels enacted during the Democrats' government monopoly of Mr. Obama's first two years as president. The Senate therefore maintains high spending via continuing resolutions, not whole new budgets as the Constitution requires.

Because of Senate rule-breaking and President Obama's unwillingness to reduce the size of government, the only opportunity Republicans have to cut spending comes when a debt limit ceiling is reached, when GOP lawmakers can force Democrats to choose between a partial government shutdown or trimming down our dangerously-obese Uncle Sam.

This has produced a crisis-oriented kind of compromise – brief extensions of the debt ceiling that let wild spending continue, but on a short leash.

"The budget is a Doomsday Machine," said David Stockman, the controversial former Budget Director for President Ronald Reagan. Our current crisis-ocracy thus creates "a new fiscal cliff every few months," as we become the buffalos stampeded to the edge of each of these cliffs.

Escaping The Trap

Living amidst crisis-driven economics and politics is stressful and can produce unanticipated consequences – from heart attacks to mental and social breakdown.

While President Obama was using the Newtown shooting tragedy as a crisis to impose gun control, *Forbes* Magazine columnist Louis Woodhill offered three important ideas to reduce the fear that pushes people to acquire more guns. He urged President Obama to stop using crises to circumvent the Constitution, and instead to do more to suppress crime so people will feel safer.

Mr. Woodhill's third suggestion showed deep understanding of how government via crisis-ocracy is harming us – and can be reversed: "Stabilize the dollar," he wrote.

"Inflation, and even the possibility of inflation, creates anxiety," he wrote. "People sense (correctly) that inflation threatens their survival. Hyperinflation can cause not only economic disaster, but also a collapse of law and order."

"Faced with a dollar subject to the whims of [Fed Chairman] Ben Bernanke and Barack Obama, people will buy more guns," wrote Woodhill. "Returning to a stable, gold-defined dollar would, among other things, reduce the demand for firearms," he concluded.

Amen. And so, too, would a return to civilized politics and an end to openly ideological class warfare bullying by an imperious president who relishes ruling by decree, demonization of opponents, and outright intimidation.

Because the politicians tax us by devaluing and debasing our dollars, few are eager to return to the honest, gold-defined dollar that made America great, prosperous and free. So long as we denominate our lives and hold our savings in the form of paper fiat dollars, we will will render onto Caesar a growing share of our labors and suffer more stress and fear at one cliff after another.

We have an alternative. We can create our own personal and family gold standard, our own liberating transformation, by exchanging politicized paper dollars for gold that the politicians cannot debase by running more off a printing press in Washington, D.C.

Gold is the historically-proven way to anchor your savings in solid value, to step back from the cliff and avoid being stampeded by fear that the dollar is about to disintegrate with each new political crisis.

Creating a personal gold standard can be a golden key to escape the crisis-ocracy trap, to live with economic security and peace-of-mind, to replace danger with opportunity.

Neuroeconomics

Louis Woodhill is rational and right, but he comes from a past era where people still engaged in thought, ideas and logical debate.

Ours is the age of Addictionomics and the hypnotic illusion that we live in a real economy based on real money. Another *Forbes* columnist, Peter Ferrara, clearly sees through this mirage economy based on fiat dollars conjured out of thin air:

"Money doesn't grow on trees, you say?" wrote Ferrara in June 2013. "That outdated notion is where you went wrong. Today's paper money IS trees." [4]

Today the aim of politicians, economists and advertisers is to bypass our shrinking rational brains and grab us by our emotions, reprogram our values, and control how we vote, spend and believe by manipulating our subconscious minds.

Did you know that President Obama during the summer of 2013 began assembling a "behavioral insights team" in the White House? [5]

Did you know that this team is recruiting behavioral psychologists, neuroeconomists and other experts who study how the irrational mind makes economic decisions, and other specialists in what influences and persuades us?

Did you know that such teams of scientific mind-altering experts from America's top universities played a major role in electing President Obama in 2008 and re-electing him despite disastrous economic Obamalaise in 2012? [6]

The key member of both campaign teams and inspiration for this new office is Harvard Law School Professor Cass Sunstein, co-author with University of Chicago Behavioral economist Richard Thaler of the provocative 2008 book *Nudge: Improving Decisions About Health, Wealth, and Happiness*. [7]

"Paternalistic Libertarianism"

Nudge argues that people in the free market often make poor decisions, and that government or other superior guides should "nudge" them to make better choices.

Nanny Statists Thaler and Sunstein call their elitist approach "paternalistic libertarianism" because it non-coercively and gently pushes people to do what Nanny Statist Progressives – the authoritarian opposite of liberty-loving Libertarians – think is best for them....to lose weight, eat healthier foods, save money, conserve energy, and so forth.

In a key chapter of *Nudge* titled "Following the Herd," Sunstein and Thaler acknowledge that they recommend three psychological techniques for "nudging" someone.

The first technique is information – structured in a "choice architecture" that provides only limited choices...because too many alternatives are stressful and tend to delay someone from making a decision.

Their second technique is peer pressure, a technique also used in small communities of the past, as well as in Communist Party cells and among Progressives to impose conformity, obedience and collectivist groupthink.

Sunstein's and Thaler's third technique for "nudging" someone is priming, subtly programming the mind with trigger words, concepts, images and cues that can move a person towards a particular response and decision.

In the hands of entirely honorable people, nudging can be relatively harmless and sometimes helpful. Used by more sinister manipulators, *Nudge*'s techniques might become a form of mind and behavioral control. And when used by self-serving government, *Nudge* might become the velvet glove that disguises an iron fist.

It could be used not to persuade people to do what is in their best interests, but it could also be used for what MIT radical intellectual Noam Chomsky calls "the manufacture of consent," to manipulate people into assenting to whatever the State or ruling political party wishes.

A "nudge" is a kind of push, and this push could come to shove.

"Nudging" Voters to Obama

When in 2008 Sunstein and Thaler assembled a team of behavioral scientists to help elect then-Senator Barack Obama, among their recruits were Duke University's Dan Ariely, author of *Predictably Irrational*, and Princeton University Nobel laureate behavioral economist Daniel Kahneman, author of *Thinking, Fast and Slow*.

This team apparently helped tailor Mr. Obama's campaign message and direct it to precisely-targeted "profiled" audiences he could win over. As Sunstein would do again in 2012, he apparently helped develop ways to "prime" potential voters with such messages and to use peer pressure techniques.

On election day, for example, many who had not yet voted were called and told how many of their neighbors had already cast ballots. This implied that the neighbors might be told if they failed to vote.

This nudged prospective Democrats into going to the polls, where most voted for Mr. Obama. This technique was credited with significantly increasing voter turnout. A similar peer-pressure "nudge" for campaign donations weeks earlier likely also boosted the campaign's cash flow.

Many local American utility companies have begun using this "nudge" peer pressure technique by telling customers how their energy conservation compares to their neighbors'. A leader in this approach is Opower.

A grateful President Obama named Sunstein to head the Federal Government's Office of Information and Regulatory Affairs, which shapes and implements regulations and information technology. Sunstein served in this influential job from September 2009 until August 2012.

In 2008 Sunstein wed radical international activist Samantha Power, chosen in 2013 by President Obama to be Ambassador to the United Nations.

Herding Humans

Inspired by Sunstein and Thaler, the ruling Conservative Party in the United Kingdom years ago created its own governmental "Behavioural Insights Team" to nudge citizens in benign directions. When asked for an example of its success, one was that nudging had increased the percentage of citizens filing their taxes on time.

In April 2013 the government announced that this office would be partially privatized, making some of its knowledge and skill at swaying people available for commercial use.

Now, purportedly at Sunstein's nudging, the Obama White House is creating a similar permanent office in the U.S. Its manipulative techniques and data base can be used to help people, or to help politicians.

Much of "nudge," remember, aims to narrow the choices those it targets are given – and to influence them socially and subconsciously. This is a far cry from rational, open debate and discussion of issues and candidates.

We each have an individual mind and a collective mind. People will do things as members of a group, team, platoon or lynch mob that they would never do as individuals.

There is a herd inside our head that can prod us to behave differently in a group, and that makes human beings susceptible to being herded, stampeded and collectivized. Nudge targets our herd mind.

Manipulating Collective Consciousness

Much of the greatness of the Western tradition of the Enlightenment is that it encouraged individualism, giving freedom to those who did not surrender to the pressure to see oneself only as a member of a tribe, race or nation.

This is a large part of the genius of Western Civilization. And this is precisely what Progressivism seeks to destroy. Karl Marx acknowledged that his aim was to return humankind to a tribal way of life in which individuality is subsumed by the collective....or, as Hillary Clinton believes, “it takes a village to raise a child.”

Two recent examples shed light on this dark side of Progressivism. In 2012, four Democratic operatives produced an 80-page pamphlet on how to persuade people to support tougher gun control. [8]

Their advice to Democratic candidates was to “always focus on emotional and value-driven arguments about gun violence” and on “feelings,” while using “emotionally-engaging images.” It recommends avoiding discussion of the law, political differences, the Second Amendment, or the National Rifle Association that might leave listeners feeling they know too little to make an informed anti-gun decision.

“Don’t break the power and undermine the value of emotionally powerful images and feelings by appearing squeamish or apologetic in presenting” tales of horrific gun violence, the pamphlet advises. This is an example of how Progressives deal with almost all issues today: use emotions and demagoguery instead of rational discussion and debate.

Holder Aims to “Really Brainwash People”

Emotions are used to trump ideas, and to herd and stampede people to support Progressive policies and demands. Everything is a crisis, from guns to global warming to the debt ceiling, addressed not to thinking individuals but to the emotional group-think collectivized herd inside our head.

What is the objective of President Obama's Administration vis-a-vis guns and the mind?

His Attorney General Eric Holder may have told us. In 1995, as a U.S. Attorney in Washington, D.C., Holder in a speech before the Women's National Democratic Club said he was announcing a campaign to "really brainwash people into thinking about guns in a vastly different way."

Yes, Eric Holder admitted that his aim was to "brainwash people." Why are we not surprised?

His remarks were carried on C-SPAN2, a video of which can be seen by following our footnote to a clickable website. [9]

Also disturbing is a paper titled "Conspiracy Theories" co-authored by Cass Sunstein in 2008. In it we learn how he would deal with those who promote conspiracy theories on the Internet and elsewhere that government finds troublesome.

"Silence" Them

Sunstein proposes "that government should engage in cognitive infiltration of the groups that produce conspiracy theories" with stealth *agents provocateurs* who would undermine their ideas with contrary ideas. [10]

Sunstein's idea of an appropriate target for surveillance and infiltration would be a group "whose members believe that the federal government, say, is a hostile and morally repellent organization that is taking over the country, akin to a foreign invader...."

"Government," Sunstein and his co-author Adrian Vermeule of Harvard Law School wrote, "is faced with suppliers of conspiracy theories, and might aim at least in part to persuade, debias, or silence those suppliers."

Yup, he said "silence" them.

Government agents, they write, can introduce "cognitive diversity" into conspiracy web chat rooms and other communication centers because "polarization tends to decrease when divergent views are voiced..."

Ah, it reminds us of President Obama's Secretary of the Interior Sally Jewell, who in Summer 2013 told a gathering "I hope there are no 'warming deniers' in the Department of the Interior."

Secretary Jewell presumably made this intimidating, anti-science statement to frighten any honest scientists in her employ out of daring to dispute the Progressive Obama climate dogma and orthodoxy designed to justify immensely higher taxes and much more powerful government.

She clearly implied that dissenters would lose their jobs and then their heads to demonstrate that Progressives tolerate no deviation from the ideological party line.

The Borg

Perhaps Professor Sunstein should tell Secretary Jewell about the mind-opening virtue of allowing "cognitive diversity." Oh, wait, Progressives allow no diversity contrary to their own collectivist ideology, which is not unlike that of *Star Trek: The Second Generation*'s Progressive-collectivist species "The Borg."

Even the left-wing webzine *Salon.com* reacted with horror to Sunstein's "spine-chilling proposal," because he had a powerful government job as a controller of government information policy and is a close confidant to President Obama. [11]

How reassuring it was in August 2013 to read that President Obama had selected a panel of experts to review allegations that his National Security Agency had been collecting data about and spying on potentially millions of Americans – and to notice that one of Mr. Obama's hand-picked experts to do this honest, even-handed investigation of what might be a massive abuse of American rights and privacy is Cass Sunstein. [12] On April 14, 1999, Sunstein and co-author Stephan Holmes wrote a *Chicago Tribune* column titled "Why We Should Celebrate Paying Taxes."

"In what sense is the money in our pockets and bank accounts fully 'ours'?" they asked. "Did we earn it by our own autonomous efforts? Could we have inherited it without the assistance of probate courts? Do we save it without support from bank regulators....?"

"Without taxes there would be no liberty," Sunstein and Holmes wrote. "Without taxes there would be no property. Without taxes, few of us would have any assets worth defending...."

"Most importantly, the dependency of individual freedoms on collective contributions has not sufficiently penetrated the American debate over our basic rights....," they wrote. "You cannot be for rights and against government because rights are meaningless unless enforced by government.... *There is no liberty without dependency*." [Emphasis added] [13]

The voice of the Progressive rings loudly in this article, disparaging the individual, and confusing dependency on the collective with individual liberty.

When Progressives Outlaw Freedom...

Unlike Sunstein, who has benefited mightily from being part of Washington's ruling elite, millions of other Americans have learned the hard way that *because* of taxes, many of us have few assets worth defending.

Libertarians have a traditional reply to Progressive Statists like Professor Sunstein who seem mistakenly to believe that Americans' "unalienable" rights come from government, not God: "When Progressives outlaw freedom, only outlaws will be free."

Of course an American can be for human rights and against government. How else could we have overthrown the government of King George III to re-establish our rights? Perhaps Professor Sunstein has been worshipping the State too blindly.

Incidentally, do you remember President Obama in 2012 telling hardworking business owners: "You didn't build that...?"

Could Mr. Obama have learned this collectivist sophistry from his comrade and appointee Mr. Sunstein, who in his 1999 article wrote: "In what sense is the money in our pockets and bank accounts fully 'ours'? Did we earn it by our own autonomous efforts?"

Progressives for 100 years have used such rationalizations to justify taking more and more from the earnings of America's makers. As long as the pie was growing, there was enough to fatten makers and takers alike.

Today, however, the pie is shrinking, and a bloated Uncle Sam is shoving others aside so he can grab more and more of what is left.

People are starting to see our Potemkin economy for what it is. The Money Mesmerism that fooled so many is no longer entrancing. Our Voodoo Economics no longer pins down the paper "doll" in the U.S. Dollar.

The easy-money Gimme Pigs and Federal Reserve stimulus Zombies still come for free handouts when Progressives call, but the candy is losing its sweetness when every night in Detroit is Halloween.

The old tricks and treats of Quantitative Easing and Zero Interest are losing their magic when fewer and fewer are producting anything.

With withdrawal symptoms starting and sobriety returning, Progressives can no longer keep their game going through fraud and empty promises as they have until now. Nobody believes in them anymore. The dependence, however, remains.

"They're addicted to the 'crack' known as QE [Quantitative Easing]," is how veteran Fox Business News reporter and author Charles Gasparino in June 2013 described it.

All that the Progressives now have left is force – financial repression and the governance of snatch and grab, regulate and control. They can no longer rule as "addictators" because this drug is losing its potency from chronic overuse.

Even if they survive with their power intact, the only road into the future for collectivism is downhill. One way or another, we are watching the grim end of the Progressive 100-Year detour, and people turning right towards home.

Will the America of Founding giants, pioneers and faith revive and return? Or has a century of Progressive addiction and dictation made recovery of what once we were impossible?

The answer to this is in your hands. Which future do you want?

The Perennial Progressive / Socialist Agenda

"Three years after the end of the second world war, the drums are beating for a third. Civil liberties are being destroyed. Millions cry out for relief from unbearably high prices. The American way of life is in danger.

"The root cause of this crisis is Big Business control of our economy and government.

"With toil and enterprise the American people have created from their rich resources the world's greatest productive machine. This machine no longer belongs to the people. Its ownership is concentrated in the hands of a few...an invisible government....

"The...old parties, obedient to the dictates of monopoly.... refuse to negotiate a settlement of differences with the Soviet Union.... They move to outlaw the Communist Party....
"They build the Federal Bureau of Investigation into a political police with secret dossiers on millions of Americans....

"They shackle American labor with the Taft-Hartley Act at the express command of Big Business, while encouraging exorbitant profits through uncontrolled inflation....

"The Progressive Party will work through the United Nations for a world disarmament agreement to outlaw the atomic bomb... and...to destroy existing stockpiles of atomic bombs....

"The Progressive Party will initiate such measures of public ownership as may be necessary to put into the hands of the people's representatives the levers of control essential to the operation of an economy of abundance....

"The Progressive Party demands the overhaul of the tax structure according to the...ability to pay.... We propose to enact effective excess profits and undistributed profits taxation."

– Progressive Party Platform, 1948 [A]

Chapter Six
Financial Repression

"The bottom line is we're not broke,
there's plenty of money,
it's just [that] the government doesn't have it.

– Rep. Keith Ellison
(D.-Minnesota) speaking before
Progressive Democrats of America
July 25, 2013

Detroit has become a symbol of Progressivism's failure, yet at the same time another major birthplace of the global automobile industry has been thriving.

Welcome to southern Germany's auto cities: Munich, home of the Bavarian Motor Works BMW; just to its north Ingolstadt, home of Audi; and less than 150 miles west, Stuttgart, the home of Porsche and Mercedes.

Stuttgart is "the heart of Germany's middle-class prosperity," wrote *Time* financial reporter Rana Foroohar in August 2013. [1] The small and mid-size family-owned export companies here produce high-tech equipment for the automotive and other industries.

Here the "per capita GDP is a whopping $84,000, more than double that of Berlin," she reports. Such *Mittelstand* firms employ 60 percent of Germany's workers and produce more than half of the nation's total economic output.

Much of Germany's prosperity, along with the world-renowned quality of its automobiles, has been produced in and around the Stuttgart-Ingolstadt-Munich axis – as once was the case with American production in and around Detroit.

Euro-Peons

Germany has an intense work ethic, devotion to quality, and sound economics. These are things Detroit largely lost in its Great Withdrawal, an exodus of more than a million achievers.

During the 20th Century, Germany in two World Wars came close to conquering Europe. Both times it was driven back in part by American might embodied in our industrial heartland centered on Detroit.

In 1999, Germany began its third attempt to conquer the continent, this time via trade and economics. Its main weapon of choice has been a new currency launched that year called the Euro.

In previous books we have identified the Euro as Germany's Deutschmark in disguise, because through its position as the dominant economy in Europe Germany can largely control the Euro.

Germany's objective was to establish economic hegemony over the rest of Europe. Its aim was to turn the peoples of other nations there, who could not match Germany's wealth and productivity, into "Euro-peons."

In 2013, German policy decided to make an example of one of the smallest of the 17 nations in the Eurozone, whose members gave up their own currencies and adopted the Euro.

The shock waves from that event set off tremors around the world. Those with ears to hear recognize it as a warning that in many nations – including the United States – those who have bank accounts are at risk of government seizing all or a large part of their savings.

Welcome to Cyprus

The ancient Greeks believed that their goddess of love and beauty, Aphrodite, first came ashore on the eastern Mediterranean island of Cyprus.

The valuable metal that ancient Greeks mined there took its name from the island, *aes Cyprium*, later shortened to *Cuprum*, then *copper*.

Cyprus, with its rich farmland and balmy Southern California-like climate, has been coveted by conquerers for thousands of years. The latest are Turkish troops who seized the northern third of the island in 1974, later proclaimed it the Turkish Republic of Northern Cyprus, and remain today as 18 percent of the partitioned island's roughly one million people.

Until 2013, the 77 percent of Cypriots who are of Greek ancestry naively assumed that what they had earned by the sweat of their brow and saved in local banks was their money. They then received a terrifying wake-up call that could soon be coming to your local bank.

Cypriots awoke on March 18 to find their banks closed, local ATMs drained of cash, and their savings and checking accounts inaccessible. Their bewilderment and outrage soon boiled over in angry street protests.

Imagine how you would feel if you were suddenly locked out of your bank and bank accounts. How would you pay your bills or buy food for your family if you had set nothing aside for emergencies? How and why did this happen?

The European Central Bank implicitly backed a 100,000 Euro guarantee so people would not pull their bank deposits. In Cyprus, the top deposits above this amount took a 45.5 percent "haircut." This averted potential bank runs and a Great Withdrawal, even though the ECB lacks the reserves to make its guarantee good in a crisis.

Bankrupt

The Republic of Cyprus in January 2008 joined the Eurozone and accepted the Euro as its currency, just in time for its economy to be pulled down by the Great Recession that later that year hit much of Europe and the U.S.

Like their Eurozone kin in Greece, the Greek Cypriots had a fragile economy but strong credit – because lenders assumed that Germany would bail out any Eurozone nation's debt to protect the Euro.

The Cypriots borrowed heavily and invested heavily in Greece. When, with Eurozone encouragement, Greece stopped paying on its bonds, the banks of Cyprus lost billions. By March 2013 the two biggest banks of Cyprus were near bankruptcy.

The Greek Cypriot government and Cyprus' once-respected banks desperately needed a bailout and made a deal to get at least 10 Billion Euros from the "troika" – the European Commission, European Central Bank, and International Monetary Fund (IMF).

Angela Merkel Is Not Pleased

The Eurozone was intended to have a disciplined common currency that should give Germany an advantageous trading position with neighboring, Euro-using nations. [2]

What German policy miscalculated was that some Eurozone nations, especially the PIIGS – Portugal, Italy, Ireland, Greece and Spain – would be offered large loans by banks that assumed Germany would ultimately pay any such debt to keep Euro nations from defaulting. The PIIGS were intoxicated by the multi-billion-dollar credit cards they were offered as Eurozone members, and they spent like drunken teen-agers, running up huge debts that they could not pay when the global economy slid into recession.

From Germany's point of view, the result has been a nightmare of more than $600 Billion worth of bailouts.

To get this money, the Cypriot government agreed to ante up another 5.8 Billion Euros itself – to be raised by imposing a progressive "levy" on all island bank accounts...6.75 percent on accounts up to 100,000 Euros, 9.9 percent on accounts above 100,000 Euros, and 15 percent on accounts above 500,000 Euros.

The Eurocrats of the troika blessed this deal to confiscate a hefty chunk of all Republic of Cyprus bank accounts, despite the Cypriot government guarantee against loss of up to 100,000 Euros in all bank accounts – similar to the Federal Deposit Insurance Corporation protection for American bank accounts.

Like American Progressives, these Eurocrats assumed that governments' needs are always superior to individual rights.

(Old-fashioned Americans are usually shocked when they read the European Declaration of Rights, because every specified human right ends with a clause saying that it can be ignored whenever government "needs" to do so. Thank heaven that American rights are what our Declaration of Independence called "unalienable" and come from the Creator, not from expedient, self-serving governments and politicians.)

This Cypriot confiscation was exactly what the newly-elected President of Cyprus had explicitly promised only two weeks earlier that he would never do. Imagine, after this promise, learning that a hunk of money equivalent to several years' interest would be seized from your savings.

Why, furious citizens shouted, were ordinary people being robbed to cover the debts to foreign bankers – especially German bankers – incurred by Cypriot politicians and banks?

The troika, it seemed, had invaded Cyprus – like so many other invaders over millennia – and was looting the savings of ordinary citizens, merely because politicians needed the money and therefore felt entitled to take it.

The United States is the biggest funder of one third of this troika, the International Monetary Fund (IMF), but President Barack Obama did not threaten to withhold IMF funds unless it halted this bank robbery in Cyprus. By his silence, the President became an accomplice of the looters.

Pickpocket Progressives

American politicians have systematically looted all bank accounts in the United States for the past 100 years.

This has, with some historic exceptions, been done not by openly seizing all or part of the money in citizen bank accounts – but by stealth, the debasing of the dollar's value through deliberate inflation as stealth taxation.

In our 2011 book *The Inflation Deception*, we quoted economic historian G. Edward Griffin's explanation of how the wealth-eroding power of manufactured inflation has been, and is, used as a means of confiscation, a de facto invisible tax:

> *"Inflation has now been institutionalized at a fairly constant 5% per year. This has been determined to be the optimum level for generating the most revenue without causing public alarm. A 5% devaluation applies, not only to the money earned this year, but to all that is left over from previous years. At the end of the first year, a dollar is worth 95 cents. At the end of the second year, the 95 cents is reduced again by 5%, leaving its worth at 90 cents, and so on. By the time a person has worked 20 years, the government will have confiscated 64% of every dollar he saved over those years. By the time he has worked 45 years, the hidden tax will be 90%. The government will take virtually everything a person saves over a lifetime."*

Inflation can also be an ideological weapon used to wage class warfare, redistribute wealth, and overthrow nations and economic systems, as liberal British economist John Maynard Keynes explained in his 1919 book *The Economic Consequences of the Peace*:

"Lenin is said to have declared that the best way to destroy the Capitalist System was to debauch the currency," wrote Keynes. "By a continuing process of inflation, governments can confiscate, secretly and unobserved, an important part of the wealth of their citizens...."

"As the inflation proceeds and the real value of the currency fluctuates wildly from month to month," Keynes continued, "all permanent relations between debtors and creditors, which form the ultimate foundation of capitalism, become so utterly disordered as to be almost meaningless; and the process of wealth-getting degenerates into a gamble and a lottery."

"Lenin was certainly right," Keynes concluded. "There is no subtler, no surer means of overturning the existing basis of society than to debauch the currency. The process engages all the hidden forces of economic law on the side of destruction, and does it in a manner which not one man in a million is able to diagnose."

Inflation is a key method by which the wealth of the people they rule has been confiscated by Progressive bureaucrats in Washington, D.C., and by Social Democrat Eurocrats in Brussels. Inflation is achieved simply by printing vast quantities of fiat paper money – dollars or Euros – and spending them into the economy to dilute and debase the value of currency workers have earned and saved.

Financial Repression

For thousands of years, successful cultures taught that thrift was good, and that it was far better to be a saver than a spendthrift. To paraphrase Benjamin Franklin, a penny saved is a penny earned. In cultures where people postponed their pleasures and saved their money, the resulting accumulation of capital led to investment and prosperity.

Keynes wrote instead of savings as "the paradox of thrift." Economies, he taught, are expanded not by saving – which slows down the flow of money – but by spending, which accelerates the passing of money from one pair of hands to the next.

Prosperity, Keynes wrote, requires "animal spirits" of optimism, risk-taking and entrepreneurship...and requires trust that those who succeed will not have their earnings or savings confiscated.

Unlike most economists, Keynes practiced the theories he preached, making one fortune by investing, losing it, and then making a second large fortune. Unlike Mr. Obama, Keynes knew that increasing taxes in a down economy, or government looting of private savings accounts, would mortally wound the animal spirits needed to improve the economy for everybody.

In Cyprus we witnessed European welfare states dying because they have killed off the freedom and animal spirits that centuries ago made Europe prosperous and a source of enlightenment to the world.

In recent years, the Federal Reserve has used a cynical policy that prods savers to withdraw their bank accounts and invest them instead in higher-risk ventures such as stocks to stimulate the economy.

Economists have a formal term for the Fed policy: "Financial Repression." [3]

Fed policy can drive up or down the rates both of inflation in the economy and of interest that banks pay those with savings accounts.

Lately the Fed has deliberately driven down the rate banks pay to savers below the rate of inflation – classic financial repression – which means that people with savings accounts are losing money every day they leave their money in the bank.

Real world inflation of at least 7 percent each year is eating up the value of dollars in bank accounts faster than the bank's interest payments of 1 or 2 percent are increasing it. And your savings' purchasing power spirals down the drain even faster when bank fees nibble away at your principal in these accounts, and then government taxes the pittance you are paid.

Traditional savers are conservative, prudent, careful people who sleep better with their life savings secure. These are the values that built America.

The trouble is, many traditional Americans are being robbed blind by politicians and economic manipulators who, through inflation, are expropriating 5 percent or more of the wealth of working Americans via the stealth tax of inflation.

Most Americans have had far more expropriated quietly from the value of their savings accounts than even the greediest Cypriot politicians schemed to snatch directly via a one-time fee on citizen savings accounts.

Are you ready for a future where the old will be too poor to retire and must work until they drop in harness? Are you ready for a future where the young will have no place to advance up the job promotion ladder clogged by seniors who cannot retire? Are you ready for a declining society where a majority of takers and spenders devour a dwindling minority of makers and savers? This is the alternative future we can see in the crystal ball of Cyprus.

The Coming Savings Grab

Does anyone doubt that today's rapacious, spending-addicted Progressive politicians would hesitate to confiscate your life savings not only via inflation, but also directly if they had a pretext, an emergency of some kind, a plausible justification that they thought would let them get away with such a savings grab?

During President Barack Obama's first term, he massively expanded the Welfare State and dependency on government. He effectively nationalized one-sixth of the economy via Obamacare, seized control of several major banks and two of the nation's three biggest car companies. He expropriated 90 percent of a trillion dollars' worth of student loans. He increased the Federal Government's share of our Gross Domestic Product by 25 percent, and added $5.8 Trillion to our nation's debt – which now exceeds America's entire annual production, public and private.

As President Obama's second term unfolds, he will need enormous amounts of money to pay for his unrestrained big-spending and ever-bigger government agenda.

His next takeover target is almost certainly the $18.5 Trillion that Americans have saved in their personal Individual Retirement Accounts (IRAs), 401(K) plans, and pension accounts that hold U.S. Dollars and paper securities.

The Last Private Money

These are among the biggest pools of private money left in America, and our spendaholic Progressive politicians are eager for any excuse to siphon this treasure into the government's coffers.

In 2010 President Obama's Treasury and Labor Departments, as well as then-ruling congressional Democrats, were openly discussing ways to confiscate private retirement accounts and put in their place government "Annuities" backed by Treasury or other government securities, as the American Enterprise Institute reported.

Progressives apparently see such confiscation of savings as a way to enrich government, stimulate the economy and redistribute wealth. Progressives think it is unfair and unequal that self-reliant, responsible citizens defer their pleasure to create savings accounts with their hard-earned, hard-saved money.

Progressive plans to grab your savings were moved to the political back burner after Republicans won control of the House of Representatives in November 2010. Any economic crisis, however, could give the President a pretext to impose, and Republicans a reason to acquiesce to, these prepared plans overnight by Executive Order.

Between 41 cents and 46 cents of every dollar the Federal Government now spends is borrowed money, even as the "full faith and credit" of the government behind our faith-based U.S. Dollar is waning. The People's Republic of China and Japan used to be eager to buy U.S. debt, making it America's #1 export. Today such lenders are backing away, and 90 percent of American Treasury obligations are now purchased by the Federal Reserve – America's own quasi-private Central Bank.

A major factor in today's sick economy is that governments in both Europe and the United States have turned regulatory power into *de facto* government ownership and politicization of the banks....and therefore of the economy, which seems less and less to follow the old values of free market Capitalism and private property.

The government is literally paying today's credit card bills in our left pocket with more credit cards in our right pocket. It is adding more than a trillion dollars to our debt every year for as far as the eye can see. We are living in an Alice-in-Wonderland economy addicted not to productive work, but to the Federal Reserve conjuring ever-more free stimulus trillions out of thin air just to stave off collapse.

As of September 2013, the Fed continues to create $85 Billion each month. Chairman Bernanke has never used the word "taper" or "tapering," and neither has his most likely successor, Fed Vice Chair Janet Yellen. The Fed, of course, can alter its stimulus and call the change by some other name.

The bigger that Progressive governments get, the hungrier they get. If the Welfare State keeps growing, government will soon have to devour everything else to feed its bottomless appetite.

So what do you need to know to survive in this world of rapacious government?

Withdraw While You Can

In December 2012 a Joint Paper was issued by the Federal Deposit Insurance Corporation (FDIC) and the Bank of England (the Central Bank "Federal Reserve" of the United Kingdom). [4]

This Joint Paper shows how future failures by financial institutions deemed "too big to fail" can be paid for not with huge government bailouts, as happened in 2007-2009, but with "bail-ins," like what four months later would happen in Cyprus, that seize the assets of these institutions and their "unsecured creditors."

Who are these "unsecured creditors" whose wealth can be confiscated?

You are....*if* you have a bank account.

"Although few depositors realize it, legally the bank owns the depositor's funds as soon as they are put in the bank. Our money becomes the bank's, and we become unsecured creditors holding bank IOUs or promises to pay."

Thus wrote Ellen Brown, an attorney and Chair of the Public Banking Institute, in her March 2013 analysis of this FDIC-BOE Joint Paper titled "*It Can Happen Here: The Bank Confiscation Scheme for US and UK Depositors*." [5]

This is why the Government of Cyprus was able to seize billions from what depositors thought were their secure, private bank accounts in March 2013. [6]

This Joint Paper lays a basis for government seizing bank accounts to cover bank debts in the United States, the United Kingdom and other countries. Similar policies are being laid in the European Union, where banks in many countries are shaky, as well as in New Zealand and Canada, where approval for such "bail-ins" is included in the 2013 ruling party budget.

This is why veteran asset manager Eric Sprott titled his April 2013 analysis of this Joint Paper and Cyprus bank account seizures *Caveat Deposi-*

tor, "Depositor Beware." [7]

As private bank accounts become targets for government confiscation, banks here and abroad will become less stable. Banks will need to set aside more money, and offer higher interest rates to entice depositors to put their savings at risk as "unsecured creditors." [8]

Fewer people will want such no-longer-secure bank accounts, which will delight Keynesian government economists who see old-fashioned thrift as retarding economic growth.

As we noted, one reason the Federal Reserve has slashed interest rates is to impose "financial repression," to herd savers out of savings accounts that pay less than the rate of inflation, and into riskier investments such as stocks. [9]

Government policies will make mortgages and other loans more costly for borrowers, which could further retard business growth, hiring, and the housing market. Government's new banking regulation may kill the American free market economy while trying to "save" it.

And in the end, when private banks have all gone bust under the pressure of such regulations, government may be the only money-lender left... something Karl Marx and Friedrich Engels called for in their 1848 *Communist Manifesto*. [10]

Many believe that their accounts are insured by the government, by the FDIC. And this *might* be true if only one or two small banks fail, and if all your accounts combined add up to less than the $250,000 FDIC insured limit per institution (*not* per individual account, as many mistakenly believe).

The FDIC, however, has at most $33 Billion in current reserves plus a qualified promise of $500 Billion in Dire Emergency funding from the Federal Reserve and Treasury to cover more than $7 Trillion in insured, and more than $9 Trillion including uninsured, bank accounts.

In Cyprus, the European Central Bank initially went along with the seizing of even small government-insured accounts. Even mom-and-pop accounts are not necessarily safe. The message was clear: if government really wants the money, it will grab it. The ECB, whatever it promises, lacks the reserves to bail out depositors in the event of widespread European bank runs, a continental Great Withdrawal.

If the U.S. or global economy caves in, or a foreign cyber Pearl Harbor erases or garbles the nation's banking computers, or terrorism and panic cause a run on major banks and depression, the FDIC could run out of funds within hours.

Even if the Fed eventually conjures tens of trillions out of thin air to rescue banks and reimburse depositors, these paper fiat dollars would trigger a tidal wave of inflation and have far less purchasing power than the savings they replaced. This is similar to what happened in 1923 in Weimar, Germany. It happened more recently in Zimbabwe, formerly Southern Rhodesia, which had been the bountiful bread basket of southeastern Africa until a Progressive ruler confiscated the nation's farms and gave them to his cronies.

The current Administration has also considered actions like Argentina's in 2008, where the government confiscated the money in private retirement accounts and replaced it with government bonds worth only 29 percent of their face value.

Only solid money such as gold in private hands will stay afloat and gain value during the flood of inflation from trillions in paper money printing that our government has thus far struggled to keep dammed up.

The December 2012 Joint Paper by the FDIC and Bank of England could be evidence that they see the dam starting to crack.

Is this why they have been preparing the legal and regulatory basis for dealing with a crisis that might include the biggest government money grab in history?

This is clearly no time to put all your nest eggs in one place, especially if that place is a bank account. This is a time for prudent diversification that includes investments that neither government regulations nor money printing can easily confiscate or debase.

For a list of powerful banks and other institutions that we believe have been cooperating in this same confiscatory direction, see page 44 of the Bank for International Settlements (BIS, sometimes called the "Bank of

Banks") Basel Committee on Banking Supervision *Report and Recommendations of the Cross-border Bank Resolution Group*. [11]

The Day Your Savings Vanish

Like the people of Cyprus, you will get no advance warning, no chance to get your money out, and no choice in the matter on the day your life savings – if denominated in U.S. Dollars – vanish.

The government and its media lapdogs will simply announce that President Obama, facing a Pearl Harbor-like digital foreign attack on our banking system or other vague crisis, "acted decisively and heroically to save the savings of working Americans."

The banks and related institutions – and possibly the stock exchanges, after the 2010 NYSE "flash crash," and NASDAQ's August 2013 "flash freeze" halted trading for more than three hours – could be closed for a few days by government orders, then re-open with the actual paper money in people's pension, IRA and 401(K) accounts missing.

A legal precedent already exists for this in FDR's 1933 closing of the banks, and in his Executive Order requiring Americans to exchange their money for what quickly proved to be 70 percent less than their money's real market purchasing power.

In such a takeover today, in place of your hard-earned savings, the government could replace your old accounts with new ones based on new financial instruments that promise to pay a reliable rate of return – in effect, government annuities backed by trillions in new Treasury notes.

Those below retirement age will be required to pay stiff penalties if they attempt to withdraw the value that these accounts purportedly have. People might be prohibited from withdrawing more than a small monthly amount from the accounts at all, and even this will be in rapidly-inflating, debased dollars of falling value.

This, Americans will be told, is part of the price we all must pay for President Obama saving our savings.

The confiscated private money itself could vanish, spent almost instantly by President Obama and other Progressive politicians to fund and enlarge the Welfare State on which a huge fraction of Americans now depend.

President Obama could also use executive powers in other ways. He might, for instance, order outright wealth redistribution.

Mr. Obama could command issuance of a new currency in which one "New Dollar" would be worth 10, 100 or 1000 old dollars – much as happened with the Mexican New Peso in 1993 or the Israeli New Shekel after a period of hyperinflation in 1986. This could either snare or expropriate those possessing a larger quantity of cash than their tax filings show.

Such manipulation is easier for small national currencies than for the U.S. Dollar, which is the World Reserve Currency used by almost all nations in key transactions and as part of their own Central Bank reserves. Nevertheless, such a sudden re-valuation of the dollar could occur.

The U.S. Government and Federal Reserve are already devaluing the dollar as a way to make American export goods cheaper in the global "race to debase," known as the "currency wars" among nations.

Our deliberate debasement of the dollar is one reason why Russia increasingly trades in its currency, not dollars, with Japan. Russia and the People's Republic of China also increasingly trade in each other's currencies, not dollars, and both have sought to reduce the dollar's power and role as the Global Reserve Currency.

Similar Seizures

Confiscation of savings is no fantasy. Many recent precedents for it already exist. As previously mentioned, Argentina in 2008 effectively expropriated the money in private pension funds, leaving in its place debased government bonds with a market value only 29 percent of the bonds' face value.

In Cyprus, after the legislature was forced to back off its scheme to snatch money directly not only from large but also from small bank accounts, the politicians then proposed as their "Plan B" the idea of grabbing wealth from their nation's pension funds. [12]

A *Wall Street Journal* investigation reported that Spain has diverted roughly 90 percent of its 65 Billon Euro national Social Security Reserve Fund into risky Spanish debt. Governments in Italy and France have done likewise with pension funds. [13]

In other precedents, Bulgaria transferred approximately $60 Million in private retirement savings into a government pension scheme. Ireland levied money from the National Pension Reserve Fund to bail out banks. In 2010 Hungary demanded that citizens give the government their private savings or forfeit all state pension money they had been promised. In July 2013 Poland reportedly confiscated roughly half of citizen pension funds. [13]

Our politicians of both major parties looted and spent $2.66 Trillion from the Social Security Trust Fund, leaving paper IOUs in its place. Mr. Obama's comrades also diverted almost three-quarters of a trillion dollars from the Medicare Trust Fund to bankroll Obamacare.

Then-Secretary of the Treasury Timothy Geithner temporarily funded the government via executive branch "extraordinary measures" – from May until August 2011 by selling assets of the Civil Service Retirement and Disability Fund and the G Fund of the Thrift Savings Plan, and again in January 2013 by borrowing from the Federal Employee Pension Fund.

In 2012 California Governor Jerry Brown signed into law the first government-run retirement program for private employees, reportedly funded by requiring companies with 5 or more employees to divert 3 percent of each employee's pay to CalPERS, the California Public Employees Retirement System. This new law is expected in its first year to add $6.6 Billion to the coffers of a California government retirement system, already underfunded by as much as $500 Billion.

This is one more way to tax private sector workers' earnings to bankroll fat pensions for the public employee unions that have ruined the once-golden State of California, as the Federal Government is now doing to the country.

California has also begun declaring previous legal tax breaks invalid, then billing investors retroactively not only for taxes they legally avoided but also for penalties on imputed past taxes not paid. This violates one of the most fundamental principles of Western law – that someone cannot be punished *ex post facto* for "breaking a law" that did not yet exist when he purportedly broke it.

No wonder California is now experiencing a "reverse gold rush" of successful people fleeing to preserve their money from new sky-high taxes. By destroying this state's once-prosperous economy, politicians have shown why the animal on the California flag is a bear, not a bull.

Caveat Saver

In 1933, acting without warning (as 80 years later would happen to savers in Cyprus), President Franklin Delano Roosevelt by Executive Order 6102 closed all the banks and commenced looting private wealth. [21] FDR soon re-opened the banks after he had destroyed America's Gold Standard dollar, a major step on the downward path to today's fiat dollar with no intrinsic value whatsoever.

This is the Fed's "elastic currency" that Progressive politicians in 1913 created the Federal Reserve to "furnish." This began the Great Debasement that in 100 years has brought us to today's greatly-debased political and economic system. Immediate effect: FDR closes banks, and savers lose 70 percent of the value of their money.

To prevent future bank runs by frightened depositors, FDR signed into law federal insurance on bank deposits. The most recognized of such insurers is the FDIC, the Federal Deposit Insurance Corporation, which today promises: "Each depositor insured to at least $250,000 per insured bank."

As stated previously, some depositors mistakenly believe that their money is protected against loss because they have several accounts of under $250,000 each in the same bank. No, FDIC says it will cover only a *total* of $250,000 per bank, no matter how many different insured accounts are involved.

FDIC has generally made good on accounts even in excess of this limit when individual banks have gone bad, but it is not required to do so. If a major national collapse or run on hundreds of banks occurred, FDIC today has only about $33 Billion in reserves (along with an emergency line of credit for $500 Billion – raised from $30 Billion during the Great Recession in 2009 – that can be used only if both the U.S. Treasury and

Federal Reserve approve).

As of December 31, 2012, deposits in American domestic offices totaled roughly $9.447 Trillion, of which the FDIC estimates that $7.382 Trillion was in "insured deposits." Compared to such numbers, $33 Billion – or even $500 Billion – are tiny fractions of the accounts FDIC promises to fully insure. In a major Great Withdrawal, the FDIC would be overwhelmed. [14]

Even so, American bank accounts increased dramatically in 2012. Then, starting in January 2013, net deposits at the 25 largest U.S. lenders have had their biggest drop since the immediate aftermath of the 9/11 terrorist attacks. One reason may be surviving the New Year "Fiscal Cliff." Another may be the abrupt end of a $1.6 Trillion backstop for the FDIC known as TAG, the Transaction Account Guarantee program. TAG's demise may have led some sophisticated investors to believe their money has safer, better places to go than American banks. [15]

In today's world of fractional-reserve banking, banks lend out most of the money people deposit with them, which is how they can afford to stay in business and pay depositors interest. This system, however, means that banks simply do not have enough cash on hand to return the money of a large fraction of depositors if panic stampedes them into a run on the bank, a Great Withdrawal.

Presumably the U.S. Government and Federal Reserve would turn on the printing press in a banking collapse and would conjure out of thin air as many trillions of dollars as are needed to cover FDIC-insured deposits – but the value of these dollars would be washed away in the resulting tidal wave of high inflation.

Caveat Emptor, the ancient Roman admonition "Let the Buyer Beware," should remind people that they must exercise due diligence, even in a bank with an FDIC symbol on its door. Does your bank have a good reputation? Is it prudent? Not all financial instruments sold by or in FDIC-approved banks are FDIC-insured, and many customers have been burned by failing to understand this.

In March 1985 in Cincinnati, Ohio, many who were depositors in respected Savings & Loans such as Molitor Loan and Building Company and Charter Oaks Savings Association believed their accounts were secure.

They then heard local radio superstar Bill Cunningham (who today is a national radio and television star) warning listeners about such S&Ls: "It's time to panic. Take your cots and tents and line up. You better be the first in line, or you might not get your money." [16] Many who listened to Cunningham, and acted quickly, saved much of their savings.

In March 2013, Fox News Channel reporter Bill Hemmer, a Cincinnati native, told viewers of how, at his father's urging, his mother in 1985 rushed to Molitor and was the last one admitted before they locked their doors.

She came away with 90 percent of the family's savings from the cash-short institution. Those who arrived later got nothing, even though depositor accounts were promised to be guaranteed by ODGF, the Ohio Deposit Guarantee Fund.

Ohio's Governor closed 70 S&Ls for three days to cool the Great Withdrawal that threatened to sweep the state. [16-17] A Savings & Loan crisis shook Maryland, and frightened savers across the nation.

From 1980 until 1991, approximately 1,500 commercial and savings banks, along with 1,200 Savings & Loan associations, failed and were resolved by regulatory agencies. The loss from this cost almost $240 Billion to rectify, roughly $150 Billion of which was charged to taxpayers when Federal Savings and Loan Insurance Corporation (FSLIC) reserves funds proved insufficient. [18]

Most depositors ultimately got their money, but months passed before it happened. How would you pay your bills or mortgage or for food if this happens to you?

In our post-Cyprus world, the media calls what the Hemmer family suffered a 10 percent "haircut." For hard-pressed families in 1985 Cincinnati or 2013 Cyprus, the loss of some or all of their savings, and of all of their trust, must have felt like a scalping.

We must always remember that promised insurance did not keep Cincinnati savers safe a mere 28 years ago, and that Eurocrats initially authorized seizing not only the Cyprus bank accounts of the wealthy but also the government-insured bank accounts of middle-class families who had been promised that their money would be safe.

In today's world of debased, inflatable fiat money and debased, rapacious politicians, our savings and retirement bank accounts are not necessarily safe. You cannot trust government fiat money and insurance promises – whether from the Economic and Monetary Union [EMU] of the European Union or from the United States Government – to secure the value of your savings. [19] You must do that yourself, using things that have protected individual savings for thousands of years.

Government owns your bank account, according to the European Central Bank, the European Commission and the International Monetary Fund (IMF).

For the Mediterranean island of Cyprus, this "troika" affirmed in March 2013 that private bank accounts – originally to have included even mom-and-pop accounts of less than 100,000 Euros that had been guaranteed against loss by the Cypriot government – can be looted through a one-time levy if government needs the money.

And today's obese welfare state governments have an insatiable money hunger that grows bigger as they get fatter.

The precedent of Cyprus creates uncertainty about the legal status and individual ownership rights of *all* private property in the 17-nation Eurozone, a legal precedent that governments outside of Europe also might soon use because today's politicians are addicted to taxing and spending as never before.

In Cyprus, people could see that today's Santa Claus welfare states come into our lives not only to deliver gifts, but also to loot and steal. As renowned British journalist Ambrose Evans-Pritchard wrote, Cyprus "has finally killed the myth" that Big Government "is benign." [20]

The Cyprus Omen

Like the Black Plague that killed up to 60 percent of Europe's people seven centuries ago, a financial "Green Plague" spreading economic contagion has been unleashed by the account looting in Cyprus.

The Green Plague's first symptom is a loss of trust in government and banking. Its second symptom is a desire to withdraw one's cash and

flee....or, at a minimum, not to make additional deposits.
In the U.S., the first "immune response" to news of the bank account seizures in Cyprus was a brief triple-digit plummet in the stock market, and a double-digit surge in the price of gold.

This contagion has the potential to plunge Europe into recession or depression, an economic death spiral that in the interconnected global economy could quickly drag China and the U.S. down, too.

The precedent Cyprus has set is for government closing banks without warning, and then announcing that it is confiscating depositor money.

Cyprus also set precedents for government imposing controls that restrict how much money an account holder can withdraw or remove from the country. It allowed the government to turn liquid accounts into fixed-term accounts that depositors cannot withdraw for years without paying a substantial penalty.

Under the deal reached on March 25, Cyprus' second-biggest bank, known as Laiki or the Cyprus Popular Bank, is to be restructured into two entities, a "good" bank for insured deposits of 100,000 Euros or less, which would remain intact and be moved to the larger Bank of Cyprus, and a "bad" bank for deposits too big to be fully insured. For the "bad" bank's depositors, their "haircut" means a loss of 20 percent, 40 percent or even more of what was in their bank account.

This will not inspire confident Eurozone investing. In other struggling Eurozone economies such as Greece, Spain, Portugal and Italy, the example of Cyprus could prompt millions of local and foreign depositors to take the money out of their bank accounts before money-hungry politicians do. The memory of Cyprus will also deter others from putting new money into European banks. [21]

Cyprus is causing a deficit of trust, a loss of faith in government and financial institutions likely to last for generations. This deficit of trust could reduce growth and cast a shadow over the optimism and resilience needed to build our economic future.

"We hope people will believe us, believe the collective leadership of the European Union," the Finance Minister of Cyprus Michael Sarris told CNBC on Sunday, March 17, promising that when his nation's banks re-opened that Tuesday that people would be able to move their money out of the country. [22]

From now on, Sarris said, Cypriots "can be very confident that nothing will happen to their savings....there is [sic] no capital restrictions."

The Cypriot banks never opened on Tuesday, and when they did open on Thursday it was with draconian capital restrictions limiting daily withdrawals to 300 Euros, prohibiting the cashing of checks, and giving government the power to confiscate any significant amount of money carried by people leaving the country.

Perhaps Mr. Sarris can understand why no sane person any longer believes "the collective leadership of the European Union."

Markets were shaken all over the world when the head of the Eurogroup of 17 national Finance Ministers, Jeroen Dijsselbloem of the Netherlands, told an interviewer that what happened in Cyprus would be a "template" for future bank bailouts in Europe, i.e., that Eurocrats would again loot savings accounts before using government money to bail out banks on the verge of bankruptcy. [23]

No wonder that in an interview with *Der Spiegel*, German economist Peter Bofinger warned that what Eurocrats set out to do in Cyprus "will shake the trust of depositors across the Continent. Europe's citizens now have to fear for their money."

"The Spaniards, Italians and Portuguese may not run to the banks today or tomorrow," Bofinger continued, "but as soon as the crisis intensifies in a euro-zone country, the bank customers will remember Cyprus. They will withdraw their money and, by doing so, intensify the crisis."

Such fearful Great Withdrawals, Bofinger warned, could cause a domino effect, and every economic downturn leaves savers asking if their country is the next Cyprus. [24] The seeds of continental bank runs have been planted.

And in a Europe already technically in recession after two quarters of negative growth, the media echoes with advice like that of Member of the European Parliament and leader of the United Kingdom Independent Party (UKIP) Nigel Farage: "Get all your money out of Europe now." [25]

Cyprus, writes *Time* columnist Rana Foroohar, might "become the economic equivalent of the assassination of Austrian Archduke Ferdinand, which started World War I," by shattering the economic unity and slow recovery of Europe, which is roughly 25 percent of the global economy. [26]

"I am chilled by the realization of how similar circumstances in Europe in 2013 are to those of 100 years ago" on the eve of World War I, Luxembourg's Prime Minister Jean-Claude Juncker said in a March 11 interview with Germany's *Der Spiegel*. Juncker in 2011 said of touchy economic matters in Europe, "When it becomes serious, you have to lie." [27]

American Takings

President Jimmy Carter signed a law that gave government the means to strong-arm banks into making billions of dollars of loans to credit-unworthy individuals who were in politically-favored groups. These coerced bank loans, which have been a kind of expropriation from bank shareholders, precipitated the Great Recession that still cripples the U.S. economy.

As we explained in *Crashing the Dollar*, this Community Reinvestment Act was a Progressive ideological effort to make banks absorb much of the cost of providing housing for low income Democratic Party voters. It worked so well that today, after the crisis it set in motion, home ownership is at a 30+ year low. President Obama in 2013 was strong-arming banks to do such lending.

A major factor in today's sick economy is that governments in both Europe and the United States have turned regulatory power into *de facto* government ownership and politicization of the banks.

The political sin of Cyprus was not that its once-solid banks had faltered after it joined the Eurozone in January 2008, only months before recession hit. Nor was it the near bankruptcy of Cyprus banks and the need for a bailout of 17 Billion Euros – a trivial amount to cover for a Eurozone that since May 2010 has spent more than $600 Billion to bail out other member nations.

Cypriot banks paid much higher interest rates than mainland European banks, and held tens of billions of Euros of deposits from wealthy Russian oligarchs. German Chancellor Angela Merkel, up for re-election in September 2013, did not want German taxpayers and banks paying to protect the fortunes of Russians.

The heavy levies on large Cyprus accounts, on the other hand, would seem to fall like a "progressive" tax on the 4 percent of depositors who accounted for 60 percent of all the bank deposits – and presumably a large share of these are Russians.

As the dust of Cyprus continues to settle, however, evidence is starting to show that the biggest Russian oligarchs tended to use Cypriot banks as transit points, with hot money seldom staying there for long.

During the week the Cypriot government delayed signing an agreement with the troika, reported Reuters, many Euros in nominally-closed banks somehow left the country via still-open Cyprus-owned banks in London and Moscow, and perhaps via corporate jets. [28]

So who got caught in the Eurozone's giant cash grab of private bank accounts? Russians did, but mostly small and middling business people, not billionaires. So did ordinary families whose mom-and-pop accounts exceeded 100,000 Euros after a lifetime of scrimping, saving and earning interest...who have now lost a hefty hunk of their life savings. Those with bank loans and mortgages will still have to pay, except, of course, certain Cypriot politicians whose debts reportedly have been written off. [29] Welcome to the Progressive welfare future George Orwell foresaw in *Animal Farm*, where everyone is equal but some animals are more equal than others.

Merkel's government made it a condition of bailing Cyprus out that it could no longer be the kind of "financial center" it has been. Between 25 percent and 30 percent of Cypriots were employed by banks and the financial sector, so this Diktat means that the island's economy will now sink – and the promised Eurozone bailout will be far too little to keep Cyprus from insolvency. [30]

This could push Cyprus out of the Eurozone, into the arms of Russia, and back to its previous national currency, the Cypriot Pound. This might mean that if the current Lebanon-ruling Syrian regime allied with Russia falls, we might soon see Cyprus as the new Russian naval base in the Mediterranean. We might also see Gazprom oil rigs tapping the potentially-large oil deposits undersea in Cypriot waters, despite Turkey's objections.

It is true that Cyprus' banks housed accounts worth 716 percent – more than seven times – the nation's Gross Domestic Product (GDP), a very high ratio, yet far from the highest in Europe. (By comparison, America's proportion of bank assets to GDP is approximately 93 percent.) [31]

Luxembourg's banking sector as a share of GDP is 2,174 percent – and Luxembourg has recently told the Eurozone to keep its hands off its banking sector and accused Germany of "striving for hegemony" in the Eurozone by crushing the banking sector in Cyprus. [32]

Another Mediterranean island nation, Malta, has a banking sector to GDP ratio higher than Cyprus at 792 percent, and Ireland's is also higher at 718 percent.

It is also reportedly true that Russians and other foreigners did money laundering in Cyprus. Oddly, however, Germany says relatively little about even more money laundering being done in Malta, London and Lichtenstein.

The real political sin of Cyprus was not that its once-solid banks were near bankruptcy and needed a bailout of 17 Billion Euros – but that Cyprus was a small tax haven in a European Union hungry for more taxes, and that Cyprus' banks held tens of billions of Euros of deposits from wealthy Russian oligarchs that looked ripe for the plucking.

Ironically, in our 21st Century world the former Soviets appear to be the capitalists, and the once-capitalistic, now-welfare state Europeans are engaged in expropriating private wealth to fatten Big Government, as Communist regimes used to do. The Russians were the first to sell private passenger trips to the International Space Station, while NASA and the United States long fought to keep space the exclusive domain of government, uncontaminated by Capitalism.

The Slow Siphon

The value of American bank accounts is being drained in slow motion, as has been done for many decades, via a policy of inflation that deliberately debases the value of every dollar as an invisible *de facto* tax. As a result, today's dollar is worth less than two cents of the 1913 dollar, a cumulative inflation expropriation of $222 Trillion in today's dollars from the American people. It also, in effect, expropriates a portion of the savings of those in Europe and throughout the world who depend on the value of the U.S. Dollar.

Again, the U.S. Federal Reserve also practices "financial repression" by holding interest rates below the rate of real world inflation. This means that those who have their savings in bank accounts paying 1 percent or 2 percent interest are having their dollar-denominated wealth eaten up by government-driven and Fed-driven inflation. This facilitates the looting of savings accounts via the invisible taxation of inflation.

Cyprus Winners and Losers

Simone Foxman at *The Atlantic* numbers among the losers everyday Cypriots who now face years of austerity and hardship, and small-fry Russians caught in this trap. Democracy lost, too, she says, because 67 percent of Cypriots wanted to leave the Eurozone. [33]

The "free flow of money in Europe" is also one of her losers.

Another way to say this is that the Euro lost – and the Eurozone will never be the same, or even be long for this world, because of Cyprus.

Cyprus, in effect, split the Euro currency in two, as some northern Europeans had long proposed doing. They wanted the Eurozone divided into a kind of First Class and Second Class system in which the "lazy and profligate" southern European nations would not have currency or credit quite equal to northern Europeans.

This Eurozone Class System is precisely what events have produced in Cyprus, where tight capital controls are expected to last for years and impose limits on the flow of Cypriot Euros that will make them inferior for international business purposes to, say, German Euros with no capital controls. [34]

Germany has in a sense pushed Cyprus halfway out of the Eurozone by making the island nation use a Second Class Euro currency.

Germany can now create a Eurozone-wide class system merely by Cyprus-ifying and imposing capital controls on other southern Eurozone nations, one by one.

Among Foxman's winners are northern Eurozone policymakers, who saved billions in bailout money and made a precedent and an example of tiny Cyprus, whose GDP is smaller than Vermont's and only two-tenths of 1 percent of Europe's GDP, as a way to intimidate larger southern European nations.

The Eurozone redefined bank deposit holders as if they were shareholders in order to justify seizing their accounts. Heaven only knows how much blowback and how many unintended consequences for Europe and the Euro this will produce.

Foxman's final winner from the Cyprus bailout: The Cayman Islands, Luxembourg, and other Tax Havens, because "All that Russian money has to go somewhere."

Future Dangers

The troika of Eurocrats, the European Central Bank, and the IMF was initially willing to let Cyprus expropriate pension funds as a way to reach the threshold for a bailout – and changed their minds only when German Chancellor Angela Merkel, up for re-election in September 2013, called this unacceptable because of the harm it could do to middle-class people.

However, as noted, President Barack Obama's Administration is considering ways to confiscate the more than $18.5 Trillion of savings in American retirement accounts – 401(K)s, IRAs and pensions – by replacing them with less valuable government debt obligations used to create "annuities," a confiscation similar to what the government of Argentina in 2008 did to private pension holders. [35]

The larger our governments become, the more hungry and desperate they become for deposits of private wealth that can be devoured. Private bank accounts, retirement accounts, and pension funds are targets that spendaholic politicians in both Brussels and Washington, D.C., clearly have in their cross-hairs for expropriation.

Americans need to study Cyprus for what it reveals about emerging politician plans in Europe and the U.S. for taxing and controlling people.

Americans who act wisely today can secure their life savings against what happened to the money and bank accounts of Cyprus.

Who owns the money you have saved? You might think that you do, that your life savings are your personal property just like your home or your jewelry.

Today's politicians, however, increasingly act as if money is something created, given value, and perpetually owned by the government.

As we explain in our 2012 book *The Great Debasement: The 100-Year Dying of the Dollar and How to Get America's Money Back*, today's Leftist politicians believe in Modern Monetary Theory, which defines paper currency as a "creature of the state" created by the government for its purposes, not yours.

Today's Progressive politicians assume that, in President Obama's words, you "didn't build" your savings, that whatever money you have accumulated came from government and is subject to being taxed or otherwise confiscated out of your hands whenever government wishes to redistribute it to serve the higher collective good.

You might have earned and set aside a few dollars in your own pocket or bank account, but, according to Progressives, this wealth does not legitimately belong to you. It belongs to the State, which can reclaim this money – by force if necessary – whenever our rulers wish to redistribute to favored others what you selfishly thought were the fruits of your labor.

To Progressives, private property is an obsolete, primitive idea based on greed and selfishness. All that matters to them is the collective, as represented by the government – and their own limousines, their caviar, and their use of your money to buy their perpetual re-election as the superior ones who rule over the rest of us.

The Great Withdrawal

President Obama is eager to "spread the wealth around" that rightly belongs to achievers who have earned and saved it. Yet the more he takes from these savers, by "means testing" or a hundred other Progressive gimmicks, the more he will discourage people from saving for their own retirement – and the more he will make retirees dependent on an already-bankrupt government.

People need to wake up and see the bull's-eye, the red laser dot, where greedy, grasping money-hungry politicians are aiming for their IRAs, 401(K)s, pensions and savings accounts.

Your retirement nest egg could be targeted for political confiscation, so one prudent decision could be to "Move it or lose it." It is wise to diversify a portion of your savings into something that will not be lost if the politicians suddenly confiscate America's retirement accounts, or further debase the dollar's value to cover the stratospheric debts caused by out-of-control government spending.

The more money government takes, the bigger it gets. And the bigger government gets, the more money it needs to take from us to sustain itself and its dependents. If this expansion of the State continues, it will soon devour us all.

This all-consuming expansion of government began with the rise of Socialism in Europe and with the Progressive takeover of the United States in the election of 1912. It took President Woodrow Wilson only one year to implement both the Federal Reserve System and the Income Tax, which, just like taxes today, was passed by politicians promising that it would tax only the rich.

This began the 100-year Great Debasement of the United States, both economically and culturally, that we explain in our 2012 book *The Great Debasement*.

What happened in 2013 in Cyprus could be one of the factors moving Western civilization past the point of no return that might take us into permanent economic depression and a new Dark Age.

For the past 100 years, the Left has been driven by utopian visions of building heaven on Earth by investing all its hopes and dreams in The State. An all-powerful State, they believed, should replace free market Capitalism and even God at the center of their Brave New World.

Most Leftists have looked to Europe and its Welfare States as the locomotive pulling humankind towards this Socialist paradise.

History changed on March 25, 2013, as the European bank raid in Cyprus showed that the Social Democratic Welfare States of Europe can never again be trusted to act in a moral and civilized way.

Europeans from across the political spectrum and the continent now feel insecure and forced to contemplate withdrawing not only their money from European and American banks and turning to better kinds of exchange than paper fiat dollars, but also withdrawing 100 years' worth of the hope, trust and godless utopian faith they had deposited in government.

Socialism died on March 25, 2013.

Welfare States may stagger on, and even keep expanding for a few more years – but on Earth A.C. (After Cyprus) and Earth A.D. (After Detroit's bankruptcy), no thinking or moral person is a True Believer Socialist anymore.

Belief in Big Government suffered a mortal wound in Cyprus. The pseudo-religious cult of the political Left has no future. [36]

Those who still pretend to worship The State are now just the greedy vulture Leftovers and courtiers who feed on the carnage left by Big Government. And today's Big Government has become a predator, preying on the people it was supposed to serve.

We are at a turning point in history and will soon see whether The Great Withdrawal is a right turn that reboots Enlightenment thinking, restores free minds and free markets and a higher faith, and rescues humankind from the Great Debasement of a century of collectivist failures.

PART THREE
There Can Be Only One

Chapter Seven
Progressive Power Grab

*"We could be looking at
an historic self-collapse
of the liberal idea."*

– Daniel Henninger
of the *Wall Street Journal* [1]

Progressives are becoming desperate because, despite all they have done to hook, hypnotize and herd the American people, their hard-won power now shows signs of slipping away in a convergence of events that we call the Great Withdrawal.

Power means everything to today's radical Progressives, including President Obama, because their collectivist ideology is a substitute for lost or never-found religious faith.

Progressives have made government their God. They have no other. Ruling and imposing their ideology via the coercive power of the State is ultimately what gives meaning and purpose to their lives. What might they do to keep all that power from slipping out of their hands?

For the past 100 years, Progressives have used the power of the State trying to force their collectivist pseudo-religion onto other Americans. It is now clear that their Progressive dream has failed. America will never in the foreseeable future become a successful Progressive New Eden.

Decade after decade, polling has shown the same result – that only around 20 percent of Americans describe themselves as liberal or Leftist. Most who support Progressives merely go along, scarcely understanding the implications of this destructive ideology.

Poisonous Seeds

The good news is that Progressives have been unable to convert anywhere near a majority of Americans to their utopian cultic beliefs, which are profoundly contrary to and alien from traditional American history and culture.

The bad news is that Progressives succeeded in imposing government programs, policies and values that have turned millions of Americans into government dependents – and entitlement, free lunch and welfare junkies.

The poisonous seeds that Progressives have methodically planted in American soil may yet bring the United States down.

If Progressives are able to cling to power, and can prevent the uprooting of their seeds, then America may soon permanently become just another European-style Welfare State with chronic high unemployment, economic stagnation, and a mediocre standard of living and life.

As happened in ancient Rome, such a Progressive-caused economic and cultural death spiral will progressively weaken us. Soon the Vandals or some other wave of more energetic barbarians – perhaps Islamist terrorists, perhaps barbarians from within – will torch and pillage our cities, and carry off our last things of value.

President Barack Obama and his Progressive comrades seem determined to rule or ruin.

Mr. Obama, a veteran Chicago community organizer who worked for the radical organization ACORN, may be following the hard-left tactics of those who aim to rule by ruining.

Collapse the System

In 1966 two radical Socialists at Columbia University, where Barack Obama would study a decade later, developed a revolutionary alternative way to destroy Capitalism without the need for a violent Marxist revolution. Richard Cloward and Frances Fox Piven laid this out in an article titled "The Weight of the Poor" in the far-left magazine *The Nation*.

Their strategy, as we explained in our 2010 book *Crashing the Dollar*, was to load up government welfare rolls with as many people as possible, then train them how to demand the maximum possible benefits.

The Cloward-Piven Strategy, as radicals from ACORN to Obama have called this gambit, is intended to overload, bankrupt and break the system.

It is somewhat like a prank on college campuses during the 1950s and 1960s in which engineering students calculate how water flows in the school's sewer pipes, then synchronize the simultaneous flushing of toilets in different campus buildings to overload and break the pipes.

The sewer, having been designed to handle only light overloads, could have functioned without problem for 100 years, but is vulnerable to such deliberate sabotage.

The Cloward-Piven strategy likewise synchronizes demand to cause a welfare system overload designed to force politicians, and in particular moderate Democrats, to respond.

Whatever happens, from a radical Socialist point of view, is a win-win situation. If Democrats rush to pour more money into welfare, they will then have to raise taxes on the middle and upper classes to pay for it. This effects a greatly-increased redistribution of income to the poor and weakens Capitalism.

Such increased taxation will, sooner or later, eat up profits and destroy the capitalist system in America.

The Obamacare Two-Step

Notice how in Obamacare insurance companies are mandated to provide many additional and expensive benefits, but are restricted from raising their rates.

Mr. Obama once explained to a labor union gathering that what he wanted was "single payer," i.e., socialized medicine, but he told them "it will take us about 10 years to get there."

What he apparently meant is that Obamacare would be designed to seduce insurance companies into supporting its passage – but then would drive private insurers out of business. This would leave only government as the health insurer of last resort, thereby creating the socialized medicine President Obama said he wanted in the first place.

Obamacare adds a huge new entitlement in our system when other entitlements – Social Security, Medicare, Medicaid, and other health care combined are already eating up 45 percent of every tax dollar, and Veterans and other benefits are consuming another 19 percent. Federal, state and local governments are spending $1 Trillion each year on welfare. Entitlements keep growing and could soon devour the entire national budget unless reined in soon. [2]

President Obama seems to be using Cloward-Piven tactics with Obamacare in a two-step strategy to bring down the old cultural, political and economic order. Obamacare displaces and destroys America's healthcare system, which in many ways was the best in the world. Then, when the old system of private doctors and private insurance collapses because of crushing government regulations and mandates, it is replaced with government monopoly healthcare.

By ruining the old system, Progressives gain power to create and rule the new system. Study President Obama carefully, and you will see how he has used this tactic over and over.

Promise Them Anything

This is the magician's politics of deception and misdirection that has been practiced since at least ancient Rome. Scholar Philip Freeman in 2012 published the political advice given to Roman statesman Cicero by his brother.

Published as the book *How to Win An Election*, its 2000-year-old advice might seem familiar to President Obama: Promise them anything to win, because once you have the power, you have no need to keep any promises. [3]

Did Cicero promise voters that they could keep their own doctor, and that "Cicerocare" would make their health insurance cheaper, not more expensive?

Divide-and-Conquer is the essence of imposing a Welfare State. First, government robs us blind. Then it runs out of seeing-eye dogs, and expects us to be grateful for our dependency on government.

Did you think it an accident that government takes so much from us in taxes that we cannot save enough for our own retirement? Thus, most of us wind up dependent on the government's Socialist Security system.

In a Cloward-Piven mass attack on the welfare system, if politicians refuse to authorize all the benefits demanded, this becomes a propaganda opportunity to proselytize those denied more benefits about their victimhood and the need to overthrow the Capitalist system.

As Chicago community organizer Saul Alinsky taught in his book *Rules for Radicals*, Leftists win by polarizing people and setting them at one another's throats. This radicalizes many, making them into useful pawns, weapons who can be directed by community organizers like Alinsky and Obama.

The Divider Effect

Polarization is one of the biggest keys to understanding the Progressive strategy and tactics of President Obama and his comrades.

Those ruling the Roman Empire, and later the British Empire, were masters of the techniques of Divide-and-Conquer.

In the young United States, Americans thought of themselves as individuals and were eager to learn from others. We were a practical, pragmatic people relatively immune to polarization – except insofar as racism and slavery warped and undermined our ideals of liberty.

E Pluribus Unum – "Out of Many, One" – has been one of the unofficial mottos on America's Great Seal and money. We created one nation based on our highest ideals and respect for the freedom of others.

The Progressives set out to reverse this...and to make America's new motto "Out of One, Many."

As collectivists, Progressives despise individualism. To them, we are not unique individuals but members of collectives or groups.

Betty Jones, Progressives insist, is not an individual. She is an African-American, a female, a young single person, a Democrat. To be Politically Correct, she should think of herself only as the sum of these parts, the groups to which she belongs that define her place in our oppressive American and Western culture.

The Progressives' 13 Wars

"War is the health of the state," proclaimed Progressive author Randolph Bourne on the eve of World War I. Government, Bourne believed, is never more powerful than when it imposes martial law in wartime, silencing all critics and opponents in a "whose side are you on – ours or the enemy's?" polarization of politics.

Progressives have used cultural warfare as a way to make their political power permanent.

As they lose their ability to rule by the comparatively soft power of welfare bribery, addictionomics and "nudge," Progressives are now moving from the gentle drug-induced totalitarian politics of Aldous Huxley's *Brave New World* into the brutal surveillance and dictatorial politics of George Orwell's 1948 dystopian novel *1984*.

Progressives, to create and entrench their power, have created at least 13 cultural wars and taken a leading role on one side in each.

The 13 Cultural Wars promoted by Progressives are familiar, once you recognize them and see how politicians use them to polarize Americans for political gain:

1. Rich versus Poor
2. Nationalist versus Internationalist
3. Capitalist versus Progressive
4. Exploiter versus Exploited
5. Individualist versus Progressive/Collectivist
6. White versus Black & Hispanic
7. Men versus Women
8. Single versus Married
9. Gay versus Intolerant
10. Young versus Old
11. Hip versus Square
12. Stupid versus Bright
13. Religious versus Non-religious

Early Progressive Teddy Roosevelt railed against "hyphenated Americans," yet such collectivist loyalty is precisely what today's Progressives prefer: that we hyphenate ourselves by group as Gay-Americans, African-Americans, and so forth. The goal in using these and other polarizing categories is, of course, to drive wedges between people that politicians can exploit.

Gaming the Gullible

Thus, the Progressive radical group Occupy Wall Street – also known as "Anarchists For Bigger Government" – preached that America was locked in a culture war between "the 1 Percent" of wealthy people and the rest of us, the 99 percent who earn less.

This is raw class warfare, the bread and butter of Progressivism, that uses some of humankind's least attractive negative impulses – envy and jealousy – to polarize our politics.

In our age of multiculturalism – "out of one, many" – our children are taught that nationalism and its concomitant patriotism are so yesterday, so unfashionable and divisive. In his famous Berlin speech, candidate

Barack Obama in 2008 described himself as a "citizen of the world."

Mr. Obama might not have been born in a log cabin in Kenyatucky, Africa. However, his self-identified status as a "citizen of the world" is not a qualification under the U.S. Constitution to be an American President – unless your name is Barack Hussein Obama.

Progressive Hate Harvest

White versus Black has also long been a staple of Progressive campaigns, which pit one race against another. What makes this odd for Progressive Democrats, of course, is that theirs was historically the political party of the slaveowners, the Ku Klux Klan, Jim Crow and Bull Connor. Every Southern segregationist who used clubs, fire hoses and dogs against civil rights marchers in the 1960s was a registered Democrat.

The only thing that the Democratic Party has changed are the racial and ethnic groups they favor. The deliberate division of America along racial lines, fomenting hatred and anger so that divide-and-conquer tactics could elect Democrats – this remains exactly the same, and sows the same kind of racial polarization, discord, anger and latent violence.

President Obama played the racial polarization card in the fatal Florida shooting of African-American teenager Trayvon Martin, which became an issue at precisely the moment Mr. Obama desperately needed to take the public spotlight off his potential involvement in the scandals of Benghazi, the Internal Revenue Service behaving politically, and his National Security Agency spying on Americans.

Democrats have successfully pulled off one of the most amazing propaganda coups in history – persuading 95 percent of African-Americans to vote for the party that enslaved their ancestors instead of for the Republican Party of the Great Emancipator, Abraham Lincoln, who freed their ancestors. Astonishing!

Married to Uncle Sam

Progressive Democrats have for decades positioned themselves as the party of young single women – the party that defends their access to contraception, abortion, and income via a welfare approach bureaucrats have called GARS, "Government Assuming the Role of Spouse." This casts Uncle Sam in a whole new light.

The votes of young single women were essential in President Obama's successful 2012 re-election. So, too, were African-Americans, who turned out to vote in 2012 in higher proportion than White Americans....a triumph of the Democratic Party's use of psychological "nudge" techniques to increase Black voter turnout.

By siding with the homosexual community, Mr. Obama won over a group whose votes are concentrated in urban areas that Democrats almost automatically carry. Democrats may not need gay votes to be victorious, but they urgently need gay money. Gays may be 2 percent of America's population, but they make up 20 percent of President Obama's major fundraisers.

Rahm Emanuel, the Progressive Mayor of Chicago and President Obama's first Chief of Staff, once collectivistically said: "Gays are the next Jews of fundraising." [4]

Progressives also target their appeal to those who, like themselves, regard themselves as smarter than mere successful business people.

Such self-important people can be swayed by movie stars, pseudo-intellectuals and the latest fashions in ideas and causes. What is more persuasive than illiterate airhead celebrities mouthing Progressive propaganda scripted for them about global climate change or green energy?

Godless Progressives, from atheist British scholar Richard Dawkins to Democratic Party fundraiser and HBO comic Bill Maher, preach that atheists are "brights" and imply that religious believers are therefore less than bright. As with many other culture war issues, these polarizing views are used where they hit susceptible audiences.

The purpose of such tactics, always remember, is to divide Americans, pit us against each other, and thereby conquer us to secure the control of government power for Progressive collectivist Statists.

By creating such unrelenting polarization, Progressives are creating a toxic political environment that poisons millions of American minds and turns us into the Divided States of America.

The Politics of Destruction

America's Founders were familiar with divide-and-conquer politics. This is why they make no mention of political parties in the Constitution. They saw such partisan organizations as "faction," a source of division, polarization and needless hostility in a country they wanted to be more harmonious and cooperative.

The Founders would be horrified by how low and vicious Progressive politics have become. The 13 wars driven by partisans now encourage hatred verging on violence.

Even worse, in their desperate fear of losing power Mr. Obama and his comrades have begun using the U.S. Government in ways reminiscent of authoritarian rulers.

We now know, for example, that agents within the Internal Revenue Service abused power in a highly partisan way. Lois Lerner, the head of an IRS office who invoked her Fifth Amendment right to avoid self-incrimination before a congressional subcommittee, in 2010 told a college class that great "pressure" had been put on her to go after conservative Tea Party organizations.

Congressional investigations continue, but as of this writing the Washington, D.C., office of IRS chief counsel William Wilkins was apparently directly involved in looking into conservative organizations. Wilkins is one of only two Obama White House political appointees at the IRS. [5]

Many Tea Party group leaders told a congressional committee that the IRS had demanded inappropriate information of them, including confidential lists of donors and even what group leaders said in their prayers.

In the case of at least one Iowa right-to-life organization, its confidential information demanded by the IRS was illegally passed on to a pro-abortion organization that published these documents. Some of the published documents had internal IRS code on the pages, leaving no doubt that these leaked documents came from IRS files.

While the IRS swiftly granted a beneficial tax status to nearly every left-wing group seeking it, most of more than 150 conservative groups found their applied-for status delayed – in many cases, for years. The effect of this was to put a thumb on the scale in the 2010 and 2012 elections by impeding fund raising by these conservative groups...but not liberal ones.

Some of these conservative groups told Congress that after they applied to the IRS, they not only were audited by the IRS but also came under regulatory scrutiny by several other federal agencies.

Frank VanderSloot, one of eight prominent business owners who publicly supported the 2012 GOP presidential candidate Mitt Romney, told Fox News' Neil Cavuto how he had been targeted by a heavy IRS audit during the campaign, and by media accusations that he was a tax cheat. [6]

In the end he was exonerated, but only after spending $85,000 in legal and CPA costs. The IRS and media attacks on him, he suspected, were done to intimidate other business leaders out of backing Republicans.

The government gave extraordinary powers to the Internal Revenue Service because, frankly, politicians want lots of money squeezed out of taxpayers. This power has been abused in the past, e.g., when President Richard Nixon wanted audits of some he had put on an "enemies list."

On President Obama's watch, IRS agents have apparently used this power in shockingly partisan ways...the sort of government action we would expect in a Banana Republic dictatorship, but not in the United States.

In congressional testimony, Carter Hull, who has worked for the IRS for more than 40 years, said that he was directed to send Tea Party-related materials to an adviser of controversial IRS official Lois Lerner.

Hull said he was also directed to send such documents to the Office of Chief Counsel Wilkins, an Obama political appointee. Hull said that someone from this office told him to send a letter asking for more information from Tea Party groups. [7]

At the same time, evidence has continued to mount of the National Security Agency (also known as the Puzzle Palace) using its vast global and national surveillance capabilities to monitor and record the telephone and Internet communications of as many as 100 million Americans.

The NSA is charged with trying to intercept communications between terrorists in order to safeguard America against their attacks. Its monitoring might, therefore, have caused little concern.

Do not worry, they tell us. The government is merely collecting "Metadata" such as telephone numbers. More recent evidence claims otherwise, that three-quarters of private communications within the U.S. may be recorded.

For sake of argument, let's assume the optimists are right – that only such Metadata is being collected. You might have seen an insurance ad that depicted Paul Revere easily warning patriots that the Redcoats were coming via a cell phone, with no arduous Midnight Ride needed.

Kieran Healy in a blog reproduced by the webzine *Slate.com* pondered what the American Revolution would have been like if the British Redcoats had the ability to collect and analyze Paul Revere's Metadata. Conclusion: by following the data threads, the British would have been able to identify, map, trace, and perhaps snuff out the Sons of Liberty patriot network. Such Metadata could have changed world history. [8]

In August 2013 it came to light that the Department of Defense has been teaching soldiers a course on dealing with terrorists that identifies America's patriot Founders as terrorists. This should not surprise us after then-head of the Department of Homeland Security Janet Napolitano early in the Obama Administration sent a booklet to the nation's law enforcement personnel telling them to view as potential terrorists those who advocate Second Amendment rights, oppose abortion or Big Government, or are critical of President Obama.

The National Security Agency potential spying on Americans has been happening at the same time the IRS is suspected of using its power to tilt an election to help Progressives win. How can we know that the NSA was not likewise involved in partisan spying to benefit Mr. Obama?

Some argue that an innocent person has nothing to fear from Big Brother reading his emails or overhearing his telephone calls.

Those who say this do not appreciate just how many laws and bureaucratic regulations the Progressives have imposed on us. One analyst has estimated that in today's thicket of rules and laws, the average American inadvertently commits three felonies...and God only knows how many misdemeanors...every day.

If a political foe or rival can use government surveillance to monitor as the musical group The Police once sang – "Every breath you take, Every move you make, Every bond you break, Every step you take, I'll be watching you..." –then laws might be enforced against you that are used against almost nobody else.

"The more corrupt the State, the more numerous the laws," wrote the Roman historian Tacitus nineteen centuries ago. Today's over-regulated America has vast numbers of laws, and for every law there are at least 11 bureaucratic rules that have the force of law. And now, under Obamacare, we have a mandate by the government requiring you to purchase a private commercial product, insurance.

President Obama has made this even more complicated by capriciously blocking the enforcement of immigration and other laws, and by giving unions and his other favorites exemptions from some Obamacare rules. This clearly violates his oath of office promising to faithfully execute the laws, not just those parts of the law that he likes.

This thorny thicket of rules and laws is a source of great uncertainty and fear for citizens, especially business people.

Make one misstep with government regulations in esoteric realms such as environmental pollution rules, and a company can be hit with hundreds of thousands of dollars or more in fines and penalties.

Imagine being a small businessman working as a bartender at his own local saloon. A minority customer comes up to the bar, appears to have a little glow on, and orders a drink. Under today's laws, if you serve him, and later that night he is charged with drunk driving in a fatal accident, you and your bar might be legally liable for serving someone who was already inebriated. On the other hand, if you refuse to serve him, the next day you might face a lawsuit for violating his civil rights by refusing him.

In 2013 President Obama's Equal Employment Opportunity Commission sued private companies that had rejected job applicants with proven criminal records. This, said the EEOC, was discriminatory. Other regulators, however, will fine or sue companies if their employees engage in criminal behavior.

Trial lawyers are second only to labor unions among the biggest campaign contributors to Progressive politicians who flood our society with new rules and laws.

Today, as it was in Tacitus' ancient Rome, each new law or rule opens potential opportunities for trial lawyers to sue; for politicians to shake down potential donors for what amounts to "protection money" or a gratuity for government undermining their competitors; and for ideologues to use new laws or rules as a club to beat those they oppose.

Is it any wonder that 23 million Americans are unable to find needed full-time work? Or that so many would-be entrepreneurs are afraid to open their own businesses that would employ people?

At a time when many kinds of government power appear to be used politically to advance the President's partisan agenda, we can see that the power to regulate – like the power to tax – can be the political power to kill.

We propose calling extreme government regulation "regulution" when used by Progressives such as President Obama to ideologically transform society by coercion, just as a violent Marxist revolution would do.

A zealous bureaucratic regulator, by going after a targeted company again and again, can drive its legal and other costs to the breaking point, even if in the end no fines are levied for violating the government's laws and rules.

Today's radical Progressive activist lawyers, as President Obama was and is, nowadays even have a term for what they do: "Lawfare." They twist the law into a weapon and form of warfare that they use to hector, cripple, bankrupt or destroy those with whom they ideologically disagree.

In America, traditional law holds people and companies innocent until and unless they are proven guilty. This is not how the modern Progressive Regulatory State works. It often assumes you to be guilty unless you can prove yourself innocent, which puts the legal burden of proof on you.

And if you can with great effort and expense prove your innocence, do not hold your breath waiting for the regulators to reimburse your costs to do so.

The group Americans for Tax Reform has created "Cost of Government Day" to mark that day each year when you have paid the cost not only of your taxes but also of those hidden taxes that add to the cost of everything you buy and do – government regulations.

In 2011, we remember, ATR's "Cost of Government Day" fell around August 11, meaning that Americans on average had worked approximately 223 days – roughly 61 percent of the year – just to pay their taxes and the cost of government regulation.

Regulations were relatively few before the Progressive takeover of America that began with newly-elected Democratic President Woodrow Wilson taking office in 1913.

As Nanny Statists who want to control everybody's life in even the tiniest details, Progressives adore regulations, and the more the merrier.

What if Progressives had never gained power? What if government left people almost entirely to their own lives and enterprises, as Founding Fathers such as Thomas Jefferson intended?

What if America's economy was not hamstrung and frightened by a vast spider's web of sticky, tricky government "Thou Musts" and "Thou Shalt Nots"?

We got a tiny hint of what used to be from a 2013 research study by economists John Dawson of Appalachian State University in Boone, North Carolina, and John Seater of North Carolina State University in Raleigh.

Their study, titled "Federal Regulation and Aggregate Economic Growth," concluded that if America was relieved of the burden of the last six decades of accumulated regulations, then America's economy and our income would be considerably brighter. [9]

If those six decades of Progressive regulatory burden had never been strapped like a 10-ton weight onto our backs, they calculate, the median household income in America today would not be the $53,000 it is now.

Without all those Progressive regulations, the median household income in America, they calculate, would be $330,000.

The price each household in America pays each year for our nation having elected Progressives is the difference: $277,000 every year.

Progressives, just in Progressive regulatory burden alone, have made you and your family 75 percent poorer. [10]

And this does not include all the nightmarish taxes and loss of freedom that Progressives have imposed on us.

Without the past six decades of power-mad Progressive regulations, America's Gross Domestic Product (GDP) today would not be today's $16 Trillion – but each year would be $54 Trillion!

Instead of a stagnant economy with frightened investors and 23 million unemployed or underemployed, we could right now be awash in abundant prosperity, with good-paying jobs and economic security for everybody.

What we have today instead is the price we pay for the election of Big Government Progressives like President Barack Obama.

Surely, you might say, we need *some* regulations, don't we? That is not the real question. The real question is: How much are you willing to pay for regulations – $277,000 each year from every American family?

And when will you say we have enough regulation? When New York Nanny Statist Mayor Michael Bloomberg tells you he – for your own good – will not permit you to buy a glass of soft drink bigger than 16 ounces?

Progressives, remember, will support *any* increase in regulation – because it brings an increase in their power over your life.

To understand just how crazy and oppressive the Progressive Regulations are, check out the 72-page annual Competitive Enterprise Institute study *Ten Thousand Commandments 2013: An Annual Snapshot of the Federal Regulatory State* by Clyde Wayne Crews. [11]

Progressives wanted to build their own kind of prosperous and egalitarian paradise. What Progressives have created instead is an unreal economy, high and addicted on Federal Reserve stimulus money printed out of thin air. It is a society with ever-more takers and ever-fewer makers to produce actual things and profits that can pay for this. Progressives are now trying to do from sea to shining sea what they did to Detroit.

And now, with the economy close to stall speed and their public approval polls plummeting, Progressives such as President Obama are turning to the one thing collectivists know: they want to keep on centralizing power.

Sadly for them, the more power they impose, the more unpopular they become. The more they rely on controlling people through addiction and welfare dependency, the less resilient our cities and economy become to the shocks of recession, crime and terrorism.

The Progressives have run out of money. They now face an almost bottomless deficit of funds...and, even worse, a deficit of trust. Without trust, there is none of the optimism and confidence that John Maynard Keynes called "animal spirits" that investors need to put their capital at risk to revitalize the economy.

Progressive politicians have raw power, but they are no more competent to invest wisely in the economy than Josef Stalin and other historic collectivists were.

And the worse things get, the more force and coercion Progressives will have to use to stay in power.

Under President Barack Obama's Administration, the Federal Government has been moving rapidly to lock in place massive new powers of surveillance and control....to accelerate a zombie majority of dependents, to import a proletariat of immigrants because this element of Marxist revolution has never naturally existed in America, and to prop up the insanity of Obamacare.

President Obama has rushed to put in place a surveillance state with the power to intimidate and silence opponents, and to destroy those who persist in challenging it.

Mr. Obama is politicizing almost everything, including the IRS's role in impairing conservative groups and deciding who qualifies for what coverage under Obamacare.

The president has put in place Executive Orders such as EO 13603 that give him virtually unlimited power in an emergency. Who has the power to declare such a national emergency? Mr. Obama does.

The America of George Washington and Thomas Jefferson now has a president who casually decides which laws he will enforce, usurping thereby the Constitutional power of the Congress....which the Framers made the most powerful branch of government, Article One of the Constitution. The presidency to the Framers was almost an afterthought. It was the House of Representatives that embodied the will of the People...where all taxing and spending measures must originate.

The Federal Reserve has taken onto itself the powers of a central planning agency of the government. Its new Consumer Financial Protection Bureau, created by Progressive Democrats before they lost control of the House of Representatives in 2010, is funded directly by the Fed, not Congress. This agency is therefore not controllable by congressional pursestrings.

Is this the new Progressive future for the all-powerful Administrative state? This agency is considering ways to confiscate America's 401(K)s and IRAs as an ever-more-desperate Progressive White House looks for whatever money it can seize and spend.

The Fed has become the great Central Planner in the U.S. and in much of the world, an institution never envisioned by the Framers. Yet at the same time, said former Defense Secretary Donald Rumsfeld in September 2013, President Obama's "absence of leadership is a signal to the world that the United States is withdrawing..."

Progressive policy is demilitarizing America's military, while providing military weapons and tactics to our local police as if they were to be occupiers of a conquered province, with drones keeping an eye on every American backyard and an ear on every cell call.

President Barack Obama travels America to urge more gun control, yet departments in his Executive Branch of government are buying billions of rounds of bullets. Government demand for ammunition was devouring manufacturer supplies of brass, gunpowder and lead. This is leaving store shelves stripped bare of many calibers of ammunition needed by America's private hunters, target shooters, and law-abiding citizens with guns for self-defense.

Bullets have become a much more profitable investment than most stocks.

One could almost say that President Obama is turning lead into a "precious metal" that prudent investors should buy after they finish diversifying their portfolios 20 percent with gold.

Progressives continue to pursue the old Marxist model of highly-centralized control. They want the IRS, NSA, and ultimately the Obama White House to look down on everyone.

Yet the more they centralize power and must use coercion to impose their corrupt crony capitalist Progressive ideology, the more vulnerable they become to free, decentralized opponents...and the more opposition they will create.

When the Progressive house of cards falls, it will be with a mighty crash as their supporters and victims withdraw.

In a way, we almost feel sorry for Progressives.

Progressivism arose as a way to deal with the emergence of an industrial age and the rise of science.

Progressivism is already obsolete. We are now rapidly moving into a post-industrial age. Robots are taking over the tasks that once dehumanized people on Henry Ford-like assembly lines.

Yet Progressivism is still trying to assert a divisive new era, by making us pledge allegiance not to the United States and American Republic, but allegiance to racial, ethnic, sexual preference and gender identity groups. Is this what Health and Human Services Secretary Kathleen Sebelius meant in September 2013 when she described the government as "Our Federal Family"?

The West has already moved on to much higher consciousness and individualism. Any true belief in equality and diversity now recognizes that each individual can change the future. Each of us can be the seed of the future of humankind. We are more than our mere racial or ethnic or gender background.

Progressivism today has become a regressive, reactionary ideology that would drag us backward into a more primitive age.

Enlightenment free enterprise, guided by faith in things higher and more noble than government statism and collectivism, is vastly better at creating genuine progress.

Instead of forcing humankind to build pyramids to the glory of Barack Obama or Hillary Clinton, we should let individuals be free to keep most of the fruits of their labor and to build their own dreams free from statist dictates and coercive redistribution.

Progressivism has become the new form of slavery. The challenge in freeing humankind today is to leave Progressive slavery behind, to free people to pursue individual opportunities and visions.

Chairman Mao once deceptively said, "Let 100 flowers bloom. Let 100 views contend." Of course, in Communist China, when views contrary to the collectivist state bloomed as Chairman Mao told them they could, their heads were immediately cut off by a central authority determined to keep its own selfish and privileged power.

Progressives want to silence opposition because they know that in a free competition of ideas, their narrow and obsolete ideology would lose.

Never assume that the narrow-minded Progressivism that imposed eugenics and global warming dogma has a superior wisdom. Progressivism is a throwback philosophy that humankind should now throw back into the garbage bin of history.

Progressive defeat, however, is not certain. If collectivists can keep their grasp on our government, the future could look like a never-ending Great Depression – which, come to think of it, is how Keynes described the Dark Ages.

The Progressive road is literally what Hayek described – a road to serfdom and to a permanently stagnant, wretched economy of broken and ineffective government programs.

The Progressive road to serfdom is, of course, a downhill road – which means that we won't need good cars from Detroit. Gravity – a "renewable" natural resource – will pull us faster and faster, all the way down to the bottom.

From The Declaration of Independence, July 4, 1776: [B]

"The history of the present King of Great Britain is a history of repeated injuries and usurpations, all having in direct object the establishment of an absolute Tyranny over these States. To prove this, let Facts be submitted to a candid world:

"[King George III] has refused his Assent to Laws, the most wholesome and necessary for the public good. He has forbidden his Governors to pass Laws of immediate and pressing importance, unless suspended in their operation till his Assent should be obtained; and when so suspended, he has utterly neglected to attend to them....

"He has refused to pass other Laws for the accommodation of large districts of people, unless those people would relinquish the right of Representation in the Legislature, a right inestimable to them and formidable to tyrants only....

"He has dissolved Representative Houses repeatedly, for opposing with manly firmness his invasions on the rights of the people....

"He has obstructed the Administration of Justice, by refusing his Assent to Laws for establishing Judiciary powers. He has made Judges dependent on his Will alone....

"He has erected a multitude of New Offices, and sent hither swarms of Officers to harrass our people, and eat out their substance....

"He has combined with others to subject us to a jurisdiction foreign to our constitution, and unacknowledged by our laws; giving his Assent to their Acts of pretended Legislation...

"For imposing Taxes on us without our Consent....

"For taking away our Charters, abolishing our most valuable Laws, and altering fundamentally the Forms of our Governments....

"For suspending our own Legislatures, and declaring themselves invested with power to legislate for us in all cases whatsoever....

"He has excited domestic insurrections amongst us...."

Chapter Eight
The Great Withdrawal

"I didn't leave the Democratic Party.
The Democratic Party left me."

– Ronald Wilson Reagan
A former labor union president
who as a young man supported
the New Deal

The desperate Progressive Power Grab now underway can be defeated.

Instead of the new Dark Age that collectivists are frantically trying to impose, the American people could instead choose to return to the path of our nation's Founders, patriots and pioneers....a path based on sound money and sound values.

This could end the 100-Year Detour into Progressivism and re-boot our nation's original operating system – an operating system that works through freedom, faith, and individual enterprise and responsibility.

People are beginning to wake up, to break the hypnotic spell through which Progressivism has controlled American minds and markets, and to look at the real economy with open eyes.

On CNBC on August 16, 2013, for example, guest Ed Butowsky of Chapwood Investments was deep in a panel discussion about who the next Federal Reserve Chairman would be and how this would affect the market, when suddenly he paused:

"It's just amazing to me, doing this for as long as I have," said Butowsky, "how much talk we have about what's going on in Washington related to the stock market, who the new Fed chairman's going to be."

"I look forward to the day we don't care who the Fed chairman is because the free market is doing what it needs to do," said Butowsky, "and we see stock prices rise because of great earnings, not because of a Fed chairman."

"That won't happen for a while," replied CNBC host Bill Griffeth.

"Not in our lifetime," added CNBC analyst Ron Insana. [1]

Seeds of Progressivism's Extinction

The marketplace has been so politicized by Progressives, and become so influenced by government and Fed decisions, that investors routinely base their decisions on the heavy thumb of politics that controls and defines our economy and money. Yet freedom could return not just in our lifetime, but soon.

Butowsky is right. Before we can return to economic health, America needs to take a giant step towards separation of free market and State... because when politicians and the government inject themselves constantly into the economy, there really can be no free market – just a zombie economy of crony pet companies the politicians reward, punish or ignore.

"We don't have a market economy now," said Thomas Hoenig shortly before his 2011 retirement as President of the Federal Reserve Bank of Kansas City, Missouri. "I hate to use this term, but it's almost crony capitalism – who you know, how big your political donation is." [2]

Breaking 100 years of Progressive dependency, addiction and control will require detox, withdrawal symptoms and rehab...but at the end of this process we will again be the world's bright, shining city on a hill of which President Ronald Reagan spoke. We will be America again.

Progressives still believe in the ways of the early Left, when the goal was to centralize all power and command, and to create giant projects mostly to create jobs. Such dinosaur worship of bigness carries the seeds of its own extinction. The more centralized power becomes, the more vulnerable it is.

Green Shoots of Decentralization

Mr. Obama wants to "spread the wealth around," but as the old paradigm sought, to collectivize total power – the real coin of the Progressive realm – onto himself, making himself a "power Trillionaire."

The Jeffersonian paradigm, by contrast, is decentralized – and is symbolized by the Internet, originally conceived by the military as a communications network so spread out across multiple links that it could never be knocked out in time of war.

Mr. Obama has commanded that he be given an "Off" switch for this Peoples' communication system that now permits limitless alternative points of view to be expressed and shared.

It's easy to see why Progressives are frightened. The green shoots of a free, decentralized era that rejects them are springing up all around us.

The Internet gives Americans the ability to find news and information without the old Progressive media monopoly, which is disintegrating, and to create new communities of shared views and interests.

The age of 3-D printing is rising. This technology means that instead of buying things at a local store, you can acquire the electronic DNA, the assembly code, of a wide range of goods and create them in your own home.

Will government surveillance that now records your emails and telephone calls be able to detect exactly what you and a neighbor shared and "printed" out? Perhaps not, if they have to print it to find out what it is. This technology has already been used to print three-dimensional teeth aligners, engine parts, and a wide variety of other objects. Early models are already on the market.

We saw what computer downloading of shared music did to that industry. Now imagine a home device that could let people copy almost any relatively small retail item without buying it.

Such a printer armed with a sufficiently detailed command code has already been used to create a handgun that could be fired. How might such a technology transform a society that Progressives are trying frantically to disarm and control? [3]

Workers of the World Breaking Their Chains

The very heart of Progressivism is the State of Wisconsin, where the Communist Party USA once held its national convention in Milwaukee.

A recent new law in Wisconsin, however, allows workers to quit their union and keep their job. The *Milwaukee Sentinel* newspaper in July 2013 reported that public employee unions there have lost on average between 30 and 60 percent of their dues-paying members during the last two years. [4] One big union was decertified in 2013.

Blue-collar union membership nationwide has plummeted from the early 1950s, when nearly one American worker in three belonged to a union, to today's sinking six percent of the workforce.

The one growing sector of the union movement has been among government workers, the very kind of white collar people in Wisconsin who are quitting their unions in droves.

No wonder the AFL-CIO and its comrades advocate "card check," a way of unionizing workplaces while denying workers their traditional right to a secret ballot vote whether they want to unionize. Progressives are "pro-choice" on only one issue, and against any freedom of choice where they could lose.

If union workers across the country were given the same free choice as Wisconsin workers, members could vote with their feet to end their union membership in a Great Withdrawal.

Such a withdrawal would be a transformative event for America, because unions with their coerced member dues are the biggest campaign contributors to President Obama and Democratic candidates.

A mass exodus is underway from high-tax, high-regulation Progressive states such as California and New York. Even the Hollywood film industry now shoots more and more of its movies away from Hollywood, where union demands and government taxes have cut too deeply into the profits of Progressive moviemakers.

Thousands relocated as part of the Free State Project to move enough Libertarians to the State of New Hampshire to influence its politics.

A record number of Americans have been moving overseas, and in a record percentage of cases renouncing their U.S. citizenship, in part to avoid the taxes our country levies on foreign earnings.

"Americans renouncing U.S. citizenship surged sixfold" over the previous year during the Second Quarter of 2013, reported *Bloomberg*. This is what Cato Institute economist Daniel J. Mitchell calls "going Galt," after the hero who goes on tax strike against the government in Ayn Rand's novel *Atlas Shrugged.*

The United States is "the only nation in the Organization for Economic Cooperation and Development that taxes citizens wherever they reside."

Several Progressive states such as New Jersey have become "Death Spiral States" that seek to impose heavy taxes on those moving out. [5] The Progressive message this sends is clear: you exist to serve the government, not the other way around.

An October 2012 Rasmussen Poll found that 60 percent of those interviewed said that the Federal Government is not ruling with the consent of the governed. The very legitimacy of President Obama's Progressive governing is now being questioned by a strong majority of Americans. In a May 2013 Fairleigh Dickinson University Poll, 29 percent of respondents said that "armed revolution" might be necessary to protect liberties. [6]

Not surprisingly, economic growth and job creation are occurring in pro-free enterprise states such as Texas, North Dakota and other low-tax states that Americans are withdrawing to, not from.

Clearly, the old Progressive paradigm of centralized power and control has failed. The former editor of the journal *Foreign Policy*, Moises Naim, ponders what will replace it in his 2013 book *The End of Power: From Boardrooms to Battlefields and Churches to States, Why Being in Charge Isn't What It Used to Be.*

The emerging age, as Naim sees it, is one in which "micropowers can topple tyrants" and decentralized groups will shape history. This is not obsolete, discredited Progressivism, but the "creative destruction" of economist Joseph Schumpeter restoring our Republic along free market lines.

In this time of change, it is more important than ever to be diversified and prepared for desperate steps that President Obama might take to hang onto and centralize power. You likely do not want to leave the United States, but it is now prudent to hedge your investments so you at least partly "secede" from the U.S. Dollar and could survive if this currency loses much of its value.

The spirit of America's Founders was to spread the power around, and to leave individuals free to pursue their own dreams – not be collectivized into sacrificing their life and liberty to build a pyramid to Pharaoh Obama or other Progressives who may come along after him such as former Secretary of State Hillary Rodham Clinton, if not defeated at the polls.

Liberty Amendments

We applaud former Reagan Administration adviser, legal scholar and Landmark Legal Foundation President, talk radio star and best-selling author Mark Levin for his 2013 bestseller *The Liberty Amendments: Restoring The American Republic.*

In this book, Levin calls on the states to amend the U.S. Constitution by invoking their until-now-unused power to do so. This power, spelled out in Article Five of the U.S. Constitution, authorizes states to amend the Constitution directly via a convention called by two-thirds of the states and by approval of pre-set Amendments by three-fourths of the states.

"I used to have a great fear of constitutional conventions," Oklahoma Senator Tom Coburn said in response to reading Levin's book. "I have a great fear now of not having one."

"I have no illusions about the political difficulty in rallying support for amending the Constitution by this process," writes Levin. [8]

He understands that many who now fatten at the Progressive public trough will oppose changing a system that today gives them privileges and advantages.

Enacting any of Levin's Liberty Amendments would require the support of 38 states in a country where today at least 12 states are almost irredeemably dominated by Progressives. Even so, in 1984 President Ronald Reagan won re-election in 49 of the 50 states.

Our Framers' vision endures in this amendment process, so the votes of low-population states such as Wyoming and New Hampshire count equally with those of the Welfare States New York and California.

Among Levin's proposed Amendments are ceilings on how much the Federal Government could spend – 17.5 percent of GDP – and how much it could tax – 15 percent of any person's income.

Levin's Amendments would prohibit all expansive use of the Constitution's Commerce Clause, and would protect private property from abusive use of the Takings Clause as happened in Poletown at the Detroit Mayor's direction.

"Property Privacy"

We hereby offer some additional Amendment ideas concerning money and economics for your and Mr. Levin's consideration:

1. Switch to a National Sales Tax such as the Fair Tax or some similar simpler tax as the main source of Federal Government revenue, which would give taxpayers far more privacy and choice about when and how much tax they pay.

As an essential part of this change, we must eliminate any risk of taxpayers getting hit by two major taxes at the same time by abolishing the 16th Amendment, which allowed the 1913 enactment of the Federal Income Tax. This Progressive income tax is what Karl Marx and Friedrich Engels proposed in their 1848 *Communist Manifesto* as one of ten ways to destroy free enterprise and Capitalism. Extend the Constitution's prohibition against income taxation to state and local governments as well.

Progressive "Wealth Registration"

2. Establish "property privacy" as a standard that would prohibit the federal, state and local governments from recording or tracking the income, savings, purchases and wealth production of citizens or others legally in the country. This would restore to Americans economic freedom akin to that enjoyed by people in Hong Kong and other prosperous financial centers.

Frankly, in a free society the government should be prohibited from knowing how much income or wealth you and your family have. If Progressives love equality as much as they say, then tax us all equally and stop trying to use government surveillance and power to redistribute wealth from one person to another.

Many Americans today understand that gun registration is merely a Progressive prelude to gun confiscation by the government, as it was in Nazi, fascist, Communist and other collectivist nations.

Why do these same Americans not recognize that the income tax and its massive violation of financial privacy is a form of "wealth registration," a Progressive prelude to the wholesale confiscation – either gradual or sudden – of citizens' income, wealth and inheritance?

Tax revenues, as the Framers understood, should be limited to tariffs and imposts, or what today we might think of as sales or value-added taxes. The key is that citizens choose when and how much tax to pay by buying things. These original constitutional taxes were not based on the government knowing how much you earned, saved or inherited. The Constitution included language to make an income tax unconstitutional.

The highest typical tax signed into law by America's Framers was the tax on landed property, the deed to which was registered with and had its ownership presumably protected by the government. Who owned which piece of land was therefore already known by the government.

In an ideal future, all such property tax would also be abolished, because it charges citizens *de facto* "rent" on their own property. The property tax implicitly asserts that all property belongs to the State, the Universal Landlord, and that we little homeowners are merely its tenants who can be evicted for non-payment of property tax.

No Corporate Taxation Without Representation

3. Abolish all corporate taxes. The same Progressives who demand ever-higher taxes on corporations have tried to deny free speech to corporations, to stifle their ability to join the media debate in defense of their own interests and points of view, especially in ways that influence elections.

A key slogan of the American Revolution was "no taxation without representation." Until and unless corporations are granted the same free speech and voting rights as citizens, they should not be taxed as separate entities.

This is especially egregious insofar as corporations are owned by people, who must also pay income tax. When the income of their enterprise is taxed once at the corporate level and then again when it comes down to the corporation owners at a personal level, the result is double taxation of their investment, effort and success.

Most taxes on corporations and the rich are passed on in the form of higher prices to consumers. The politicians cleverly force corporations to be the government's unpaid tax collectors, and to be the lightning rods for public anger over high prices that instead should be directed at greedy politicians. In the end, Progressivism shafts the lower and middle classes.

America already has the heaviest corporate income tax rates – above 35 percent – of any major nation. The fact that many companies can jump through legal hoops to reduce this tax a bit does not make them free. It merely turns them into companies that must jump through government hoops to keep more of what they have earned. This is not liberty, nor is it the way to have an optimally prosperous economy. Progressives should be told to stop thinking that the solution to every problem is another tax increase. No nation has ever taxed itself into prosperity.

4. Abolish the Federal Reserve System, a central banking system that gives the government *de facto* control of money and credit in the United States, is something that Marx and Engels proposed to destroy the bourgeoisie and Capitalism. (In fact, of Marx's and Engels' 10 measures, nine have entirely or in part been put into law in the United States by Progressives.)

5. Restore a gold standard as the basis for American money and currency. Unlike today's paper fiat money, a gold standard is real money onto itself that carries no counter-party risk, i.e., the need for some outside entity to give it value. Gold as money is almost entirely self-regulating. Gold needs no Federal Reserve to fiddle with America's money supply or interest rates, unlike today's economy based on fiat money and artificial values.

Currency Competition

How important is this kind of sound, honest money?

"It is impossible to grasp the idea of sound money if one does not realize that it was devised as an instrument for the protection of civil liberties against despotic inroads on the part of governments," wrote Austrian economist Ludwig von Mises in his 1912 book *The Theory of Money and Credit*. "Ideologically, [sound money] belongs in the same class with political constitutions and bills of rights."

Parents and grandparents should teach their descendants what real money, solid money is, both by their example and through gifts as a child or grandchild grows.

This provides a secure nest egg and stimulates the curiosity and survival skills needed to succeed in today's tough economy. This is why we helped put together video spots in which a nine-year-old girl explains facets of the economy. You can watch some of these videos via the Internet at www.swissamerica.com/media2.php.

6. Allow currency competition, as Nobel laureate economist Friedrich A. Hayek proposed, so that citizens could use whichever currency or medium – including precious metals, barter, new innovative electronic currencies, or their own personal currency – they prefer in any transaction.

This would give today's printers and minters of the U.S. Dollar, the Euro, the Chinese Yuan, the Japanese Yen and other kinds of fiat money incentives not to debase their currencies by overprinting. This would tend to make the global economy far freer and more stable, and would make many currencies more reliable as storehouses of value and purchasing power.

Today, instead, global "currency wars" have become a "race to debase" as countries deliberately devalue their currencies to make their export goods cheaper in foreign markets.

7. Foster tax competition by requiring that taxes in the United States may never be higher than the lowest effective tax rate in the lowest-taxed country of a list of 50 of the world's most "free" economies.

It ought to be America's policy to be a "tax haven" for all who flee other nations in search of personal and economic freedom – as most of our ancestors did.

Becoming the world's best tax haven would again turn the United States into a magnet attracting the most productive and successful people and their investments from throughout the world, a Great Influx as we enjoyed more than a century ago before collectivist Progressives came to power here.

Redistributing Taxpayers

Such a seedbed of freedom and opportunity would again make the U.S. the most prosperous nation on Earth. Such tax competition would also help to liberate taxpayers everywhere, because other governments would feel pressure to cut taxes to prevent their most successful citizens from leaving.

In his eagerness to turn free Americans into Euro-peons indentured to the Entitlement State, Mr. Obama has joined Europeans in trying to destroy all tax havens such as Cyprus so that taxpayers have no place to flee for freedom from oppressive taxation.

"High tax rates don't redistribute income. They redistribute taxpayers," wrote George Gilder. "Some go to their yachts, some to poor countries. [Tennis star] Bjorn Borg doesn't live in Sweden, of course. He lives in Malta," a tax haven.

It would be splendid if such tax cutting put our obese and gluttonous

Uncle Sam on a diet. Trimming taxes should slim our government down, at least relative to the rest of the economy.

Truth be told, however, the government could become far richer than it is today by taxing a smaller share of a vastly larger pool of national productivity and prosperity. Even money-hungry Progressive politicians could gain by letting the rest of us be free.

We should amend the Constitution to prohibit any and all laws requiring U.S. citizens to pay taxes to the U.S. Government on income or wealth earned outside the United States.

Contrary to this, the Obama Administration has suggested that it wants to eliminate the current limited deductibility of foreign taxes from U.S. taxes owed. Instead of deductions, Mr. Obama apparently would like to impose outright double taxation on U.S. citizen and U.S. company earnings abroad.

President Obama's open, visceral class warfare against private business and achievers discourages foreign investors from coming here. This Progressive hostility to market freedom also gives successful American entrepreneurs and companies good reasons to leave the United States.

Alternatives to Collectivism

To counter the Progressives' effort to nationalize and control everything, we ought to support the privatization, decentralization and free choice of almost everything.

To understand why, consider an April 2013 interview on the BBC show "HARDtalk." [9] The guest, Tufts University philosopher and atheism advocate Daniel Dennett, was asked why secularism was sweeping Europe, leaving Christian churches nearly empty – yet in the United States, Christianity is thriving.

One likely reason, Dennett said, may be marketplace competition, which has made American churches healthier and more dynamic than those in Europe. European countries created official State churches, and for centuries provided them with privileged legal status and subsidies extracted from all taxpayers.

Thomas Jefferson abhorred such government religions. To "compel a man to furnish contributions of money for the propagation of opinions which he disbelieves and abhors, is sinful and tyrannical," he penned in his Statute of Virginia for Religious Freedom."

(We think of Jefferson's words every time we see or hear anti-capitalist propaganda being broadcast with our tax dollars on the government networks PBS, the Progressive Broadcasters of Socialism, and NPR, National Progressive Radical-radio.

This is sinful, tyrannical...and, coincidentally, violates the charter of their overseer, the Corporation for Public Broadcasting...one more of the many laws our Progressive rulers violate every day.)

The First Amendment

In Europe, as Welfare-State governments lost the faith of their people, faith also waned in those churches tied to the State.

In the United States, by contrast, our Constitution's First Amendment explicitly prohibits any such "establishment of religion" by the government.

Even after America's Revolution, State churches lingered in some states. In New England, for example, the Congregational Church offshoot of the Puritans – who came in 1620 seeking freedom to practice their religion – had become the State church. Jefferson was denounced from many pulpits for proposing to end this tradition of churches that benefited from government privilege and money. Today, more than 200 years later, we can see that Jefferson saved America's vibrant tradition of faith from what happened in Europe.

This separation of Church and State, Dennett and other scholars such as Baylor University sociologist Rodney Stark suggest, helped protect churches in America from the taint and corrupting influence of government.

Religious liberty gave Americans the freedom to choose the preacher or approach that spoke to their hearts and minds.

As a result, in recent years America's "mainstream" Progressive denominations that embrace left-liberal ideology have seen their memberships plunge – while attendance at evangelical mega-churches has soared as believers voted with their feet for churches that worship God, not government.

Thomas Jefferson willed that on his tombstone he be remembered only – "and not a word more" – as the author of America's Declaration of Independence, the father of the University of Virginia, and the author of the Statute of Virginia for Religious Freedom. [10]

Our Land of Giants

Jefferson, of course, was more. He was also a best-selling author and celebrated scientist in both the United States and Europe. He was a member of the Virginia legislature and the Continental Congress. He was Governor of the State of Virginia. He was America's ambassador to France, Secretary of State and Vice President of the United States. And – we almost forgot – Jefferson was for two terms President of the United States.

He wanted not even one of these high political honors mentioned on his tombstone. As Jefferson said, he wished to be remembered "only for what I have done for the People, not what the People have done for me."

Jefferson said that he viewed his retirement from politics as a promotion because he was going from being a servant of the People to again being one of the People, the real rulers that those in government were supposed to serve. He was, wrote Jefferson, "leaving office with hands as clean as they are empty."

Such are the giants who founded America, next to whom our Progressive rulers such as President Obama stand less than 1/10th of an inch high.

"When little men cast large shadows, you know the sun is setting," went a popular saying from the 1960s. Few American leaders have ever been smaller, or cast a larger, more ominous shadow over America, than President Obama.

Yet as Benjamin Franklin suggested, we have the power to determine whether America's sun is setting or rising. Our nation is still able to produce leaders such as President Ronald Reagan, who inspires us to again make it "Morning in America."

Separations

Ultimately it is in our hands to take back the power from Progressives, roll back the huge government they have tried to impose as our master, withdraw and detox from the Progressive Brave New World drugging and mind control they have done, and re-boot the operating system of America's Framers.

When Jefferson wrote in a private letter about creating a "wall of separation" between Church and State, his Enlightenment view was light years beyond the neo-feudal elitist ideology of today's Progressives.

Progressives worship the State and, as socialists, want government to occupy every inch of the public square. They reason that since Church and State must be separate, and the State must be everywhere, therefore religion should not be allowed anywhere.

Jefferson, by contrast, believed in his motto: "Rebellion to Tyrants is Obedience to God." He wanted the State to be very, very, very small and occupy only a tiny distant corner of the public square. This would leave ample room for churches and faith to be everywhere else.

Understand this: The Progressives' power-mad ideology poisons everything it touches. It insists on politicizing and controlling everything.

We need to withdraw from this Progressive toxicity in order to heal America before this poison kills our nation and our children's future.

If Thomas Jefferson were here today, he would cheer today's dawn of The Great Withdrawal by saying that we need, in principle, many more kinds of separation from the Progressives' European values. We need:

Separation of Church and State – to protect human rights and our highest values from the State.

Separation of Economy and State – because government is devouring America's Makers and replacing them with parasitic Takers.

Separation of Money and State – because we need currency backed by something solid such as gold, as the Framers specified, so that Progressives cannot rob or control us by printing trillions of paper fiat dollars out of thin air. Under a gold standard, money is self-regulating and needs no Federal Reserve to manipulate interest rates or money supply.

Separation of Business and State – because free markets provide vastly better goods at lower prices than does today's society with government interjecting its power, rules, mandates and taxes everywhere. Most regulation can be done by the private sector and institutions such as Underwriters Laboratory, whose UL label on your new lamp or appliance certifies that they tested its wiring for safety.

Separation of Commerce and State – because government should automatically presume that the private, not the public, sector leads in our society. If private companies wish to do space exploration or build hotels on Mars, for example, government should get out of their way and stop acting as if humankind's future in outer space must be entirely socialist, i.e., government owned. Our settlement of space should be on a capitalist model of private property and profit, not a socialist model in which all human activity will be controlled by government permits. This New Frontier should be more like America's Old Frontier....a place of individual freedom. Our leading starship should not be named the Enterprise...but the Free Enterprise.

Separation of Locality and State – because, as the Framers specified, the strongest government should be local, and the next strongest statewide. The Framers' vision of Federalism wanted what little government we have to be small and close to the People, so that those in government are directly responsive to the People and behave as servants, not masters. Your local police should not be armed like storm troopers by the central government in Washington, D.C.

Separation of Science and State – because politicized science today is being manipulated to expand the power and wealth of government. The bigger the government gets, the smaller our freedom becomes. Science that is funded and directed by Progressive politicians will be corrupted to serve the agenda of those politicians.

Major institutions and the United Nations still honor pseudo-scientists whose private emails exposed in "climategate" revealed their boast of being able to "hide the decline" in global temperatures.

These warming alarmists were caught red-handed telling one another proudly that they successfully concealed measurements that indicated climatic cooling, not warming. So why have these betrayers of science not been drummed out of the scientific community, and why has not every study that cited their data been discredited and discarded? This shows clearly that the warming alarmists are not true scientists but Progressive political shills. This is what happens when government funds, and politics corrupts, science.

Separation of Nation and State – because people, as a matter of human rights, should be free to leave the government under which they live without penalty or loss of the value of their property. In formal use, nation means the people of a land, and State means the government ruling that land. People should have the right to withdraw freely from the State that rules, regulates and taxes them.

Removing the poison of Progressive politics from these fields, and privatizing 10,000 more, will make our society far healthier, happier, freer and more prosperous.

These suggestions might seem radical – because they are.

This is what the United States shaped by our revolutionary Founders was like before the Progressives imposed a monster European-style government with tentacles that now reach into every corner of our lives. Once, long ago, the central government actually left us alone.

One of Thomas Jefferson's proudest boasts was that under his presidency, the average American almost never saw a tax collector. No Progressive income tax skimmed the cream off what you earned before you even received your pay. The gold dollars you received actually grew in value when you saved them.

Americans did not live in fear that Federal Government bureaucrats could capriciously harass or destroy them. We did not spend our lives on our knees begging and paying for government permits, licenses and approvals at every turn.

Unlike the Progressive ideology, the American Dream is not a *utopia* – a word coined from Greek roots by Sir Thomas More that means "No Place."

The original American Dream existed for most of 137 years. It worked, attracting those seeking freedom and opportunity from around the world. It is proven and could work again.

Charter City

Can Detroit be saved? Veteran journalist John Fund has his doubts, and in September 2013's *American Spectator* he proposed selling Detroit lock-stock-and-barrel to Canada, if our next-door neighbor is willing to take it. [11]

CNBC host Larry Kudlow, a former Federal Reserve Bank of New York economist and official in President Ronald Reagan's Office of Management and Budget, believes that the kind of Enterprise Zones proposed by the late Congressman Jack Kemp could help revitalize Detroit.

An Enterprise Zone reduces taxes, and sometimes regulations, in specific neighborhoods to make investment there more attractive. Such a policy would need to roll back large amounts of government greed and power to succeed in Detroit – a precedent its Progressive politicians might be reluctant to permit.

Enterprise Zones work best, of course, when the area around them remains burdened with higher taxes and heavier regulations. Such zones, ironically, could give politicians a rationalization for *not* easing their tight regulatory grip or tax greed near an Enterprise Zone.

Another innovative idea comes from New York University economist Paul Romer, who would expand the successful idea of charter schools to whole "charter cities" where free market economics are unfettered and citizens are free to move in or out.

"Why not turn abandoned Detroit into New Detroit, a business-friendly charter city where taxes are low and regulation light?" asks American Enterprise Institute economist James Pethokoukis, who applauds Romer's idea. [12]

As a one-industry town, Detroit for decades tried to deal with the decline of America's automobile business by building office complexes, sports arenas, and a monorail. Even in bankruptcy, this city agreed to build yet another sports complex.

Detroit instead should have been "trying to attract smart, wealthy, entrepreneurial people," wrote Harvard University economist Edward Glaeser in his book *Triumph of the City*.

The ideal, of course, would be to restore America to what it once was – an Enterprise Zone of low taxes and small government from sea to shining sea.

Do not hold your breath waiting for Progressives to return the power and freedom that they have spent a century relentlessly taking away from the American people.

Belle Isle

In his 2013 book *Belle Isle: Detroit Game Changer*, real estate executive Rodney Lockwood proposes to transform an uninhabited 928-acre island in the Detroit River between the United States and Canada into a city-state with "its own laws, customs and currency, under United States supervision as a Commonwealth."

Lockwood's Belle Isle would have no personal or corporate income tax and would impose few regulations on free enterprise. It would quickly become "the 'Midwest Tiger,' rivaling Singapore and Hong Kong as an economic miracle." In low-tax free market Macau, one can reportedly obtain citizenship and a Macau Passport simply by spending $1 Million for a local residence.

Investors would pay Detroit $1 Billion to buy Belle Isle, and the Motor City would reap billions more in spillover profit from having this global center of wealth, opportunity and investment next door.

To become one of Belle Isle's 35,000 citizens, an applicant would have to pass a background check and pay a one-time fee of roughly $300,000 – a bargain for American achievers who today are hit hardest by Progressive income taxes.

Citizens of the Commonwealth of Belle Isle could also escape the hidden tax called inflation that we explored in our 2011 book *The Inflation Deception*.

Ayn Rand-fan Lockwood's city-state would have its own presumably-gold-backed currency named the "Rand." This independent currency's value would be undiminished by Federal Reserve or Federal Government printing of paper money out of thin air that over the past 100 years has shrunk today's dollar to less than two pennies of the 1913 gold-backed dollar's value.

Ayn Rand in her 1957 novel *Atlas Shrugged* describes a Great Withdrawal of the greatest achievers from a Progressive society much like ours today – with the kind of authoritarians and self-righteous Leftists she witnessed seizing control when she was a young girl in Russia about to flee from the Bolshevik takeover.

Prophetically, Rand in *Atlas Shrugged* depicts Starnesville, a once-great Midwestern industrial city that was home to the Twentieth Century Motor Company, a company and Detroit-like city ruined by socialism.

Belle Isle. Now *that* alternative future away from Progressivism could be a free "enterprise zone" worthy of consideration!

The Pro-stressive Health Hazard

However, even if you choose to stay and pay in America, you should change your thinking about Progressivism. You should start withdrawing your support and acceptance from the Progressives' expanding Governmentality.

Here's yet another reason why: Progressivism is hazardous to our health.

Progressivism has addicted, weakened and impaired the rational thought of more than just our economy and stock market speculators.

The Progressives' high taxes, regulation, manipulation, intimidation and oppressive use of the Internal Revenue Service and other government agencies have become a major cause of uncertainty, fear and stress for many millions of Americans.

Stress, as scientists are learning, causes many societal and personal ills.

Stress raises a person's risk of suffering cancer, heart attack, stroke, sleep disorders, mental health, and likely even overweight.

Thus, our Progressive government becoming obese and throwing its weight around could be part of the reason why two-thirds of Americans are now overweight and at greater health risk.

Thus, Obamacare – which Progressives have promoted as a way to improve our health – is instead causing anxiety and tax stress that could be making Americans sicker.

Perhaps Paul Krugman of the *New York Times* was not entirely joking when in January 2013 he told an audience that balancing the budget for Obamacare might require the help of its death panels. These panels, made up of appointed non-physicians, have the power to ration and cut off health care to patients based on their age and other factors.

Progressivism wants ever-larger government, which is also unhealthy for our species.

"If government were a product, selling it would be illegal," writes famed author P.J. O'Rourke. "Government is a health hazard. Governments have killed many more people than cigarettes or unbuckled seat belts ever have." [13]

Under today's Progressive President Barack Obama, the government seems to have been turned into a partisan weapon directed against non-Progressives. As late-night comedian Jay Leno joked, no one could tell how much tax a Powerball Lottery winner owes, because the IRS did not yet know whether she was a Republican or a Democrat.

With recent news showing how the IRS was tilting against Republicans, this joke drew loud, if bitter, laughter from Leno's audience. Since NBC announced that Leno would soon be replaced, the veteran comic told many more jokes critical of Democrats – and his ratings skyrocketed above more liberal competitors on other networks.

In an American Welfare and Entitlement State where partisan politics now routinely use the government to punish the Makers for the benefit of the Takers, it's clear why achievers feel stress and anxiety. They have been targeted and are being looted by Progressive pirates.

Yet the Takers also suffer in today's coercive Progressive re-engineering of society.

The Bears

Visitors to Yellowstone National Park have for many decades seen signs telling them not to feed the bears. One reason for this policy is that giving free food to the Bears encourages them to expect, and when denied to take, the food that humans have with them. This increases the danger that humans face from being near these bears.

This policy is also intended to help protect the bears. When young bears grow up being given handouts of food, they, just like humans, can readily learn to be Takers and not Makers.

Such bears may become adept at mooching and snatching from people, but they never learn to be highly-skilled hunters in the wild.

These bears would lose the ability to survive on their own. Free human food would transform these majestic creatures that have long survived by finding their own food into domesticated pets dependent on, and addicted to, tourist junk food handouts.

The Progressive Welfare State likewise damages the health and well-being of both the Makers and Takers it exploits. It transforms society, dividing us into a class of serfs whose dreams for their own children are confiscated in ever-higher taxes...and a class of domesticated pets of the State who must remain dependent and unsuccessful to keep their government benefits coming.

Progressivism has produced a profoundly unhealthy society, a land of broken and stolen dreams in which people are kept small so the government can grow ever bigger.

It is time to withdraw from this unhealthy Progressivism, and to rediscover our path back to the values of America's Founders – a path back to a world where keeping the government small gave Americans the ability to become as large as their ability, determination and hard work could make them.

As collectivists, Progressives turn almost every political difference into a confrontation of "Us versus Them," of culture wars.

Progressives seek to cure racism, for example, yet their prescription for doing this is racial polarization. They are Balkanizing Americans into thinking of themselves and others not as individuals but as members of racial groups.

Progressives, having imposed their collectivist idea of race, then use government policies to distribute financial and other benefits to those in racial groups they favor, and to deny such benefits to those in other racial categories.

What idea might do a better job eradicating racism? We should recognize that race is a man-made construct of artificial collectivist categories. No "black" or "white" gene that defines our race exists.

Restoring America's Foundation

What matters are individuals, each unique and possessing the potential to become the seed of what humankind's future can be.

It should not surprise us that Adolf Hitler was both a racist and a socialist, for these two collectivist views of the world are very nearly identical. Both define and exhalt collective definitions of humankind. Both racists and collectivists despise the individual and see the world comprised only of groups.

And both have used their collectivist view as a divide-and-conquer way to radicalize supporters and demonize opponents. It's no coincidence that the Democratic Party was the political party of the slaveowners, the Ku Klux Klan, Jim Crow and Bull Connor.

This Progressive political party still gets its power from polarization, from promoting racial, class, gender and other identities and using these to set Americans at each others' throats.

Progressivism, at its core, is a primitive, reactionary philosophy of bringing people together by tearing them apart. Humankind must grow beyond this ancient conflict-based kind of society.

The United States offers a higher, more genuinely progress-making vision for our world's future. The Framers laid the basis for a society of freedom, a society of individual prosperity achieved through voluntary cooperation of the free marketplace. This society works not through a concocted, polarized clash of "Us versus Them," but through the cooperative, non-coercive interchange of green, silver and gold.

It is vital to recognize that we live in a Yo-Yo – "You're on Your own" – world.

Like the Little Red Hen in the fable, you need to take decisive steps to protect your family's life savings in the turbulence now rapidly approaching. [14]

If the kind of profligate politicians who have ruled Detroit for more than four decades cannot be removed from power via the ballot box, then Americans may need to find new ways to "vote with our feet" against oppressive government – as our ancestors did by withdrawing from unfree lands and coming to America, and then by winning America's withdrawal from the British Empire – to escape the Progressive eclipse of freedom and opportunity.

Are you ready to live under a Progressive-ruled United Statism like today's Detroit as we spiral down into a new Dark Age?

Or are you ready to turn onto a different road, a highway on which the Great Withdrawal from addiction to big government – a government that has been misdirected and has grown far beyond its enumerated Constitutional powers – could return America to a Golden Age for our nation, our children and our grandchildren?

"You and I have a rendezvous with destiny," said Ronald Reagan. "We'll preserve for our children this, the last best hope of man on Earth, or we'll sentence them to take the last step into a thousand years of darkness." [15]

Epilogue:
A Roadmap Home

"I predict future happiness for Americans
if they can prevent the government
from wasting the labors of the people
under the pretense of taking care of them."

– Thomas Jefferson

What can we do to rescue and restore our Republic and our individual liberty? The first step in finding our way home is to understand where we are.

The Progressive ideology that took America on a 100-Year Detour away from our founding values has burned out. Its promised utopia in Detroit and elsewhere failed disastrously.

Progressivism is now brain-dead and devoid of new ideas. It is a hollow shell of debt and propaganda – propped up by printing trillions in paper money out of thin air, and by a zombie fake democracy of millions of government dependents addicted to this conjured magic money.

Progressive politicians such as President Barack Obama are desperate because the dawn is almost here. Millions are awakening from the Left's hypnotic spell and hallucination.

A Great Withdrawal of people from Progressivism is underway. As this happens, the power of Progressive Big Government is melting...melting... like the wicked witch in the Wizard of Oz.

For most of 100 years Progressives ruled us by debasing our currency and values, by turning millions into welfare junkies, by breaking our self-reliant legs and then offering us a government crutch, and by using psychological techniques to herd us like animals by creating fake crises. These old methods of "soft" power are now starting to fail as people awaken.

Our Progressive rulers are now showing their true colors by using intimidation and force. Look at Mr. Obama's brutal use of government regulation, his massive surveillance of and dossiers on nearly every American, his attempts to curtail Second Amendment power in the hands of the People, his politicizing of the Internal Revenue Service to stifle Tea Party free speech, and his naked power grabs of America's private automotive, energy, student loan, banking and healthcare sectors.

The good news is that Mr. Obama is doing this because he sees Progressive power slipping away and is terrified. Power is now up for grabs, a jump ball that gives us a chance to take America back from Nanny Statist Progressives.

Americans can join this Great Withdrawal by taking power from Progressives in many ways. Record numbers are "voting with their feet," leaving the country to seek freedom in a new land, as their ancestors once did by coming here.

Millions are withdrawing from Progressive states like California and moving to free market states with no income tax like Texas and Florida, thereby shifting both economic and long-term political power in America.

Even if you stay put, you can reduce the power Progressives have had to tax you secretly via inflation. You can secede from their manipulated currency by diversifying a portion of your savings into gold, the kind of honest hard money that the Founders specified in our Constitution.

Progressives created Big Government to make We the People small. What Tocqueville understood is that Americans remained free by having voluntary non-governmental institutions such as private charities and mutual aid groups. This is why Mr. Obama has tried to restrict private charitable donations, to create dependence only on government.

When we are big and self-reliant, we can make government small again. Assert – and teach your children and grandchildren – the values of self-reliance, honest money, honor, integrity, faith and community. These are the necessary foundations on which American independence and liberty were built. These are the values that will mark and pave our road home, a journey that we shall continue in our next book.

"Whether you believe you can do a thing or not, you are right."

– Henry Ford.

A Time of Great Withdrawals

1. High-achiever Americans are renouncing their U.S. Citizenship and moving out of the country in record numbers, while at the same time the Obama Administration has ceased enforcing laws that would deter poor, uneducated people from coming here.

2. American companies are moving their operations overseas via foreign corporate partners and refusing to repatriate trillions of dollars in foreign earnings, to avoid the highest corporate tax rate of any major nation on Earth.

3. Residents of many of America's most "Progressive" states and cities continue their withdrawal to escape oppressive taxation and regulation by moving elsewhere. California, for example, is experiencing a "reverse gold rush" of residents taking their gold and skills to states such as Texas. Detroit has been devastated by such a Great Withdrawal of more than one million skilled people.

4. Unionized public workers even in Progressive states such as Wisconsin, given a chance by new law to leave their union without penalty, have been quitting in huge numbers.

5. Americans have been withdrawing from the work force in such large numbers that today the U.S. has the lowest job participation rate in almost 30 years. In particular, 30 percent of adult American men are neither working nor seeking employment.

6. Americans are withdrawing from the old liberal-biased mainstream media and turning instead to Internet and cable media that share their world view.

7. Savers have been withdrawing their bank savings accounts and bond fund holdings in large numbers. Those who look closely are seeing a slow-motion bank run that could, if a crisis happens, turn into a rapid bank run and domino effect of economic collapse.

8. Germany and several other nations have asked to take back their large gold reserves from the depository vault of the Federal Reserve Bank of New York.

9. Polls show that voters now feel a deficit of trust and are withdrawing their approval for Progressive policies and politicians in both of America's old ruling political parties.

10. The Federal Reserve hints that it may be on the verge of withdrawing, gradually, some of the more than $1 Trillion every year in stimulus it has been injecting into the U.S. economy. With the stock market and other speculators hooked on this addictive stimulus, reducing their accustomed dose of the easy money drug could trigger severe withdrawal symptoms and send the economy into deep recession or depression.

Footnotes

Opening Pages:

[1] Alexis de Tocqueville, *Democracy in America*, Book II, Part 4, Chapter 6 (translated by Harvey C. Mansfield and Delba Winthrop). Chicago: University of Chicago Press, 2000. See also Harvard University economic historian Niall Ferguson's comments on this Tocqueville passage in his book *The Great Degeneration: How Institutions Decay and Economies Die*. New York: Penguin Press, 2013. Pages 123-124.

[2] Mark Binelli, "How Detroit Became the World Capital of Staring at Abandoned Old Buildings," *New York Times*, November 9, 2012. URL: http://www.nytimes.com/2012/11/11/magazine/how-detroit-became-the-world-capital-of-staring-at-abandoned-old-buildings.html?pagewanted=all&_r=0

[3] Francis Fukuyama, *The End of History and the Last Man.* New York: Free Press/Macmillan, 1992.

Chapter One:
Welcome to Debtroit

[1] Mark Steyn, "Detroit Surrenders As If It Had Been Invaded," *Investor's Business Daily*, July 19, 2013. URL: http://news.investors.com/ibd-editorials-viewpoint/071913-664503-decaying-detroit-declares-bankruptcy.htm

[2] Tyler Durden, "25 Facts About The Fall Of Detroit That Will Leave You Shaking Your Head," *ZeroHedge*, July 21, 2013. URL: http://www.zerohedge.com/print/476669; Rachel Alexander, "Detroit: The Left's Model for Success," *TownHall.com*, July 22, 2013. URL: http://townhall.com/columnists/rachelalexander/2013/07/22/detroit-the-lefts-model-for-success-n1645905/page/full

[3] Monica Davey, "Financial Crisis Just a Symptom of Detroit's Woes," *New York Times*, July 8, 2013. URL: http://www.nytimes.com/2013/07/09/us/financial-crisis-just-a-symptom-of-detroits-woes.html?pagewanted=all&_r=0

[4] See "Will Obama Bail Out Detroit?" *Wall Street Journal* video, July 26, 2013. See also John Stossel, "What's Up With Detroit?" Fox Business Channel, July 25, 2013.

[5] Megan McArdle, "How Detroit Drowned in a Sea of Troubles," *Bloomberg*, July 25, 2013. URL: http://www.bloomberg.com/news/print/2013-07-25/how-detroit-drowned-in-a-sea-of-troubles.html

[6] Rana Foroohar, "Broken City: How Detroit's Epic Bankruptcy Could Help the Rest of the Country," *Time*, August 5, 2013.

[7] Chris Edwards, "Detroit's High Property Taxes," *Townhall.com*, July 29, 2013. URL: http://finance.townhall.com/columnists/chrisedwards/2013/07/29/detroits-high-property-taxes-n1651149

[8] Thomas Sowell, "Whites and Blacks Flee California," *LewRockwell.com*, March 29, 2011. URL: http://www.lewrockwell.com/2011/03/thomas-sowell/whites-and-blacks-flee-california/

[9] Edward Helmore, "'Detroit Will Rise Again': Glimmers of Defiance After City's Bankruptcy," *The Guardian/The Observer*, July 20, 2013. URL: http://www.guardian.co.uk/world/2013/jul/20/bankrupt-detroit-pins-hopes-creative-hub

[10] Craig R. Smith and Lowell Ponte, *The Great Debasement: The 100-Year Dying of the Dollar and How to Get America's Money Back.* Phoenix: Idea Factory Press, 2012. Pages 59-60.

[11] Wilber C. Rich, *Coleman Young and Detroit Politics: From Social Activist to Power Broker*. Detroit: Wayne State University Press, 1989.

[12] George Corsetti, "Poletown, Revisited," *CounterPunch*, September 18-20, 2004. URL: http://www.counterpunch.org/2004/09/18/poletown-revisited/print

[13] Richard A. Epstein, *Takings: Private Property and the Power of Eminent Domain.* Cambridge, Massachusetts: Harvard University Press, 1985.

[14] Ze'ev Chafets, *Devil's Night and Other True Tales of Detroit*. New York: Random House, 1990.

[15] Craig R. Smith and Lowell Ponte, *Crashing the Dollar: How to Survive a Global Currency Collapse*. Phoenix: Idea Factory Press, 2010. Pages 20-24.

[16] John Tamny, "The Unions Didn't Bankrupt Detroit, But Great American Cars Did," *Forbes*, July 21, 2013. URL: http://www.forbes.com/sites/johntamny/2013/07/21/the-unions-didnt-bankrupt-detroit-but-great-american-cars-did/

[17] Kate Abbey-Lambertz, "'Monument to Joe Louis': 25 Years Later, Detroit Fist Sculpture Still Incites Controversy," *Huffington Post*, February 16, 2012. URL: http://www.huffingtonpost.com/2012/02/16/monument-to-joe-louis-fist-sculpture-25-years_n_1275709.html

[18] Mark Steyn, "Detroit Surrenders As If It Had Been Invaded," *Investor's Business Daily*, July 19, 2013. URL: http://news.investors.com/ibd-editorials-viewpoint/071913-664503-decaying-detroit-declares-bankruptcy.htm

[19] Craig R. Smith and Lowell Ponte, *Crashing the Dollar: How to Survive a Global Currency Collapse*. Phoenix: Idea Factory Press, 2010. Pages 52-53.

[20] Ze'ev Chafets, *Devil's Night and Other True Tales of Detroit*. New York: Random House, 1990.

[21] Thomas Sowell, "Whites and Blacks Flee California," *LewRockwell.com*, March 29, 2011. URL: http://www.lewrockwell.com/2011/03/thomas-sowell/whites-and-blacks-flee-california/

[22] Michael Tanner, "Government, Not Globalization, Destroyed Detroit," *Bloomberg*, July 24, 2013. URL: http://www.bloomberg.com/news/2013-07-24/government-not-globalization-destroyed-detroit.html

[23] Tyler Durden, "25 Facts About The Fall Of Detroit That Will Leave You Shaking Your Head," *ZeroHedge*, July 21, 2013. URL: http://www.zerohedge.com/print/476669

[24] Tim Fernholz, "What Bankrupted Detroit: China? Or Robots?" *The Atlantic*, July 23, 2013. URL: http://www.theatlantic.com/business/archive/2013/07/what-bankrupted-detroit-china-or-robots/278054/

[25] Phil LeBeau, "Rare Praise: Consumer Reports Gives Chevy Impala Top Rating," *CNBC*, July 25, 2013. URL: http://www.cnbc.com/id/100912711

[26] Phil LeBeau, "Believe It or Not, Americans Are Driving Less," *CNBC*, July 27, 2013. URL: http://www.cnbc.com/id/100907911/print

[27] Bernie Woodall, Paul Lienert and Ben Klayman, "Insight: GM's Volt: The Ugly Math of Low Sales, High Costs," *Reuters*, September 10, 2012. URL: http://www.reuters.com/assets/print?aid=USBRE88904J20120910; Micheline Maynard, "Stunner: GM May Be Losing $50,000 On Each Chevrolet Volt," *Forbes*, September 10, 2012. URL: http://www.forbes.com/sites/michelinemaynard/2012/09/10/stunner-gm-may-be-losing-50000-on-each-chevrolet-volt/; Patrick J. Michaels, "Chevy Volt: The Car from *Atlas Shrugged* Motors." *Forbes*, March 16, 2011. URL: http://www.forbes.com/2011/03/16/chevy-volt-ayn-rand-opinions-patrick-michaels.html; "The Chevy Volt's $89,000 Production Cost: A Waste of Money?" *The Week*, September 11, 2012. URL: http://theweek.com/article/index/233140/the-chevy-volts-89000-production-cost-a-waste-of-money

[28] John Ransom, "Chevy Volt Heads for Fiery Crash," *Townhall.com*, July 8, 2013. URL: http://finance.townhall.com/columnists/johnransom/2013/07/08/chevy-volt-heads-for-fiery-crash-n1635710/page/full

[29] Ozzie Zehner, "Unclean at Any Speed: Electric Cars Don't Solve the Automobile's Environmental Problems," *IEEE Spectrum*, June 30, 2013. URL: http://spectrum.ieee.org/energy/renewables/unclean-at-any-speed; "Electric Cars Aren't So Environmentally Friendly," *Investor's Business Daily*, July 2, 2013. URL: http://news.investors.com/ibd-editorials/070213-662300-electric-cars-dont-cut-pollution-and-fossil-fuel-dependence.htm

[30] See "The End of Free Markets: The Rampages of Crony Capitalism in the Auto Belt" in David A. Stockman, *The Great Deformation: The Corruption of Capitalism in America*. New York: PublicAffairs, 2013. Pages 613-630.

[31] "Municipal Bonds 'Hemorrhage' $1.2 Billion on Detroit Fears," *CNBC*, July 26, 2013. URL: http://www.cnbc.com/id/100916026

[32] "'Unprecedented' $80 Billion Pulled From Bond Funds," *CNBC*, July 1, 2013. URL: http://www.cnbc.com/id/100855508

[33] Lori Ann Lorocco and others, "How Your City Might Pay for Detroit's Money Mess," *CNBC*, July 232, 2013. URL: http://www.cnbc.com/id/100907423/print; "The Detroit Decision With Trillions on the Line," *CNBC*, July 22, 2013. URL: http://www.cnbc.com/id/100903908/print; "Detroit Bankruptcy Case Could Bring Unwanted Change fror Muni Market," *CNBC*, July 26, 2013. URL: http://www.cnbc.com/id/100914877/print

[34] "Detroit Not a One-off, Aftershocks Will Be Staggering: Whitney," *CNBC*, July 24, 2013. URL: http://www.cnbc.comn/id/100909014/print see also "After Detroit, Who's Next?" *Wall Street Journal*, July 22, 2013. URL: http://finance.yahoo.com/news/after-detroit—who-s-next—225606490.html

[35] Michael Tanner, "Government, Not Globalization, Destroyed Detroit," *Bloomberg*, July 24, 2013. URL: http://www.bloomberg.com/news/2013-07-24/government-not-globalization-destroyed-detroit.html

[36] Kyle Smith, "Detroit Gave Unions Keys To The City, And Now Nothing Is Left," *Forbes*, February 21, 2013. URL: http://www.forbes.com/sites/kylesmith/2013/02/21/detroit-gave-unions-keys-to-the-city-and-now-nothing-is-left/

[37] Krauthammer said these things as a panelist on Fox News Channel's "Special Report," July 22 and 23, 2013.

[38] Monica Davey and Abby Goodnough, "Detroit Looks to Health Law to Ease Costs," *New York Times*, July 28, 2013. URL: http://www.nytimes.com/2013/07/29/us/detroit-looks-to-health-law-to-ease-costs.html?pagewanted=all

[39] Brett Joshpe, "It's Not Just Detroit: City Books Around The Country Are Much Worse Than You Think," *Forbes*, July 25, 2013. URL: http://www.forbes.com/sites/brettjoshpe/2013/07/25/its-not-just-detroit-city-books-around-the-country-are-much-worse-than-you-think/

[40] Alex Rosenberg, "Why Detroit Is Good for Gold: Ron Paul," *CNBC*, July 23, 2013. URL: http://www.cnbc.com/id/100907995/print

[41] Kevin D. Williamson, "Detroit Goes Down: A Lesson for American Cities," *National Review*, July 19, 2013. URL: http://www.nationalreview.com/node/353862/print

[42] John C. Goodman, "Detroit Is A Dying Example Of How All Ponzi Schemes End." *Forbes*, July 25, 2013. URL: http://www.forbes.com/sites/johngoodman/2013/07/25/detroit-is-a-dying-example-of-how-all-ponzi-schemes-end/

[43] To hear WJR Radio's audio of this interview, go to: http://www.youtube.com/watch?v=ggwXQsZOSMo
or http://www.youtube.com/watch?v=fOZ-Etb0k0Q
See also Peter Wilson, "Don't Touch Obama's Stash," *American Thinker*, March 9, 2013. URL: http://www.americanthinker.com/2013/03/dont_touch_obamas_stash.html

[44] Karl Marx and Friedrich Engels, *The Communist Manifesto*. London: Penguin Books, 1967. Pages 104-105.

For a discussion of how President Obama's policies coincide with Marx's and Engel's 10 points to destroy the bourgeoisie, see Mark Hendrickson, "Obama and Marx's Ten-Point Platform (Part I)," *FrontPage Magazine*, July 31, 2013. URL: http://frontpagemag.com/2013/mark-hendrickson/obama-and-marxs-ten-point-platform-part-i/; and Mark Hendrickson, "Obama and Marx's Ten-Point Platform (Part II)," *FrontPage Magazine*, August 1, 2013. URL: http://frontpagemag.com/2013/mark-hendrickson/obama-

and-marxs-ten-point-platform-part-ii/. President Obama has also issued Executive Orders that empower him to seize direct control of all communications, transportation and other resources in the nation in an emergency. Who can declare such an emergency? He can.

Previous Progressive presidents imposed these Communist Manifesto policies by various means.

A Progressive income tax is already in place, and its rates can be quickly increased to make it confiscatory.

Inheritance can already be subject to a heavy "death tax" on money that was previously taxed.

Large companies such as General Electric have become crony capitalist enterprises that largely behave as extensions of State policy.

As the largest factor in food production, mechanized corporate agribusiness has reduced the proportion of those farming the land from 40 percent in 1900 to approximately two percent of America's population today. The government heavily subsidizes and regulates many facets of agribusiness.

Both business and land-use controls by dozens of public agencies such as the Environmental Protection Agency constitute "regulatory takings," giving government the power to control the use of every piece of private property in the country.

(Many Progressives apparently have recognized that Hitler and Mussolini were smarter than Marx and Engels...because by the fascist-Nazi manner of intense regulation of nominally-private property and business, government can have all the control it wishes *and* be able to squeeze property tax from those it permits to keep a mostly-meaningless piece of paper called a deed to property. If government expropriates the land, Marxist-style, then no private "owner" is left to pay property tax.)

Money and credit have largely come under the control of the Federal Reserve, whose chairman and co-chairman are Presidential appointees; other banks have been *de facto* nationalized by "regulatory taking," by regulations so strict that they make our nominally-private banks difficult to distinguish from government-owned banks.

The government under President Obama has asserted its power to seize ownership of two of America's Big Three motor vehicle companies, of the insurance industry via "regulatory taking," and of 90 percent of the $1 Trillion student loan program.

Even prior to Obamacare, government regulated the entire healthcare industry and controlled roughly half of its total funding via Medicare, Medicaid and the Veterans Administration.

Chapter Two:
Spinning Our Wheels in Quicksand

[1] Steven Malanga, "The Indebted States of America," *City Journal*, Summer 2013. URL: http://www.city-journal.org/printable.php?id=9420

[2] "Federal Aid to State Budgets" [Map]. Washington, D.C.: The Tax Foundation, 2012. URL: http://taxfoundation.org/sites/taxfoundation.org/files/docs/fed_aid_to_states_large.png

[3] Ayn Rand, *Capitalism: The Unknown Ideal*. New York: Signet Books, 1967. Greenspan's essay appears on pages 96-101. An online text of Greenspan's essay "Gold and Economic Freedom" can be found at: URL: http://www.constitution.org/mon/greenspan_gold.html

[4] See "Federal Taxes Paid vs. Spending Received by State," Washington, D.C.: The Tax Foundation, 2007. URL: http://taxfoundation.org/tax-topics/federal-taxes-paid-vs-spending-received-state; Dave Gilson, "Most Red States Take More Money From Washington Than They Put In," *Mother Jones* Magazine, February 16, 2012. URL: http://www.motherjones.com/politics/2011/11/states-federal-taxes-spending-charts-maps; Dean Lacy, "Blame FDR and LBJ for 'Moocher' Paradox in Red States," *Bloomberg*, September 19, 2012. URL: http://www.bloomberg.com/news/print/2012-09-19/blame-fdr-and-lbj-for-moocher-paradox-in-red-states.html

[5] Paul Toscano, "Rick Santelli: 'I Don't Believe' Government Inflation Numbers," *CNBC*, August 14,

2013. URL: http://www.cnbc.com/id/100962243/print

[6] James D. Hamilton, "Off-Balance-Sheet Federal Liabilities" (monograph). San Diego: University of California San Diego, July 17, 2013. URL: http:dss.ucsd.edu/~jhamilto/CATO_paper.pdf

[7] Elizabeth Harrington, "101M Get Food Aid from Federal Gov't; Outnumber Full-Time Private Sector Workers," *Cybercast News Service*, July 8, 2013. URL: http://cnsnews.com/news/article/101m-get-food-aid-federal-gov-t-outnumber-full-time-private-sector-workers

[8] Tyler Durden / Michael Snyder, "More Than 101 Million Working Age Americans Do Not Have A Job," *ZeroHedge.com*. April 8, 2013. URL: http://www.zerohedge.com/news/2013-04-08/more-101-million-working-age-americans-do-not-have-job

[9] "A Record 21.6 Million Millenials Live with Mom and Dad," *CNBC*, August 2, 2013. URL: http:www.cnbc.com/100932822/print

[10] Ann Carrns, "College Students Don't View Debt as Burden," *New York Times*, June 15, 2011. URL: http://bucks.blogs.nytimes.com/2011/06/15/college-students-surprising-attitude-toward-debt/

[11] Michael K. Farr, "Taking Stock of S&P Earnings," *CNBC*, August 8, 2013. URL: http://www.cnbc.com/id/100950149; "Financials Near to Regaining S&P 500's Top Spot," *Reuters*, August 11, 2013. URL: http://www.cnbc.com/id/100954470

Chapter Three:
The 100-Year Detour

[1] Paul Rahe, "Progressive Racism," *National Review*, April 11, 2013. URL: http://www.nationalreview.com/node/345274/print

[2] "The Pill" [WGBH/PBS Documentary in the "American Experience" series] descriptor sheet: "People & Events: Eugenics and Birth Control." URL: http://www.pbs.org/wgbh/amex/pill/peopleevents/e_eugenics.html

[3] Peter C. Engelman, "Margaret Sanger," article in *Encyclopedia of Leadership*, Volume 4, George R. Goethals et al. (Editors), SAGE, 2004.

[4] Sanger in *The Pivot of Civilization*, page 181; quoted in Charles Valenza, "Was Margaret Sanger a Racist?" *Family Planning Perspectives*, January-February 1985, Page 44.

[5] Richard A. Epstein, *How Progressives Rewrote the Constitution*. Washington, D.C.: Cato Institute, 2006, page 107.

[6] Ibid., page 108.

[7] Paul R. Ehrlich, John P. Holdren and Anne H. Ehrlich, *Ecoscience: Population, Resources, Environment*. San Francisco/New York: W.H. Freeman, 1978. See pages 786-788; Ben Johnson, "Obama's Biggest Radical," *FrontPage* Magazine, February 27, 2009. URL: http://archive.frontpagemag.com/Printable.aspx?Artid=34198

[8] David Leonhardt, "Men, Unemployment and Disability," *New York Times*, April 8, 2011. URL: http://economix.blogs.nytimes.com/2011/04/08/men-unemployment-and-disability/?_r=0

[9] Nicholas Eberstadt, "The Astonishing Collapse of Work in America," Washington, D.C.: American Enterprise Institute, July 10, 2013. URL: http://www.aei.org/article/economics/the-astonishing-collapse-of-work-in-america/ ; for a critique of Eberstadt's analysis, see Richard S. Salsman, "What's So Bad About Women Replacing Men In The Workforce?" *Forbes*, July 30, 2013. URL: http://www.forbes.com/sites/richardsalsman/2013/07/30/whats-so-bad-about-women-replacing-men-in-the-workforce/

[10] Nicholas Eberstadt, *A Nation of Takers: America's Entitlement Epidemic*. West Conshohocken, Pennsylvania: Templeton Press, 2012.

[11] Helen Smith, *Men on Strike: Why Men Are Boycotting Marriage, Fatherhood, and the American Dream – and Why It Matters*. New York: Encounter Books, 2012.

[12] Charles Murray, *Coming Apart: The State of White America, 1960-2010*. New York: Crown Forum, 2012.

[13] Richard A. Epstein, *How Progressives Rewrote the Constitution*. Washington, D.C.: Cato Institute, 2006. Pages 66-68. 119. *Wickard v. Filburn* 317 U.S. III (1942).

[14] Felix Frankfurter, *The Commerce Clause Under Marshall, Taney and Waite*. New York: Quadrangle, 1964. The first edition of Justice Frankfurter's book appeared during the New Deal in 1937.

[15] John Halpin and Conor P. Williams, "Progressive Traditions: The Progressive Intellectual Tradition in America, Part One of the Progressive Tradition Series." Center for American Progress, April 14, 2010. URL: http://www.americanprogress.org/issues/progressive-movement/report/2010/04/14/7677/the-progressive-intellectual-tradition-in-america/

[16] Thomas G. West, "The Progressive Movement and the Transformation of American Politics," Heritage Foundation, Paper #12 in their First Principles Series. July 18, 2007.

[17] Ibid.

[18] Ibid.

[19] Craig R. Smith and Lowell Ponte, *The Great Debasement: The 100-Year Dying of the Dollar and How to Get America's Money Back*. Phoenix: Idea Factory Press, 2012. Pages 71-73.

[20] Epstein, *op cit.*, page 94.

[21]Mark R. Levin, *The Liberty Amendments: Restoring the American Republic*. New York: Threshold Editions/Simon & Schuster, 2013, Pages 90-91.

[22] Michael Tanner, *The American Welfare State: How We Spend Nearly $1 Trillion a Year Fighting Poverty – and Fail."* Washington, D.C.: Cato Institute / *Policy Analysis* Number 694, April 11, 2012. URL: http://www.cato.org/sites/cato.org/files/pubs/pdf/PA694.pdf

[23] Mark Leibovich, *This Town: Two Parties and a Funeral – Plus Plenty of Valet Parking – in America's Gilded Capital*. New York: Blue Rider Press/Penguin Group, 2013.

[24] "Woodrow Wilson Asks 'What Is Progress?'" (1912), Heritage Foundation. URL: http://www.heritage.org/initiatives/first-principles/primary-sources/woodrow-wilson-asks-what-is-progress

Chapter Four:
Addictionomics

[1] Richard H. Dillon, *Meriwether Lewis*. New York: Coward-McCann, 1965. Page 137.

[2] C.G. Jung, *Memories, Dreams, Reflections*. New York: Vintage/Random House, 2011. In this 1961 book, the pioneering Swiss psychoanalyst recounts his collaboration and break with the founder of modern psychoanalysis, Sigmund Freud.

[3] An audio recording of Huxley's speech can be found via "Aldous Huxley – The Ultimate Revolution – a Blueprint to Enslave the Masses at Community Audio. URL: http://archive.org/details/AldousHuxley--TheUltimateRevolution--ABlueprintToEnslaveTheMasses

[4] Jason Zweig, *Your Money & Your Brain: How the New Science of Neuroeconomics Can Help Make You Rich*. New York: Simon & Schuster, 2007. Page 53.

[5] George A. Akerlof and Robert J. Schiller, *Animal Spirits: How Human Psychology Drives the Economy, and Why It Matters for Global Capitalism*. Princeton, NJ: Princeton University Press, 2009. Page 47; for perspective on today's money as a unit of account, see Richard W. Rahn, "A Constant Unit of

Account," *Cato Journal*, Vol. 30 No. 3 (Fall 2010). Pages 521-533.

[6] Craig R. Smith and Lowell Ponte, *Crashing the Dollar: How to Survive a Global Currency Collapse.* Phoenix: Idea Factory Press, 2010. Pages 157-158.

[7] Hilke Plassmann, John O'Doherty, Baba Shiv, and Antonio Rangel, "Marketing actions can modulate neural representations of experienced pleasantness," *PNAS* (*Proceedings of the National Academy of Sciences of the United States of America*), Vol. 105 No. 3 (January 22, 2008). pp. 1050-1054. URL: http://www.pnas.org/content/105/3/1050.full.pdf+html

[8] Bernd Weber, Antonio Rangel, Matthias Wibral, and Armin Falk, "The medial prefrontal cortex exhibits money illusion," *PNAS* (*Proceedings of the National Academy of Sciences of the United States of America*), Vol. 106 No. 13 (March 31, 2009). pp. 5025-5028. URL: http://www.pnas.org/content/106/13/5025.full.pdf+html

See also Jianjun Miao and Danyang Xie, "*Monetary Policy and Economic Growth Under Money Illusion*," Boston University Department of Economics Working Papers Series # wp2007-045. October 29, 2009.

See also Markus K. Brunnermeier and Christian Julliard, "Money Illusion and Housing Frenzies," *Review of Financial Studies*, Volume 21 #1 (January 2008). Pages 135-180. NBER Working Papers 12810.

[9] I Timothy 6:10 (English Standard Version).

[10] Among the many books on this topic, see George Gilder, *Wealth and Poverty*. New York: Basic Books, 1981; David S. Landes, *The Wealth and Poverty of Nations: Why Some Are So Rich and Some So Poor*. New York: W.W. Norton, 1998; Jared Diamond, *Collapse: How Societies Choose to Fail or Succeed*. New York: Viking / Penguin, 2005; and Hernando de Soto, *The Mystery of Capital: Why Capitalism Triumphs in the West and Fails Everywhere Else*. New York: Basic Books, 2000.

[11] "The Cause and Cure of Inflation," in Milton Friedman, *Money Mischief: Episodes in Monetary History*. New York: Harcourt Brace, 1992. Pages 214-219.

[12] Peter Morici, "Easy Money is the Opiate of the American Economy," *CNBC*, July 16, 2013. URL: http://www.cnbc.com/id/100889431/print

Chapter Five:
The Herd Inside Our Heads

[1] Richard A. Posner, *The Crisis of Capitalist Democracy*. Cambridge, Massachusetts: Harvard University Press, 2010.

[2] Craig R. Smith and Lowell Ponte, *The Inflation Deception: Six Ways Government Tricks Us...And Seven Ways to Stop It!* Phoenix: Idea Factory Press, 2011, pages 28-31.

[3] Ibid., pages 34-35. For Keynesian multiplier, see page 57. For Meyer quote, see "Former Fed Governor Meyer: Velocity of Money Means Nothing," *CNBC*, July 9, 2013. URL: http://www.cnbc.com/id/100873633/print

[4] Peter Ferrara, "The Magic, Fairy Dust Naivete That Is Progressive Economics," *Forbes*, June 16, 2013. URL: http://www.forbes.com/sites/peterferrara/2013/06/16/the-magic-fairy-dust-naivete-that-is-progressive-economics/

[5] "A 'Nudge' To Tyranny" (Editorial), *Investor's Business Daily*, August 1, 2013. URL: http://news.investors.com/ibd-editorials/080113-666080-with-the-nudge-big-brother-never-had-it-so-good.htm; David Martosko, "Federal 'Nudge Squad' Led by 20-Something Wunderkind Gears Up to Change Americans' Behaviors – For Our Own Good," *London Daily Mail*, July 30, 2013. URL: http://www.dailymail.co.uk/news/article-2381478/Federal-nudge-squad-led-20-wunderkind-gears-change-Americans-behaviors--good.html

[6] Benedict Carey, "Academic 'Dream Team' Helped Obama's Effort," *New York Times*, November 12,

2012. URL: http://www.nytimes.com/2012/11/13/health/dream-team-of-behavioral-scientists-advised-obama-campaign.html?pagewanted=all; Rich Thau and Celeste Gregory, "Nudging Conservatives to Harness Behavioral Science," *The American* / The Journal of the American Enterprise Institute, May 3, 2013. URL: http://www.american.com/archive/2013/may/nudging-the-right-to-harness-behavioral-science

[7] Richard H. Thaler and Cass R. Sunstein, *Nudge: Improving Decisions About Health, Wealth, and Happiness*. New Haven, Connecticut: Yale University Press, 2008.

[8] Frank O'Brien, John Neffingere, Matthew Kohut and Al Quinlan, *Preventing Gun Violence Through Effective Messaging* (monograph). 2012; for a link to this pamphlet as well as commentary, see Larry Bell, "Exploiting Tragedies, Dem's Gun Grab Guidelines Emphasize Emotional Assaults Over Facts," *Forbes*, August 25, 2013. URL: http://www.forbes.com/sites/larrybell/2013/08/25/exploiting-tragedies-dems-gun-grab-guidelines-emphasize-emotional-assaults-over-facts/

[9] Joel B. Pollak, "The Vetting – Holder 1995: We Must 'Brainwash' People On Guns," *Breitbart.com*, March 18, 2012. URL: http://www.breitbart.com/Big-Government/2012/03/18/Holder-Fight-Guns-Like-Cigarettes

[10] Cass R. Sunstein and Adrian Vermeule, "Conspiracy Theories" (Monograph), January 17, 2008. URL: http://ssrn.com/abstract=1084585
The full paper can be downloaded at no cost from this Abstract website.

[11] Glenn Greenwald, "Obama Confidant's Spine-Chilling Proposal: Cass Sunstein Wants the Government to 'Cognitively Infiltrate' Anti-Government Groups," *Salon.com*, January 15, 2010. URL: http://www.salon.com/2010/01/15/sunstein_2/print

[12] Mike Levine, "White House Picks Panel to Review NSA Programs," ABC News, August 21, 2013. URL: http://abcnews.go.com/blogs/politics/2013/08/white-house-picks-panel-to-review-nsa-programs/

[13] Stephan Holmes & Cass R. Sunstein, "Why We Should Celebrate Paying Taxes," *Chicago Tribune*, April 14, 1999. URL: http://home.uchicago.edu/~csunstei/celebrate.html

Chapter Six:
Financial Repression

[1] Rana Foroohar, "How Germany Can Save the Euro," *Time*, August 19, 2013.

[2] Charles Moore, "Southern Europe Lies Prostrate Before the German Imperium," *London Daily Telegraph*, March 22, 2013 URL: http://www.telegraph.co.uk/news/worldnews/europe/cyprus/9948545/Southern-Europe-lies-prostrate-before-the-German-imperium.html; Mike Shedlock, "Merkel's Vision: 'United States of Germany,'" *Townhall.com*, March 26, 2013.

[3] Carmen M. Reinhart, "Financial Repression Back to Stay," *Bloomberg*, March 11, 2012. URL: http://www.bloomberg.com/news/2012-03-11/financial-repression-has-come-back-to-stay-carmen-m-reinhart.html; Carmen M. Reinhart and M. Belen Sbrancia, "The Liquidation of Government Debt," National Bureau of Economic Research (NBER) Working Paper # 16893. March 2011. URL: http://www.imf.org/external/np/seminars/eng/2011/res2/pdf/crbs.pdf; Alberto Giovanni and Martha De Melo, "Government Revenues from Financial Repression," *American Economic Review*, Vol. 83 #4 (September 1993). URL: http://www.jstor.org/discover/10. 2307/2117587 uid=3739560&uid=2&uid=4&uid=3739256&sid=21101221127691; Buttonwood, "Carmen Reinhart and Financial Repression," *The Economist*, January 10, 2012. URL: http://www.economist.com/blogs/buttonwood/2012/01/debt-crisis/print; Member of the European Parliament Nigel Farage, "Europe Is About to Impose Extreme Repression," *King World News* (Interview), June 22, 2012. URL: http://kingworldnews.com/kingworld- news/KWN_DailyWeb/Entries/2012/6/22_Nigel_Farage_-_Europe_is_About_to_Impose_Ex- treme_Repression.html

[4] "Resolving Globally Active, Systemically Important, Financial Institutions: A Joint Paper by the Federal Deposit Insurance Corporation and the Bank of England" (monograph), December 10, 2012. URL: http://www.fdic.gov/about/srac/2012/gsifi.pdf

[5] Ellen Brown, "It Can Happen Here: The Bank Confiscation Scheme for US and UK Depositors," *Global Research*, March 29, 2013. *Global Research* is a journal of the Centre for Research on

Globalization in Montreal, Canada.

[6] Reuters, "Bank Seizure Plans Focus on Absorbing Losses -- Regulators," *Chicago Tribune*, December 9, 2012; Julia Werdigier, "U.S. and U.K. Propose Plan to Deal With Bank Failures," *New York Times*, December 10, 2012; William L. Watts, "U.S., U.K. Regulators Take on 'Too Big to Fail' Banks," *MarketWatch/Wall Street Journal*, December 10, 2012; Pinsent Masons Law Firm, "US and UK Publish Cross-Border Proposals for Winding Up Global Financial Services Firms," *Out-Law.com*, December 10, 2012.

[7] Eric Sprott, "Caveat Depositor," *MarketFolly.com*, April 4, 2013.

[8] Robert Peston, "The Cost of Making Big Banks Safe," *BBC News*, December 10, 2012.

[9] Carmen M. Reinhart, "Financial Repression Back to Stay," *Bloomberg*, March 11, 2012. URL: http://www.bloomberg.com/news/2012-03-11/financial-repression-has-come-back-to-stay-carmen-m-reinhart.html; Carmen M. Reinhart and M. Belen Sbrancia, "The Liquidation of Government Debt," National Bureau of Economic Research (NBER) Working Paper # 16893. March 2011. URL: http://www.imf.org/external/np/seminars/eng/2011/res2/pdf/crbs.pdf; Alberto Giovanni and Martha De Melo, "Government Revenues from Financial Repression," *American Economic Review*, Vol. 83 #4 (September 1993). URL: http://www.jstor.org/discover/10. 2307/2117587 uid=3739560&uid=2&uid=4&uid=3739256&sid=21101221127691; Buttonwood, "Carmen Reinhart and Financial Repression," *The Economist*, January 10, 2012. URL: http://www.economist.com/blogs/buttonwood/2012/01/debt-crisis/print; Member of the European Parliament Nigel Farage, "Europe Is About to Impose Extreme Repression," *King World News* (Interview), June 22, 2012. URL: http://kingworldnews.com/kingworld- news/KWN_DailyWeb/Entries/2012/6/22_Nigel_Farage_-_Europe_is_About_to_Impose_Ex- treme_Repression.html

[10] Karl Marx and Friedrich Engels, *The Communist Manifesto*. London: Penguin Books, 1985, page 104. Item #5 of Marx's and Engel's list of 10 policies to destroy a capitalist society is "Centralization of credit in the hands of the State, by means of a national bank with State capital and an exclusive monopoly."

[11] Basel Committee on Banking Supervision, *Report and Recommendations of the Cross-border Bank Resolution Group*. Basel, Switzerland: Bank for International Settlements, March 2010. URL: http://www.bis.org/publ/bcbs169.pdf

[12] Jason Ma, "Cyprus Eyes Pension Fund Grab As Time Runs Out," *Investor's Business Daily*, March 21, 2013. URL: http://news.investors.com/economy/032113-648900-cyprus-may-seize-pension-funds-in-solidarity-fund.htm?ref=MoreArticles

[13] Stephanie Gruner Buckley, "Spain Is Running Out of People to Borrow From After Raiding Its Own Pensions Piggy Bank," *Quartz/Atlantic Monthly*, January 4, 2013. URL: http://qz.com/40640/spain-is-running-out-of-people-to-borrow-from-after-raiding-its-own-pensions-piggy-bank/; Dagmara Leszkowicz and Chris Borowski, "Poland Reduces Public Debt Through Pension Funds Overhaul," *Reuters*, September 4, 2013. URL: http://www.reuters.com/article/2013/09/04/poland-pensions-idUSL6N0H02UV20130904

[14] "FDIC – Statistics on Depository Institutions Report (2013). URL: http://www2.fdic.gov/SDI/rpt_Financial.asp or http://www2.fdic.gov/SDI.main4.asp

[15] Dakin Campbell, "U.S. Bank Deposits Drop Most Since 9/11 Terror Attacks," *Bloomberg*, January 23, 2013. URL: http://www.bloomberg.com/news/2013-01-23/u-s-deposits-post-biggest-drop-since-9-11-as-fdic-ends-support.html; Michelle Clark Neely, "Is the End Near for the Popular Transaction Account Guarantee Program?" St. Louis: St. Louis Federal Reserve Bank, Summer 2012. URL: http://www.stlouisfed.org/publications/cb/articles/?id=2266; Tyler Durden, "With $1.6 Trillion in FDIC Deposit Insurance Expiring, Are Negative Bill Rates Set To Become The New Normal?" *ZeroHedge*, September 24, 2012. URL: http://www.zerohedge.com/print/455854

[16] Adrienne Bosworth and others, "The Crisis: Fifteen Days that Shook Cincinnati," *Cincinnati Magazine*, May 1985. Page 39. URL: http://books.google.com/books?id=Rx8DAAAAMBAJ&pg=PA38&lpg=PA38&dq=Molitor+Savings+Cincinnati&source=bl&ots=4mpIYcWZCx&sig=uJtnbNbM1kvUq4aO57Ai5BrNuM8&hl=en&sa=X&ei=qxhVUYjnAaeViQKTioDADA&sqi=2&ved=0CC0Q6AEwAA#v=onepage&q=Molitor%20Savings%20Cincinnati&f=false

[17] *Ibid.*; "Ohio Governor Shuts 70 S&Ls for Three Days," *Associated Press/Los Angeles Times*, March 17, 1985. http://articles.latimes.com/print/1985-03-17/news/mn-35244_1_home-state-savings-bank

[18] George Kaufman, "The U.S. Banking Debacle of the 1980s: A Lesson in Government Mismanagement," The Foundation for Economic Education-FEE/*The Freeman*, April 1, 1995. URL: http://www.fee.org/the_freeman/detail/the-us-banking-debacle-of-the-1980s-a-lesson-in-government-mismanagement#axzz2P6VySTTV [Full disclosure: co-author Lowell Ponte has been a Contributing Editor at FEE's *Ideas on Liberty* Magazine aka *The Freeman*]; "The Savings and Loan Crisis and Its Relationship to Banking," Vol. 1 Chapter 4 of *History of the Eighties, Lessons for the Future*," Washington, D.C.: Federal Deposit Insurance Corporation/FDIC, 1997. URL: http://www.fdic.gov/bank/historical/history/167_188.pdf

[19] Clifford F. Thies and Daniel A. Gerlowski, "Deposit Insurance: A History of Failure," *Cato Journal*, Vol 8 No. 3 (Winter 1989). URL: http://www.cato.org/sites/cato.org/files/serials/files/cato-journal/1989/1/cj8n3-8.pdf; Kam Hon Chu, "Deposit Insurance and Banking Stability," *Cato Journal*, Vol. 31 No. 1 (Winter 2011). URL: http://www.cato.org/sites/cato.org/files/serials/files/cato-journal/2011/1/cj31n1-7.pdf; Ambrose Evans-Pritchard, "Cyprus Has Finally Killed Myth that EMU is Benign," *London Daily Telegraph*, March 27, 2013. URL: http://www.telegraph.co.uk/finance/comment/ambroseevans_pritchard/9957999/Cyprus-has-finally-killed-myth-that-EMU-is-benign.html

[20] Ambrose Evans-Pritchard, "Cyprus Has Finally Killed Myth that EMU is Benign," *London Daily Telegraph*, March 27, 2013. URL: http://www.telegraph.co.uk/finance/comment/ambroseevans_pritchard/9957999/Cyprus-has-finally-killed-myth-that-EMU-is-benign.html

[21] Wolfgang Munchau, "Europe Is Risking a Bank Run," *Financial Times*, March 17, 2013 URL: http://www.ft.com/intl/cms/s/0/b501c302-8cea-11e2-aed2-00144feabdc0.html#axzz2OcZ4q0n2; George Friedman, "Europe's Disturbing Precedent in the Cyprus Bailout," *Stratfor Geopolitical Weekly*, March 26, 2013. URL: http://www.stratfor.com/weekly/europes-disturbing-precedent-cyprus-bailout

[22] Deepanshu Bagchee, "Cyprus Finance Minister: We Hope People Will Believe Us," *CNBC*, March 17, 2013. URL: Http://www.cnbc.com/100560892

[23] "Cyprus Bailout: Dijsselbleom Remarks Alarm Markets," *BBC News*, March 25, 2013. URL: http://www.bbc.co.uk/news/business-21920574?print=true; William L. Watts and Sarah Turner, "Markets Drop on Fear Cyprus Deal Is New Blueprint," *MarketWatch/Wall Street Journal*, March 25, 2013; Luke Baker, "Cyprus to Shape Future Euro Bank Rescues: Eurogroup Head," *Reuters*, March 25, 2013; Helena Smith and others, "Cyprus Bailout: Savings Raid 'Could Happen Elsewhere,'" *The Guardian*, March 25, 2013; Bruno Waterfield, "Cyprus Bail-Out: Savers Will Be Raided to Save Euro in Future Crises, Says Eurozone," *London Daily Telegraph*, March 25, 2013; Rob Williams, "Cyprus Deal Is Model for Future Bailouts Says Top European Official as Banks are Told to Open," *The Independent*, March 25, 2013; Steve Goldstein, "Dijsselbloem Shocker Is U.S.'s Template, Too," *MarketWatch/Wall Street Journal*, March 25, 2013. URL: http://articles.marketwatch.com/2013-03-25/commentary/37999129_1_insurance-fund-uninsured-depositors-nova-bank

[24] "German Economist: 'Europe's Citizens Now Have to Fear for Their Money" (interview with economist Peter Bofinger), *Der Spiegel/SpiegelOnline*, March 18, 2013. URL: http://www.spiegel.de/international/europe/interview-with-german-economist-peter-bofinger-on-perils-of-cyprus-bailout-a-889594.html

[25] Karl Whelan, "It's Official: The Eurozone Is In Recession," *Forbes* Magazine, November 15, 2012; Marco Gioannangeli and Tracey, "Get All Your Money Out of Europe Now," *London Daily Express*, March 24, 2013. URL: http://www.express.co.uk/news/uk/386559/Get-all-your-money-out-of-Europe-now; Robert Watts, "Ukip Urges Brits to Withdraw Their Money From Spanish Banks," *London Daily Telegraph*, March 23, 2012; Armin Mahler, "Savers Be Warned – Your Money's Not Safe," *Der Spiegel/SpiegelOnline*, March 25, 2013; Simon Kennedy, "Saaving Cyprus Means Nobody Safe As Europe Breaks More Taboos," *Bloomberg*, March 25, 2013.

[26] Rana Foroohar, "Continental Commitment Issues," *Time*, April 1, 2013. URL: http://www.time.com/time/magazine/article/0,9171,2139173,00.html

[27] Jean-Claude Juncker Interview "The Demons Haven't Been Banished," *Der Spiegel/SpiegelOnline*, March 11, 2013. URL: http://www.spiegel.de/international/europe/spiegel-interview-with-luxembourg-

prime-minister-juncker-a-888021.html; Charles Forelle, "Luxembourg Lies on Secret Meeting," *Wall Street Journal*, May 9, 2011. URL: http://blogs.wsj.com/brussels/2011/05/09/luxembourg-lies-on-secret-meeting/

[28] Annika Breidthardt and others, "Insight: Money Fled Cyprus As President Fumbled Bailout," *Reuters*, March 25, 2013 URL: http://www.reuters.com/article/2013/03/25/us-eurozone-cyprus-muddle-insight-idUSBRE92O0TM20130325; Rick Moran, "How Much Cash Fled Cyprus Prior to Bailout Deal?" *American Thinker*, March 26, 2013. URL: http://www.americanthinker.com/blog/2013/03/how_much_cash_fled_cyprus_prior_to_bailout_deal.html; Tyler Durden, "Have the Russians Already Quietly Withdrawn All Their Cash From Cyprus?" *ZeroHedge.com*, March 25, 2013. URL: http://www.zerohedge.com/print/471901; Tyler Durden, "Cyprus – The Answer Is Uniastrum," *ZeroHedge.com*, March 28, 2013. URL: http://www.zerohedge.com/print/472062

[29] Margarita Papantoniou, "Cypriot Politicians' Loans Written Off," GreekReporter.com, March 29, 2013. URL: http://greece.greekreporter.com/2013/03/29/cypriot-politicians-loans-written-off/

[30] Carsten Volkery, "Last Minute Deal: The End of the Cypriot Banking Sector," *Der Spiegel/ SpiegelOnline*, March 25, 2013. URL: http://www.spiegel.de/international/europe/cyprus-to-shrink-bank-sector-under-last-minute-bailout-deal-a-890731.html

[31] Jason Ma, "Eurozone Signals Deposit Grab In Future Bank Bailouts," *Investor's Business Daily*, March 25, 2013. URL: http://news.investors.com/economy/032513-649274-cyprus-template-bank-depositors-bondholders-losses.htm; Moran Zhang, "Cyprus Crisis 2013: Are US Depositors' Money Safe With the Bank?" *International Business Times*, March 31, 2013. URL: http://www.ibtimes.com/cyprus-crisis-2013-are-us-depositors-money-safe-bank-1161807

[32] "Hands Off Our Banking Sector, Luxembourg Tells Euro Zone," *Reuters*, March 27, 2013. URL: http://www.cnbc.com/100596002

[33] Simone Foxman, "Cyprus Bailout: Winners and Losers," *The Atlantic*, March 25, 2013. URL: http://www.theatlantic.com/international/archive/2013/03/cyprus-bailout-winners-and-losers/274340/

[34] Joe Weisenthal, "If This Economist Is Correct, Then The Value of a 'Cypriot Euro' Could Be Weak For Years," *Business Insider*, March 27, 2013. URL: http://www.businessinsider.com/economist-cypriot-capital-controls-could-last-years-2013-3

[35] Carter Dougherty, "Retirement Savings Accounts Draw U.S. Consumer Bureau Attention," *Bloomberg*, January 18, 2013; Ken Blackwell and Ken Kluklowski, "Obama's Power Grabs Create an Imperial Presidency," *CNSNews*, June 18, 2012. URL: http://cnsnews.com/blog/ken-blackwell/obama-s-power-grabs-create-imperial-presidency; Gary DeMar, "Obama Administration to Go After Retirement Accounts," *Godfather Politics*, November 23, 2012. URL: http://godfatherpolitics.com/8220/obama-administration-to-go-after-retirement-accounts/
Jerome R. Corsi, "Now Obama Wants Your 401(K): Treasury, Labor on Path to Nationalize Retirement," *WND.com*, November 25, 2012. URL: http://www.wnd.com/2012/11/now-obama-wants-your-401k/; Newt Gingrich and Peter Ferrara, "Class Warfare's Next Target: 401(K)," *Investor's Business Daily* / American Enterprise Institute, February 18, 2010. URL: http://www.aei.org/article/society-and-culture/class-warfares-next-target-401k-savings/; John White, The Feds Want Your Retirement Accounts," *American Thinker*, February 22, 2013.

Chapter Seven:
Progressive Power Grab

[1] Daniel Henninger said this on the *Wall Street Journal Report* show on Fox News Channel, August 17, 2013.

[2] Romina Boccia and others, "Federal Spending by the Numbers, 2013: Government Spending Trends in Graphics, Tables, and Key Points," Washington, D.C.: Heritage Foundation, Special Report # 140 (August 20, 2013). URL: http://www.heritage.org/research/reports/2013/08/federal-spending-by-the-numbers-2013

[3] Quintus Tullius Cicero, *How to Win An Election: An Ancient Guide for Modern Politicians.* Princeton, New Jersey: Princeton University Press, 2012.

[4] Timothy P. Carney, "'Gays Are The Next Jews of Fundraising,'" *Washington Examiner*, June 26, 2013. URL: http://washingtonexaminer.com/gays-are-the-next-jews-of-fundraising/article/2532413

[5] "IRS Official Testifies that Political Appointee's Office Involved in Tea Party Screening," FoxNews.com, July 18, 2013. URL: http://www.foxnews.com/politics/2013/07/18/irs-lawyer-testifies-that-political-appointee-office-involved-in-tea-party/#ixzz2dLJIcdZN
or http://www.foxnews.com/politics/2013/07/18/irs-lawyer-testifies-that-political-appointee-office-involved-in-tea-party/

[6] Jamie Weinstein, "Frank VanderSloot: 'I'm Not the Only' Major Mitt Romney Donor Audited," *Daily Caller*, May 14, 2013. URL: http://dailycaller.com/2013/05/14/frank-vandersloot-im-not-the-only-major-mitt-romney-donor-audited/

[7] "IRS Official Testifies that Political Appointee's Office Involved in Tea Party Screening," FoxNews.com, July 18, 2013. URL: http://www.foxnews.com/politics/2013/07/18/irs-lawyer-testifies-that-political-appointee-office-involved-in-tea-party/#ixzz2dLJIcdZN
or http://www.foxnews.com/politics/2013/07/18/irs-lawyer-testifies-that-political-appointee-office-involved-in-tea-party/

[8] Kieran Healy, "Using Metadata to Find Paul Revere," *Slate.com*, June 10, 2013. URL: http://www.slate.com/articles/health_and_science/science/2013/06/prism_metadata_analysis_paul_revere_identified_by_his_connections_to_other.html

[9] John W. Dawson and John J. Seater, "Federal Regulation and Aggregate Economic Growth," *Journal of Economic Growth*, January 2013. URL: http://www4.ncsu.edu/~jjseater/regulationandgrowth.pdf

[10] Ronald Bailey, "Federal Regulations Have Made You 75 Percent Poorer," *Reason* Magazine, June 21, 2013. URL: http://reason.com/archives/2013/06/21/federal-regulations-have-made-you-75-per

[11] Clyde Wayne Crews, *Ten Thousand Commandments 2013: An Annual Snapshot of the Federal Regulatory State.* Washington, D.C.: Competitive Enterprise Institute, May 21, 2013. URL: http://cei.org/sites/default/files/Wayne%20Crews%20-%2010,000%20Commandments%202013.pdf

Chapter Eight:
The Great Withdrawal

[1] Transcript of this dialogue of "The Kudlow Report" was published by *CNBC* on August 16, 2013. URL: http://video.cnbc.com/gallery/?play=1&video=3000191297#eyJ2aWQiOiIzMDAwMTkxMzA4IiwiZW5jVmlkIjoiOTMxVVhoR3gvMFNGbnJjUEtIaTRvQT09IiwidlRhYiI6InRyYW5zY3JpcHQiLCJ2UGFnZSI6IiIsImdOYXYiOlsiwqBMYXRlc3QgVmlkZW8iXSwiZ1NlY3QiOiJBTEwiLCJnUGFnZSI6IjEiLCJzeW0iOiIiLCJzZWFyY2giOiIifQ==]

[2] David von Drehle, "The Man Who Said No to Easy Money," *Time* Magazine, February 14, 2011.

[3] J.D. Tuccille, "Wishful Thinking Is Control Freaks' Last Defense Against 3D-Printed Guns," *Reason* Magazine, May 8, 2013. URL: http://reason.com/blog/2013/05/08/wishful-thinking-is-control-freaks-last/print

[4] Daniel Bice, "Membership in Public Worker Unions Takes a Hit Under Act 10," *Milwaukee Journal Sentinel*, July 20, 2013. URL: http://www.jsonline.com/watchdog/noquarter/membership-in-public-worker-unions-takes-a-hit-under-act-10-b9957856z1-216309111.html

[5] Bill Frezza, "When Will Death Spiral States Impose Taxes On Fleeing Citizens?" *RealClearPolitics*, December 17, 2012. URL: http://www.realclearmarkets.com/articles/2012/12/17/when_will_death_spiral_states_impose_taxes_on_fleeing_citizens_100047.html; William Baldwin, "Do You Live In A Death Spiral State?" *Forbes*, November 25, 2012. URL: http://www.forbes.com/sites/baldwin/2012/11/25/do-you-live-in-a-death-spiral-state/; Leslie Kwoh, "N.J.'s Exit Tax: So Baffling, Even Officials Can't Explain It," *The Star-Ledger*, October 17, 2010. URL: http://www.nj.com/business/index.ssf/2010/10/nj_exit_tax_has_real_estate_at.html

[6] "60% Say Federal Government Does Not Have the Consent of the Governed," *Rasmussen Reports*, October 28, 2012. URL: http://www.rasmussenreports.com/public_content/politics/general_politics/october_2012/60_say_federal_government_does_not_have_the_consent_of_the_governed; "Poll Shows 29 Percent of Voters Think 'Armed Revolution' Might Be Needed," Fox News, May 2, 2013.

[7] Moises Naim, *The End of Power: From Boardrooms to Battlefields and Churches to States, Why Being in Charge Isn't What It Used to Be*. New York: Basic Books, 2013.

[8] Mark R. Levin, *The Liberty Amendments: Restoring the American Republic*. New York: Threshold Editions/Simon & Schuster, 2013, page 17.

[9] To see this BBC interview with Dr. Dennett, which aired April 2, 2013 on the BBC program "HARDtalk," go to URL: http://www.youtube.com/watch?v=l_h-Gkx83PM . Dennett's remarks about religion's strength in America can be seen in this interview, beginning 9 minutes and 15 seconds into the recording to 10 minutes and 33 seconds. For additional background about this idea, see Emory University sociologist Frank J. Lechner, "Rational Choice and Religious Economies" (2006: monograph) and its sources. URL: http://sociology.emory.edu/faculty/flechner/Rational%20Choice%20and%20Religious%20Economies.pdf

[10] "Jefferson's Gravestone." Web page of the The Thomas Jefferson Foundation, Inc. URL: http://www.monticello.org/site/research-and-collections/jeffersons-gravestone

[11] John H. Fund, "Don't Save Detroit – Sell It," *American Spectator*, September 2013. URL: http://spectator.org/archives/2013/08/20/dont-save-detroit-sell-it

[12] James Pethokoukis, "Remake Detroit, or Empty It," *National Review*, July 22, 2013. URL: http://www.nationalreview.com/node/354036/print

[13] Full disclosure: O'Rourke merrily quotes Lowell Ponte in his 1994 book *All the Trouble in the World: The Lighter Side of Overpopulation, Famine, Ecological Disaster, Ethnic Hatred, Plague and Poverty*.

[14] Craig R. Smith and Lowell Ponte, *The Inflation Deception: Six Ways Government Tricks Us...And Seven Ways to Stop It!* Phoenix: Idea Factory Press, 2011, pages 238-240.

[15] For a transcript of this Ronald Reagan speech "A Time For Choosing" delivered October 27, 1964, go to URL: http://www.reagan.utexas.edu/archives/reference/timechoosing.html
The video of this speech, along with transcript and audio, can be found at the website of the Ronald Reagan Foundation & Presidential Library at URL: http://www.reaganfoundation.org/tgcdetail.aspx?p=TG0923RRS&h1=0&h2=0&lm=reagan&args_a=cms&args_b=1&argsb=N&tx=1736; Its video is at URL: http://www.youtube.com/watch?v=qXBswFfh6AY

[A] To read the entire 1948 platform of the Progressive Party, go to URL:
http://www.davidpietrusza.com/1948-progressive-party-platform.html

[B] For the full official text of America's Declaration of Independence, go to URL:
http://www.archives.gov/exhibits/charters/declaration_transcript.html

Sources

Liaquat Ahamed, *Lords of Finance: The Bankers Who Broke the World.* New York: Penguin Books, 2009.

George A. Akerlof and Robert J. Schiller, *Animal Spirits: How Human Psychology Drives the Economy, and Why It Matters for Global Capitalism.*
Princeton, New Jersey: Princeton University Press, 2009.

Morris Altman, *Behavioral Economics For Dummies*. Hoboken, New Jersey: For Dummies/John Wiley & Sons, 2012.

John Anthers, *The Fearful Rise of Markets: Global Bubbles, Synchronized Meltdowns, and How to Prevent Them In The Future.* London: FT Press, 2010.

William W. Beach and others, *Obama Tax Hikes: The Economic and Fiscal Effects* (Monograph). Washington, D.C.: Heritage Foundation, 2010.

David Beckworth (Editor), *Boom and Bust Banking: The Causes and Cures of the Great Recession.* Oakland, California: Independent Institute, 2012.

Ben S. Bernanke and others, *Inflation Targeting: Lessons from the International Experience.* Princeton, New Jersey: Princeton University Press, 1999.

Peter Bernholz, *Monetary Regimes and Inflation: History, Economic and Political Relationships.* Williston, Vermont: Edward Elgar Publishing, 2006.

Peter L. Bernstein, *Against the Gods: The Remarkable Story of Risk*. Hoboken, New Jersey: John Wiley & Sons, 1998.

Mark Blyth, *Austerity: The History of a Dangerous Idea*. Oxford: Oxford University Press, 2013.

William Bonner and Addison Wiggin, *Financial Reckoning Day: Surviving the Soft Depression of the 21st Century.* Hoboken, New Jersey: John Wiley & Sons, 2004.

______________________________, *The New Empire of Debt: The Rise and Fall of an Epic Financial Bubble* (Second Edition). Hoboken, New Jersey: John Wiley & Sons, 2009.

Neal Boortz and John Linder, *The FairTax Book: Saying Goodbye to the Income Tax and the IRS....* New York: Regan Books / HarperCollins, 2005.

Neal Boortz, John Linder and Rob Woodall, *FairTax: The Truth: Answering the Critics*. New York: Harper, 2008.

Jerry Bowyer, *The Free Market Capitalist's Survival Guide: How to Invest and Thrive in an Era of Rampant Socialism.* New York: Broad Side / Harper Collins, 2011.

H.W. Brands, *The Age of Gold: The California Gold Rush and the New American Dream.* New York: Doubleday / Random House, 2002.

Arthur C. Brooks, *The Battle: How the Fight Between Free Enterprise and Big Government Will Shape America's Future.* New York: Basic Books / Perseus, 2010.

_____________, *Gross National Happiness: Why Happiness Matters for America – and How We Can Get More of It.* New York: Basic Books, 2008.

_____________, *The Road to Freedom: How to Win the Fight for Free Enterprise*. New York: Basic Books/Perseus Books, 2012.

James M. Buchanan and Richard E. Wagner, *Democracy in Deficit: The Political Legacy of Lord Keynes.* Indianapolis: Liberty Fund, 1999.

Todd G. Buchholz, *New Ideas from Dead Economists: An Introduction to Modern Economic Thought*. New York: New American Library/Penguin Books, 1989.

John Butler, *The Golden Revolution: How to Prepare for the Coming Global Gold Standard.* New York: John Wiley & Sons, 2012.

Bruce Caldwell (Editor), *The Collected Works of F.A. Hayek, Volume 2: The Road to Serfdom: Texts and Documents: The Definitive Edition.* Chicago: University of Chicago Press, 2007.

Stephen G. Cecchetti and others, *The Real Effects of Debt*. BIS Working Papers No 352. Basel, Switzerland: Bank for International Settlements, September 2011. URL: http://www.bis.org/publ/work352.pdf

Marc Chandler, *Making Sense of the Dollar: Exposing Dangerous Myths about Trade and Foreign Exchange.* New York: Bloomberg Press, 2009.

Harold Van B. Cleveland and others, *Money and the Coming World Order*, Second Edition. Greenwich, Connecticut: Lehrman Institute, 2012.

Tom A. Coburn, *The Debt Bomb: A Bold Plan to Stop Washington from Bankrupting America*. Nashville: Thomas Nelson, 2012.

Congressional Budget Office, *The Budget and Economic Outlook: Fiscal Years 2011 to 2021*. Washington, D.C.: Congressional Budget Office, January 2011. URL: http://www.cbo.gov/ftpdocs/120xx/doc12039/01-26_FY2011Outlook.pdf

Jerome R. Corsi, *America for Sale: Fighting the New World Order, Surviving a Global Depression, and Preserving U.S.A. Sovereignty.* New York: Threshold Editions / Simon & Schuster, 2009.

Crews, Clyde Wayne, Jr., *Ten Thousand Commandments: An Annual Snapshot of the Federal Regulatory State*. 2011 Edition. (Monograph). Washington, D.C.: Competitive Enterprise Institute, 2011.

Glyn Davies, *A History of Money: From Ancient Times to the Present Day*. Third Edition. Cardiff: University of Wales Press, 2002.

Glyn Davies and Roy Davies, *A Comparative Chronology of Money: Monetary History from Ancient Times to the Present Day.* (Monograph based on Glyn Davies and Roy Davies, above.) (2006) URL: http://projects.exeter.ac.uk/RDavies/arian/amser/chrono.html

Hernando de Soto, *The Mystery of Capital: Why Capitalism Triumphs in the West and Fails Everywhere Else*. New York: Basic Books / Perseus Books Group, 2000.

Donald J. Devine, *America's Way Back: Reclaiming Freedom, Tradition, and Constitution.* Wilmington, Delaware: Intercollegiate Studies Institute Books, 2013.

Peter H. Diamandis and Steven Kotler, *Abundance: The Future Is Better Than You Think.* New York: Free Press, 2012.

Jared Diamond, *Collapse: How Societies Choose to Fail or Succeed*. New York: Viking Press, 2005.

Peter F. Drucker, *Post-Capitalist Society.* New York: Harper Business, 1993.

Dinesh D'Souza, *Obama's America: Unmaking the American Dream*. Washington, D.C.: Regnery, 2012.

_____________, *The Roots of Obama's Rage*. Washington, D.C.: Regnery, 2010.

_____________, *The Virtue of Prosperity: Finding Values in an Age of Techno-Affluence.* New York: Free Press / Simon & Schuster, 2000.

Richard Duncan, *The Dollar Crisis: Causes, Consequences, Cures*. Singapore: John Wiley & Sons (Asia), 2003.

_____________, *The New Depression: The Breakdown of the Paper Money Economy.* New York: John Wiley & Sons, 2012.

Gregg Easterbrook, *The Progress Paradox: How Life Gets Better While People Feel Worse*. New York: Random House, 2003.

Mary Eberstadt, *How the West Really Lost God: A New Theory of Secularization*. West Conshohocken, Pennsylvania: Templeton Press, 2013.

Nicholas Eberstadt, *A Nation of Takers: America's Entitlement Epidemic*. West Conshohocken, Pennsylvania: Templeton Press, 2012.

Gauti B. Eggertsson, *What Fiscal Policy Is Effective at Zero Interest Rate?* Staff Report No. 402 (Monograph). New York: Federal Reserve Bank of New York, November 2009. URL: http://www.newyorkfed.org/research/staff_reports/sr402.pdf

Barry Eichengreen, *Exorbitant Privilege: The Rise and Fall of the Dollar and the Future of the International Monetary System.* Oxford: Oxford University Press, 2011.

_______________, *Global Imbalances and the Lessons of Bretton Woods* (Cairoli Lectures). Cambridge, Massachusetts: MIT Press, 2010.

_______________, *Globalizing Capital: A History of the International Monetary System* (Second Edition).

_______________, *Golden Fetters: The Gold Standard and the Great Depression, 1919-1939* (NBER Series on Long-Term Factors in Economic Development). Oxford: Oxford University Press, 1996.

Barry Eichengreen and Marc Flandreau, *Gold Standard In Theory & History.* London: Routledge, 1997.

Richard A. Epstein, *How Progressives Rewrote the Constitution*. Washington, D.C.: Cato Institute, 2006.

________________, *Takings: Private Property and the Power of Eminent* Domain. Cambridge, Massachusetts: Harvard University Press, 1985.

Niall Ferguson, *The Ascent of Money: A Financial History of the World*. New York: Penguin Press, 2008.

____________, *The Cash Nexus: Money and Power in the Modern World, 1700-2000.* New York: Basic Books, 2002.

____________, *Civilization: The West and the Rest.* New York: Penguin Books, 2011.

____________, *Colossus: The Price of America's Empire*. New York: Penguin Press, 2004.

____________, *The Great Degeneration: How Institutions Decay and Economies Die*. New York: Penguin Books, 2013.

Peter Ferrara, *America's Ticking Bankruptcy Bomb: How the Looming Debt Crisis Threatens the American Dream – and How We Can Turn the Tide Before It's Too Late.* New York: Broadside Books, 2011.

Ralph T. Foster, *Fiat Paper Money: The History and Evolution of Our Currency.* Second Edition. 2008.

Justin Fox, *The Myth of the Rational Market: A History of Risk, Reward, and Delusion on Wall Street.* New York: Harper Business, 2009.

Kevin D. Freeman, *Economic Warfare: Risks and Responses: Analysis of Twenty-First Century Risks in Light of the Recent Market Collapse* (Monograph). Cross Consulting and Services, 2009. This can be downloaded from the Internet at no cost from http://av.r.ftdata.co.uk/files/2011/03/49755779-Economic-Warfare-Risks-and-Responses-by-Kevin-D-Freeman.pdf or at no cost from http://www.freemanglobal.com/uploads/Economic_Warfare_Risks_and_Responses.pdf

George Friedman, *The Next Decade: Where We've Been...And Where We're Going*. New York: Doubleday, 2011.

Milton Friedman, *An Economist's Protest.* Second Edition. Glen Ridge, New Jersey: Thomas Horton and Daughters, 1975. Also published as *There's No Such Thing As A Free Lunch.* La Salle, Illinois: Open Court Publishing, 1975.

______________, *Capitalism & Freedom: A Leading Economist's View of the Proper Role of Competitive Capitalism.* Chicago: University of Chicago Press, 1962.

______________, *Dollars and Deficits: Inflation, Monetary Policy and the Balance of Payments.* Englewood Cliffs, New Jersey: Prentice-Hall, 1968.

______________, *Money Mischief: Episodes in Monetary History.* New York: Harcourt Brace, 1992.

______________, *On Economics: Selected Papers*. Chicago: University of Chicago Press, 2007.

______________, *Why Government Is the Problem (Essays in Public Policy).* Stanford, California: Hoover Institution Press, 1993.

Milton & Rose Friedman, *Free to Choose: A Personal Statement*. New York: Harcourt Brace Jovanovich, 1980.

______________, *Tyranny of the Status Quo.* San Diego, California: Harcourt Brace Jovanovich, 1984.

Milton Friedman & Anna Jacobson Schwartz, *A Monetary History of the United States, 1867-1960.* A Study by the National Bureau of Economic Research, New York. Princeton, New Jersey: Princeton University Press, 1963.

Francis Fukuyama, *The End of History and The Last Man*. New York: Free Press, 1992.

______________, *Trust: The Social Virtues and The Creation of Prosperity.* New York: Free Press, 1996.

James K. Galbraith, *The Predator State: How Conservatives Abandoned the Free Market and Why Liberals Should Too.* New York: Free Press, 2008.

John D. Gartner, *The Hypomanic Edge: The Link Between (A Little) Craziness and (A Lot of) Success in America.* New York: Simon & Schuster, 2005.

Charles Gasparino, *Bought and Paid For: The Unholy Alliance Between Barack Obama and Wall Street.* New York: Sentinel / Penguin, 2010.

Francis J. Gavin, *Gold, Dollars, and Power: The Politics of International Monetary Relations, 1958-1971 (The New Cold War History)*. Chapel Hill, North Carolina: University of North Carolina Press, 2007.

Nicole Gelinas, *After the Fall: Saving Capitalism from Wall Street – and Washington.* New York: Encounter Books, 2011.

Pamela Geller and Robert Spencer, *The Post-American Presidency.* New York: Threshold Editions / Simon & Schuster, 2010.

George Gilder, *Wealth and Poverty*. New York: Basic Books, 1981.

Jonah Goldberg, *Liberal Fascism: The Secret History of the American Left, From Mussolini to the Politics of Meaning*. New York: Doubleday, 2008.

______________, *The Tyranny of Cliches: How Liberals Cheat in the War of Ideas.* New York: Sentinel / Penguin, 2012.

David P. Goldman, *How Civilizations Die (And Why Islam Is Dying Too)*. Washington, D.C.: Regnery, 2011.

Jason Goodwin, *Greenback: The Almighty Dollar and The Invention of America*. New York: John Macrae / Henry Holt and Company, 2003.

Charles Goyette, *The Dollar Meltdown: Surviving the Impending Currency Crisis with Gold, Oil, and Other Unconventional Investments*. New York: Portfolio / Penguin, 2009.

Alan Greenspan, *The Age of Turbulence: Adventures in a New World*. New York: Penguin Books, 2007.

William Greider, *Secrets of the Temple: How the Federal Reserve Runs the Country*. New York: Simon & Schuster, 1989.

G. Edward Griffin, *The Creature from Jekyll Island: A Second Look at the Federal Reserve*. Third Edition. Westlake Village, California: American Media, 1998.

Alexander Hamilton, James Madison and John Jay, *The Federalist Papers*. New York: Mentor / New American Library, 1961. Pages 280-288. For an online version of James Madison's Federalist Paper No. 44, go to this URL: http://www.constitution.org/fed/federa44.htm

Keith Hart, *Money in an Unequal World*. New York: TEXERE, 2001.

Friedrich A. Hayek (Editor), *Capitalism and the Historians*. Chicago: Phoenix Books / University of Chicago Press, 1963.

________________, *Choice in Currency: A Way to Stop Inflation*. London: Institute of Economic Affairs, 1976. This can be downloaded from the Internet at no cost from http://www.iea.org.uk/sites/default/files/publications/files/upldbook409.pdf

________________, *The Counter-Revolution of Science: Studies On The Abuse of Reason*. New York: The Free Press / Macmillan / Crowell-Collier, 1955.

________________, *The Constitution of Liberty*. The Definitive Edition, Edited by Ronald Hamowy. Chicago: University of Chicago Press, 2011.

________________, *Denationalisation of Money: The Argument Refined: An Analysis of the Theory and Practice of Concurrent Currencies. Third Edition*. London: Institute of Economic Affairs, 1990. This can be downloaded from the Internet at no cost from http://mises.org/books/denationalisation.pdf

________________, *The Fatal Conceit: The Errors of Socialism*. Chicago: University of Chicago Press, 1991.

________________, *The Road to Serfdom*. Chicago: Phoenix Books / University of Chicago Press, 1944.

Henry Hazlitt, *The Failure of the "New Economics": An Analysis of The Keynesian Fallacies*. New Rochelle, New York: Arlington House, 1959.

___________, *From Bretton Woods to World Inflation: A Study of Causes & Consequences*. Chicago: Regnery Gateway, 1984. This can be downloaded from the Internet at no cost from http://mises.org/books/brettonwoods.pdf

Robert L. Hetzel, *The Great Recession: Market Failure or Policy Failure? (Studies in Macroeconomic History)*. New York: Cambridge University Press, 2012.

______________, *The Monetary Policy of the Federal Reserve*. New York: Cambridge University Press, 2008.

David Horowitz and Jacob Laksin, *The New Leviathan: How the Left-Wing Money-Machine Shapes American Politics and Threatens America's Future*. New York: Crown Forum, 2012.

Glenn Hubbard and Tim Kane, *Balance: The Economics of Great Powers From Ancient Rome to Modern America*. New York: Simon & Schuster, 2013.

W.H. Hutt, *The Keynesian Episode: A Reassessment.* Indianapolis: Liberty*Press*, 1979.

Craig Karmin, *Biography of the Dollar: How the Mighty Buck Conquered the World and Why It's Under Siege.* New York: Crown Business, 2008.

Charles R. Kesler, *I Am the Change: Barack Obama and the Crisis of Liberalism.* New York: Broadside Books, 2012.

John Maynard Keynes, *Essays in Persuasion*. New York: W.W. Norton, 1963.

__________________, *The General Theory of Employment, Interest, and Money.* New York: Harcourt, Brace & World, 1935.

Arnold Kling, *The Case for Auditing the Fed Is Obvious.* (Monograph / Briefing Paper). Washington, D.C.: Cato Institute, April 27, 2010. URL: http://www.cato.org/pubs/bp/bp118.pdf

Gabriel Kolko, *Railroads and Regulation 1877-1916*. New York: W.W. Norton, 1970. Originally published in 1965 by Princeton University Press.

Laurence J. Kotlikoff, *Jimmy Stewart Is Dead: Ending the World's Ongoing Financial Plague with Limited Purpose Banking.* Hoboken, New Jersey: John Wiley & Sons, 2011.

Laurence J. Kotlikoff and Scott Burns, *The Clash of Generations: Saving Ourselves, Our Kids, and Our Economy*. Cambridge, Massachusetts: The MIT Press, 2012.

________________________________, *The Coming Generational Storm: What You Need to Know About America's Economic Future.* Cambridge, Massachusetts: MIT Press, 2005.

Paul Krugman, *The Return of Depression Economics and The Crisis of 2008*. New York: W.W. Norton, 2009.

Joel Kurtzman, *The Death of Money: How the Electronic Economy Has Destabilized the World's Markets and Created Financial Chaos.* New York: Simon & Schuster, 1993.

Arthur B. Laffer, Stephen Moore and Peter J. Tanous, *The End of Prosperity: How Higher Taxes Will Doom the Economy – If We Let It Happen.* New York: Threshold Editions / Simon & Schuster, 2008.

Arthur B. Laffer and Stephen Moore, *Return to Prosperity: How America Can Regain Its Economic Superpower Status.* New York: Threshold Editions / Simon & Schuster, 2010.

George Lakoff, *The Political Mind: A Cognitive Scientist's Guide to Your Brain and Its Politics*. New York: Penguin Books, 2009.

George Lakoff and Elizabeth Wehling, *The Little Blue Book: The Essential Guide to Thinking and Talking Democratic*. New York: Free Press, 2012.

John Lanchester, *I.O.U.: Why Everyone Owes Everyone and No One Can Pay.* New York: Simon & Schuster, 2010.

David S. Landes, *The Wealth and Poverty of Nations: Why Some Are So Rich and Some So Poor.* New York: W.W. Norton, 1998.

Jonathan V. Last, *What to Expect When No One's Expecting: America's Coming Demographic Disaster*. New York: Encounter Books, 2013.

Adam Lebor, *Tower of Basel: The Shadowy History of the Secret Bank that Runs the World*. New York: PublicAffairs/Perseus Group, 2013.

Lewis E. Lehrman, *The True Gold Standard – A Monetary Reform Plan Without Official Reserve Currencies*. Greenwich, Connecticut: The Lehrman Institute, 2011.

Mark Leibovich, *This Town: Two Parties and a Funeral – Plus Plenty of Valet Parking – in America's*

Gilded Capital. New York: Blue Rider Press/Penguin Group, 2013.

Louise Levathes, *When China Ruled the Seas: The Treasure Fleet of the Dragon Throne, 1405-1433.* Oxford: Oxford University Press, 1997.

Mark R. Levin, *Ameritopia: The Unmaking of America*. New York: Threshold Editions/Simon & Schuster, 2012.

___________, *The Liberty Amendments: Restoring the American Republic*. New York: Threshold Editions/Simon & Schuster, 2013.

Michael Lewis, *Boomerang: Travels in the New Third World.* New York: W.W. Norton, 2011.

____________, *Panic: The Story of Modern Financial Insanity.* New York: W.W. Norton, 2009.

Naphtali Lewis and Meyer Reinhold (Editors), *Roman Civilization: Sourcebook II: The Empire.* New York: Harper Torchbooks, 1966.

Nathan Lewis and Addison Wiggin, *Gold: The Once and Future Money.* Hoboken, New Jersey: John Wiley & Sons, 2007.

Charles A. Lindbergh, Sr., *Lindbergh on the Federal Reserve* (Formerly titled: *The Economic Pinch*). Costa Mesa, California: Noontide Press, 1989.

Deirdre N. McCloskey, *Bourgeois Dignity: Why Economics Can't Explain the Modern World.* Chicago: University of Chicago Press, 2010.

Heather MacDonald, *The Burden of Bad Ideas: How Modern Intellectuals Misshape Our Society.* Chicago: Ivan R. Dee, 2000.

Bethany McLean and Joe Nocera, *All the Devils Are Here: The Hidden History of the Financial Crisis.* New York: Portfolio/Penguin, 2010.

Karl Marx and Friedrich Engels, *The Communist Manifesto*. London: Penguin Classics, 1985.

John Mauldin and Jonathan Tepper, *Endgame: The End of the Debt Supercycle and How It Changes Everything.* Hoboken, New Jersey: John Wiley & Sons, 2011.

Martin Mayer, *The Fed: The Inside Story of How the World's Most Powerful Financial Institution Drives the Markets.* New York: Free Press, 2001.

Michael Medved, *The 5 Big Lies About American Business: Combating Smears Against the Free-Market Economy.* New York: Crown Forum, 2009.

David I. Meiselman and Arthur B. Laffer (Editors), *The Phenomenon of Worldwide Inflation*. Washington, D.C.: American Enterprise Institute, 1975.

Gavin Menzies, *1421: The Year China Discovered America.* New York: Harper Perennial, 2002.

____________, *1434: The Year a Magnificent Chinese Fleet Sailed to Italy and Ignited the Renaissance.* New York: Harper Perennial, 2009.

Brendan Miniter (Ed.), *The 4% Solution: Unleashing the Economic Growth America Needs.* New York: Crown Business / George W. Bush Institute, 2012.

Hyman P. Minsky, *John Maynard Keynes*. New York: McGraw-Hill, 2008.

______________, *Stabilizing an Unstable Economy.* New York: McGraw-Hill, 2008.

Ludwig von Mises, *The Anti-Capitalist Mentality.* Princeton, New Jersey: D. Van Nostrand Company, 1956.

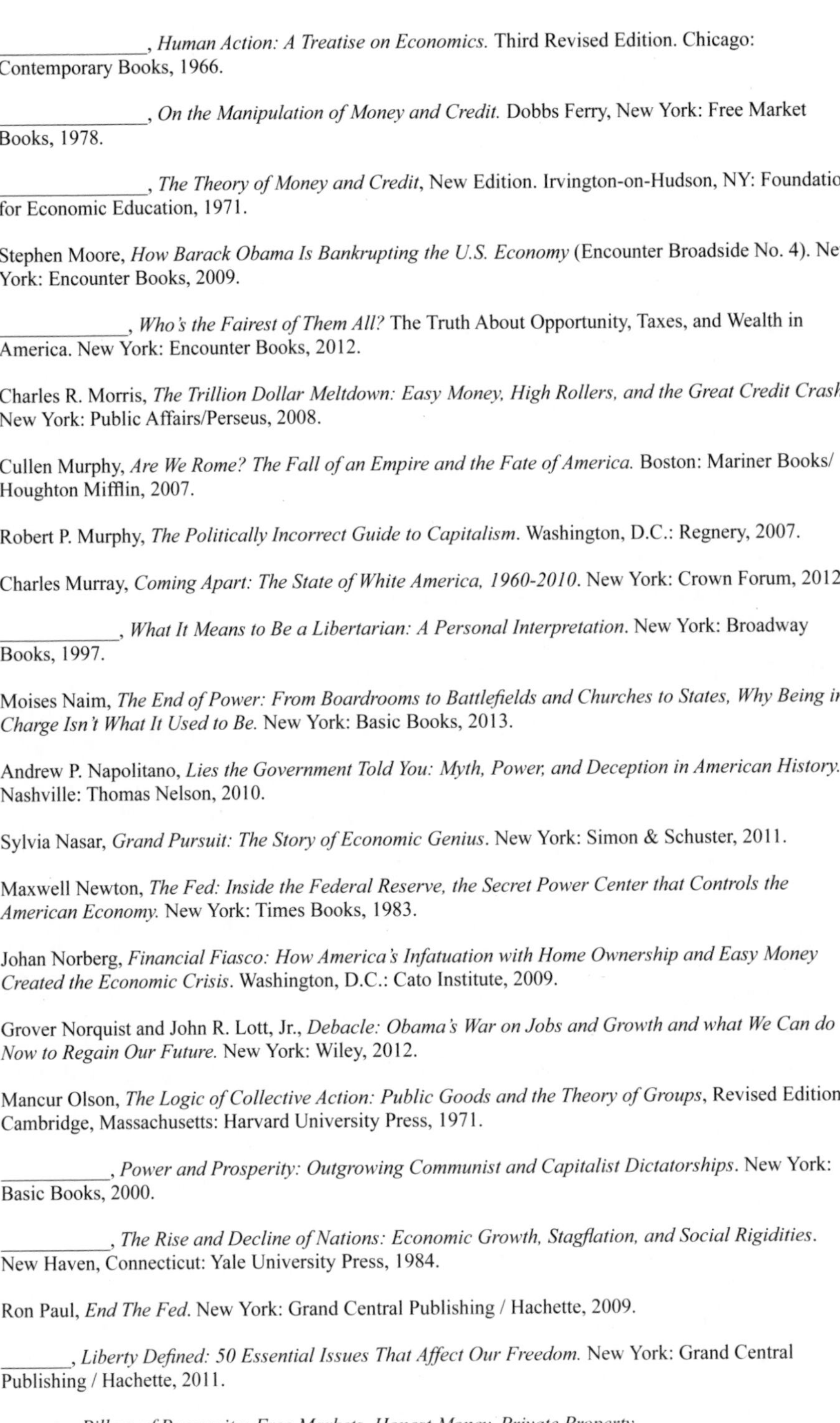

______________, *Human Action: A Treatise on Economics.* Third Revised Edition. Chicago: Contemporary Books, 1966.

______________, *On the Manipulation of Money and Credit.* Dobbs Ferry, New York: Free Market Books, 1978.

______________, *The Theory of Money and Credit*, New Edition. Irvington-on-Hudson, NY: Foundation for Economic Education, 1971.

Stephen Moore, *How Barack Obama Is Bankrupting the U.S. Economy* (Encounter Broadside No. 4). New York: Encounter Books, 2009.

____________, *Who's the Fairest of Them All?* The Truth About Opportunity, Taxes, and Wealth in America. New York: Encounter Books, 2012.

Charles R. Morris, *The Trillion Dollar Meltdown: Easy Money, High Rollers, and the Great Credit Crash.* New York: Public Affairs/Perseus, 2008.

Cullen Murphy, *Are We Rome? The Fall of an Empire and the Fate of America.* Boston: Mariner Books/ Houghton Mifflin, 2007.

Robert P. Murphy, *The Politically Incorrect Guide to Capitalism*. Washington, D.C.: Regnery, 2007.

Charles Murray, *Coming Apart: The State of White America, 1960-2010*. New York: Crown Forum, 2012.

___________, *What It Means to Be a Libertarian: A Personal Interpretation*. New York: Broadway Books, 1997.

Moises Naim, *The End of Power: From Boardrooms to Battlefields and Churches to States, Why Being in Charge Isn't What It Used to Be.* New York: Basic Books, 2013.

Andrew P. Napolitano, *Lies the Government Told You: Myth, Power, and Deception in American History.* Nashville: Thomas Nelson, 2010.

Sylvia Nasar, *Grand Pursuit: The Story of Economic Genius*. New York: Simon & Schuster, 2011.

Maxwell Newton, *The Fed: Inside the Federal Reserve, the Secret Power Center that Controls the American Economy.* New York: Times Books, 1983.

Johan Norberg, *Financial Fiasco: How America's Infatuation with Home Ownership and Easy Money Created the Economic Crisis*. Washington, D.C.: Cato Institute, 2009.

Grover Norquist and John R. Lott, Jr., *Debacle: Obama's War on Jobs and Growth and what We Can do Now to Regain Our Future.* New York: Wiley, 2012.

Mancur Olson, *The Logic of Collective Action: Public Goods and the Theory of Groups*, Revised Edition. Cambridge, Massachusetts: Harvard University Press, 1971.

__________, *Power and Prosperity: Outgrowing Communist and Capitalist Dictatorships*. New York: Basic Books, 2000.

__________, *The Rise and Decline of Nations: Economic Growth, Stagflation, and Social Rigidities*. New Haven, Connecticut: Yale University Press, 1984.

Ron Paul, *End The Fed*. New York: Grand Central Publishing / Hachette, 2009.

_______, *Liberty Defined: 50 Essential Issues That Affect Our Freedom.* New York: Grand Central Publishing / Hachette, 2011.

_______, *Pillars of Prosperity: Free Markets, Honest Money, Private Property.* Ludwig von Mises Institute, 2008.

_______, *The Revolution: A Manifesto*. New York: Grand Central Publishing / Hachette, 2008.

Ron Paul and Lewis Lehrman, *The Case for Gold: A Minority Report of the U.S. Gold Commission.* Ludwig von Mises Institute, 2007. This can be downloaded from the Internet at no cost from http://mises.org/books/caseforgold.pdf

Michael G. Pento, *The Coming Bond Market Collapse: How to Survive the Demise of the U.S. Debt Market*. Hoboken, New Jersey: John Wiley & Sons, 2013.

Peter G. Peterson, *Running On Empty: How the Democratic and Republican Parties Are Bankrupting Our Future and What Americans Can Do About It.* New York: Farrar, Straus and Giroux, 2004.

Kevin Phillips, *Bad Money: Reckless Finance, Failed Politics, and the Global Crisis of American Capitalism*. New York: Viking Press, 2008.

___________, *Boiling Point: Democrats, Republicans, and the Decline of Middle-Class Prosperity.* New York: Random House, 1993.

Lowell Ponte, *The Cooling*. Englewood Cliffs, New Jersey: Prentice-Hall, 1976.

Richard A. Posner, *The Crisis of Capitalist Democracy*. Cambridge, Massachusetts: Harvard University Press, 2010.

_______________, *A Failure of Capitalism: The Crisis of '08 and the Descent into Depression*. Cambridge, Massachusetts: Harvard University Press, 2009.

Virginia Postrel, *The Future and Its Enemies: The Growing Conflict Over Creativity, Enterprise, and Progress.* New York: Free Press, 1998.

Raghuram G. Rajan, *Fault Lines: How Hidden Fractures Still Threaten the World Economy.* Princeton, New Jersey: Princeton University Press, 2010.

Joshua Cooper Ramo, *The Age of the Unthinkable: Why the New World Disorder Constantly Surprises Us And What We Can Do About It*. New York: Little Brown / Hachette, 2009.

Ayn Rand, *Atlas Shrugged.* New York: Plume, 1999. (Reprint Edition)

________, *Capitalism: The Unknown Ideal (With additional articles by Nathaniel Branden, Alan Greenspan, and Robert Hessen).* New York: Signet / New American Library, 1967.

Carmen M. Reinhart and Kenneth S. Rogoff, *This Time Is Different: Eight Centuries of Financial Folly.* Princeton, New Jersey: Princeton University Press, 2009.

James Rickards, *Currency Wars: The Making of the Next Global Crisis*. New York: Portfolio/Penguin, 2011.

Barry Ritzholtz with Aaron Task, *Bailout Nation: How Greed and Easy Money Corrupted Wall Street and Shook the World Economy*. Hoboken, New Jersey: John Wiley & Sons, 2009.

Wilhelm Roepke, *A Humane Economy: The Social Framework of the Free Market*. Chicago: Henry Regnery Company, 1960. This can be downloaded from the Internet at no cost from http://mises.org/books/Humane_Economy_Ropke.pdf

Murray N. Rothbard, *America's Great Depression*. Fifth Edition. Auburn, Alabama: Ludwig von Mises Institute, 2000. This can be downloaded from the Internet at no cost from http://mises.org/rothbard/agd.pdf

_________________, *The Case Against the Fed.* Second Edition. Auburn, Alabama: Ludwig von Mises Institute, 2007. A version of this book can be downloaded from the Internet at no cost from http://mises.org/books/Fed.pdf

_________________, *A History of Money and Banking in the United States: The Colonial Era to World*

War II. Auburn, Alabama: Ludwig von Mises Institute, 2002. This can be downloaded from the Internet at no cost from http://mises.org/Books/HistoryofMoney.pdf

________________, *The Mystery of Banking*. Second Edition. Auburn, Alabama: Ludwig von Mises Institute, 2008. This can be downloaded from the Internet at no cost from http://mises.org/Books/MysteryofBanking.pdf

________________, *What Has Government Done to Our Money?* Auburn, Alabama: Ludwig von Mises Institute, 2008. This can be downloaded from the Internet at no cost from http://mises.org/Books/Whathasgovernmentdone.pdf

________________, *For a New Liberty: The Libertarian Manifesto* (Revised Edition). New York: Collier Books / Macmillian, 1978.

Michael Rothschild, *Bionomics: The Inevitability of Capitalism.* New York: John Macrae / Henry Holt and Company, 1990.

Nouriel Roubini and Stephen Mihm, *Crisis Economics: A Crash Course in the Future of Finance.* New York: Penguin Books, 2010.

Robert J. Samuelson, *The Good Life and Its Discontents: The American Dream in the Age of Entitlement 1945-1995.* New York: Times Books, 1995.

________________, *The Great Inflation and Its Aftermath: The Transformation of America's Economy, Politics and Society.* New York: Random House, 2008.

Peter D. Schiff and Andrew J. Schiff, *How an Economy Grows and Why It Crashes.* Hoboken, New Jersey: John Wiley & Sons, 2010.

Detlev S. Schlichter, *Paper Money Collapse: The Folly of Elastic Money and the Coming Monetary Breakdown.* New York: John Wiley & Sons, 2011.

Robert L. Schuettinger and Eamonn F. Butler, *Forty Centuries of Wage and Price Controls: How NOT to Fight Inflation.* Washington, D.C.: Heritage Foundation, 1979. This can be downloaded from the Internet at no cost from http://mises.org/books/fortycenturies.pdf

Barry Schwartz, *The Paradox of Choice: Why More Is Less.* New York: Ecco / Harper Collins, 2004.

George Selgin and others, *Has the Fed Been a Failure?* Revised Edition. (Monograph). Washington, D.C.: Cato Institute, 2010.

Hans F. Sennholz (Editor), *Inflation Is Theft.* Irvington-on-Hudson, New York: Foundation for Economic Education, 1994. A copy of this book may be downloaded at no cost from FEE's website at http://fee.org/wp-content/uploads/2009/11/InflationisTheft.pdf See also: Hans F. Sennholz, "Inflation Is Theft," *LewRockwell.com*, June 24, 2005. URL: http://www.lewrockwell.com/orig6/sennholz6.html

Amity Shlaes, *The Forgotten Man: A New History of the Great Depression.* New York: Harper Collins, 2007.

___________, *The Greedy Hand: How Taxes Drive Americans Crazy And What to Do About It.* New York: Random House, 1999.

Julian L. Simon, *The Ultimate Resource.* Princeton, New Jersey: Princeton University Press, 1981.

Mark Skousen, *Economics of a Pure Gold Standard.* Seattle: CreateSpace, 2010.

____________, *The Making of Modern Economics: The Lives and Ideas of the Great Thinkers*. Second Edition. Armonk, New York: M.E. Sharpe, 2009.

Craig R. Smith, *Rediscovering Gold in the 21st Century.* Sixth Edition. Phoenix: Idea Factory Press, 2007.

___________, *The Uses of Inflation: Monetary Policy and Governance in the 21st Century* (Monograph). Phoenix: Swiss America Trading Company, 2011.

Craig R. Smith and Lowell Ponte, *Crashing the Dollar: How to Survive a Global Currency Collapse.* Phoenix: Idea Factory Press, 2010.

___________________________, *The Great Debasement: The 100-Year Dying of the Dollar and How to Get America's Money Back.* Phoenix: Idea Factory Press, 2012.

___________________________, *The Inflation Deception: Six Ways Government Tricks Us...And Seven Ways to Stop It!* Phoenix: Idea Factory Press, 2011.

___________________________, *Re-Making Money: Ways to Restore America's Optimistic Golden Age.* Phoenix: Idea Factory Press, 2011.

Helen Smith, *Men on Strike: Why Men Are Boycotting Marriage, Fatherhood, and the American Dream – and Why It Matters*. New York: Encounter Books, 2012.

Guy Sorman, *Economics Does Not Lie: A Defense of the Free Market in a Time of Crisis.* New York: Encounter Books, 2009.

George Soros, *The Age of Fallibility: Consequences of the War on Terror.* New York: Public Affairs, 2007.

__________, *The Bubble of American Supremacy: the Cost's of Bush's War in Iraq.* London: Weidenfeld & Nicolson, 2004.

__________, *George Soros on Globalization*. New York: Public Affairs, 2005.

__________, *The New Paradigm for Financial Markets: The Credit Crisis of 2008 and What It Means*. New York: Public Affairs, 2008.

__________, *Open Society: Reforming Global Capitalism*. New York: Public Affairs, 2000.

__________, *The Soros Lectures at the Central European University.* New York: Public Affairs, 2010.

Thomas Sowell, *Basic Economics: A Common Sense Guide to the Economy.* Third Edition. New York: Basic Books/Perseus Books Group, 2007.

____________, *A Conflict of Visions: Ideological Origins of Political Struggles*. New York: William Morrow, 1987.

____________, *Dismantling America.* New York: Basic Books, 2010.

____________, *Economic Facts and Fallacies.* Second Edition. New York: Basic Books, 2011.

____________, *The Housing Boom and Bust.* Revised Edition. New York: Basic Books, 2010.

____________, *Intellectuals and Society*. New York: Basic Books/Perseus Books, 2009.

____________, *Marxism: Philosophy and Economics*. New York: William Morrow, 1985.

____________, *On Classical Economics.* New Haven, Connecticut: Yale University Press, 2007.

____________, *The Quest for Cosmic Justice*. New York: Free Press/Simon & Schuster, 1999.

____________, *The Vision of the Anointed: Self-Congratulation as a Basis for Social Policy.* BasicBooks/HarperCollins, 1995.

Mark Steyn, *After America: Get Ready for Armageddon.* Washington, D.C.: Regnery, 2011.

_________, *America Alone: The End of the World As We Know It*. Washington, D.C.: Regnery, 2008. *[Full*

Disclosure: Steyn quotes Lowell Ponte in this book.]

Joseph E. Stiglitz, *Freefall: America, Free Markets, and the Sinking of the World Economy*. New York: W.W. Norton, 2010.

_______________, *Globalization and Its Discontents*. New York: W.W. Norton, 2002.

David A. Stockman, *The Great Deformation: The Corruption of Capitalism in America*. New York: PublicAffairs/Perseus Books Group, 2013.

Paola Subacchi and John Driffill (Editors), *Beyond the Dollar: Rethinking the International Monetary System.* London: Chatham House / Royal Institute of International Affairs, 2010. URL: http://www.chathamhouse.org/sites/default/files/public/Research/International%20Economics/r0310_ims.pdf

Cass R. Sunstein, *A Constitution of Many Minds: Why the Founding Document Doesn't Mean What It Meant Before*. Princeton, New Jersey: Princeton University Press, 2011.

_______________, *Simpler: The Future of Government*. New York: Simon & Schuster, 2013.

Ron Suskind, *Confidence Men: Wall Street, Washington, and the Education of a President*. New York: Harper Collins, 2011.

Charles J. Sykes, *A Nation of Moochers: America's Addiction to Getting Something for Nothing.* New York: St. Martin's Press, 2012.

Nassim Nicholas Taleb, *Antifragile: Things That Gain from Disorder*. New York: Random House, 2012.

___________________, *The Bed of Procrustes: Philosophical and Practical Aphorisms.* New York: Random House, 2010.

___________________, *The Black Swan: Second Edition: The Impact of the Highly Improbable: With a New Section: "On Robustness and Fragility."* New York: Random House, 2010.

___________________, *Fooled by Randomness: The Hidden Role of Chance in Life and in the Markets*. New York: Random House, 2005.

Peter J. Tanous and Jeff Cox, *Debt, Deficits and the Demise of the American Economy.* Hoboken, New Jersey: John Wiley & Sons, 2011.

Richard H. Thaler and Cass R. Sunstein, *Nudge: Improving Decisions About Health, Wealth, and Happiness*. New York: Penguin Books, 2009.

Johan Van Overtveldt, *Bernanke's Test: Ben Bernanke, Alan Greenspan and the Drama of the Central Banker.* Chicago: B2 Books/Agate Publishing, 2009.

Damon Vickers, *The Day After the Dollar Crashes: A Survival Guide for the Rise of the New World Order.* Hoboken, New Jersey: John Wiley & Sons, 2011.

William Voegeli, *Never Enough: America's Limitless Welfare State*. New York: Encounter Books, 2010.

M.W. Walbert, *The Coming Battle: A Complete History of the National Banking Money Power in the United States*. Chicago: W.B. Conkey Company, 1899. Reprinted by Walter Publishing & Research, Merlin, Oregon, 1997.

David M. Walker, *Comeback America: Turning the Country Around and Restoring Fiscal Responsibility*. New York: Random House, 2009.

Jude Wanniski, *The Way the World Works*. New York: Touchstone / Simon & Schuster, 1978.

Jack Weatherford, *The History of Money: From Sandstone to Cyberspace*. New York: Crown Publishers, 1997.

Carolyn Webber and Aaron Wildavsky, *A History of Taxation and Expenditure in the Western World.* New York: Simon & Schuster, 1986.

Janine R. Wedel, *Shadow Elite: How the World's New Power Brokers Undermine Democracy, Government and the Free Market.* New York: Basic Books / Perseus Books Group, 2009.

Eric J. Weiner, *The Shadow Market: How a Group of Wealthy Nations and Powerful Investors Secretly Dominate the World.* New York: Scribner, 2010.

Diana West, *American Betrayal: The Secret Assault on Our Nation's Character*. New York: St. Martin's Press, 2013.

_________, *The Death of the Grown-Up: How America's Arrested Development Is Bringing Down Western Civilization*. New York: St. Martin's Press, 2007.

Drew Westen, *The Political Brain: The Role of Emotion in Deciding the Fate of the Nation*. Washington, D.C.: PublicAffairs, 2008.

R. Christopher Whalen, *Inflated: How Money and Debt Built the American Dream.* Hoboken, New Jersey: John Wiley & Sons, 2010.

Lawrence H. White, *Is The Gold Standard Still the Gold Standard among Monetary Systems?* (Monograph). Washington, D.C.: Cato Institute, February 8, 2008. URL: http://www.cato.org/pubs/bp/bp100.pdf

Meredith Whitney, *Fate of the States: The New Geography of American Prosperity*. New York: Portfolio, 2013.

Peter C. Whybrow, *American Mania: When More Is Not Enough*. New York: W.W. Norton, 2005.

Addison Wiggin and William Bonner, *Financial Reckoning Day Fallout: Surviving Today's Global Depression.* Hoboken, New Jersey: John Wiley & Sons, 2009.

Addison Wiggin and Kate Incontrera, *I.O.U.S.A.: One Nation. Under Stress. In Debt.* Hoboken, New Jersey: John Wiley & Sons, 2008.

Benjamin Wiker, *Worshipping the State: How Liberalism Became Our State Religion*. Washington, D.C.: Regnery, 2013.

Aaron Wildavsky, *How to Limit Government Spending...*, Berkeley, California: University of California Press, 1980.

John Williams, Hyperinflation 2012: Special Commentary Number 414. Shadow Government Statistics (Shadowstats), January 25, 2012. URL: http://www.shadowstats.com/article/no-414-hyperinflation-special-report-2012

Jonathan Williams (Editor), *Money: A History*. New York: St. Martin's Press, 1997.

David Wolman, *The End of Money: Counterfeiters, Preachers, Techies, Dreamers – and the Coming Cashless Society.* Boston: Da Capo Press / Perseus Books, 2012.

Thomas E. Woods, Jr., *Meltdown: A Free-Market Look at Why the Stock Market Collapsed, the Economy Tanked, and Government Bailouts Will Make Things Worse.* Washington, D.C.: Regnery Publishing, 2009.

_________________, *Nullification: How to Resist Federal Tyranny in the 21st Century.* Washington, D.C.: Regnery Publishing, 2010.

_________________, *Rollback: Repealing Big Government Before the Coming Fiscal Collapse.* Washington, D.C.: Regnery Publishing, 2011.

Thomas E. Woods, Jr., and Kevin R.C. Gutzman, *Who Killed the Constitution?: The Federal Government*

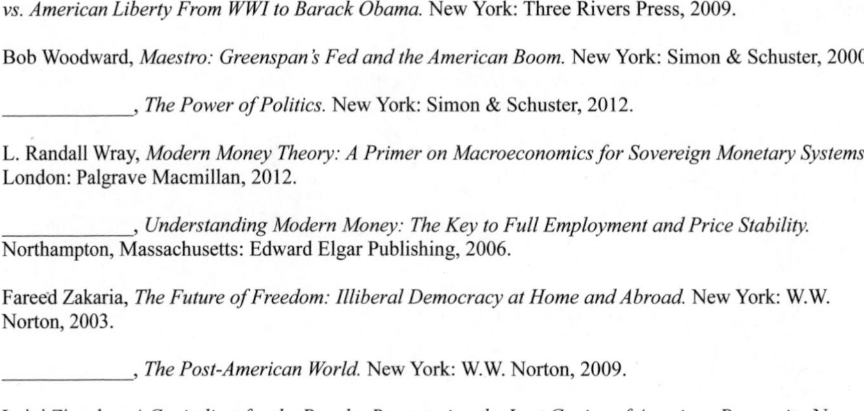

vs. American Liberty From WWI to Barack Obama. New York: Three Rivers Press, 2009.

Bob Woodward, *Maestro: Greenspan's Fed and the American Boom.* New York: Simon & Schuster, 2000.

_____________, *The Power of Politics.* New York: Simon & Schuster, 2012.

L. Randall Wray, *Modern Money Theory: A Primer on Macroeconomics for Sovereign Monetary Systems.* London: Palgrave Macmillan, 2012.

_____________, *Understanding Modern Money: The Key to Full Employment and Price Stability.* Northampton, Massachusetts: Edward Elgar Publishing, 2006.

Fareed Zakaria, *The Future of Freedom: Illiberal Democracy at Home and Abroad.* New York: W.W. Norton, 2003.

_____________, *The Post-American World.* New York: W.W. Norton, 2009.

Luigi Zingales, *A Capitalism for the People: Recapturing the Lost Genius of American Prosperity.* New York: Basic Books/Perseus Books, 2012.